# R.F.C. H.Q.

# R.F.C. H.Q.

The command & organisation of the
British Air Force during the
First World War in Europe

Maurice Baring

LEONAUR

*R.F.C. H.Q.*
*The command & organisation of the*
*British Air Force during the*
*First World War in Europe*
by Maurice Baring

First published under the title
*R.F.C. H.Q.*

Leonaur is an imprint
of Oakpast Ltd

ISBN: 978-0-85706-072-3 (hardcover)
ISBN: 978-0-85706-071-6 (softcover)

**http://www.leonaur.com**

# Contents

"Also *Doch*!"                                                      9

Farnborough to Maubeuge *via* "Port B"                            15

The Retreat and the Advance                                      23

Fère-En-Tardenois                                                36

The Move to the North and St. Omer                               44

With the First Division                                          57

St. Omer up to the First Push                                    63

Another Entr'acte at St. Omer and Another Push                  69

St. Omer Once More, and Italy                                    75

St. Omer and Another Offensive                                   83

London and Back Again                                            94

Preparations for the Somme Battle                               106

Fienvillers—The Battle of the Somme                             116

Further Operations on the Somme                                 129

The End of the Battle of the Somme and After                    141

St. André Again—The Spring Offensive                            150

Preparations for the Summer Offensive                           163

The Summer Offensive                                            171

The Second Summer Offensive                                     177

St. Omer—Fienvillers—ST. André                                  185

The Independent Air Force                                        204

DEDICATED

TO

R.F.C. H.Q.

*Make a note of that, Baring*
*Flying Corps Saying.*

# PART 1. 1914

## CHAPTER 1

# "Also *Doch!*"

*May-August*, 1914.

In May, 1914, I was travelling in Russia with a Russian friend of mine. When we reached Warsaw station, where you not only used to change, but where the railway itself continued on a different gauge, my friend talked of the military and strategical causes of this change of gauge, of further railway changes that were contemplated, and from this the talk veered to the European situation.

We talked of the *Entente*, of the Balkan situation, of the Russian army, of the German army, of the policy of the German Government, and my friend developed at some length his views on the European situation, and as to what would happen in the immediate future in the Balkans and elsewhere.

At one moment I interrupted him and said: "But if you are right in your diagnosis of the situation a European war is inevitable."

"I think there will be a European war," my friend answered, "this year."

Then we talked of other things. We parted company at Moscow. He went north, and I went south; and I did not give a thought to this conversation till some weeks later. I went to the country; and the European situation faded from my mind.

That was the first inkling of the possibility of an immediate war which appeared on the horizon of my consciousness.

I entirely forgot it during the whole of the month of June, which I spent in peaceful solitude in the centre of Russia, undisturbed and unvisited by any newspapers.

The second inkling I had of the possibility of war was at the Friedrichstrasse station at Berlin, where I arrived on June 30th at six o'clock in the morning from Russia. I bought a newspaper, and there printed in black letters, isolated, and taking the whole front page, was the sinister news that the Archduke Ferdinand had been assassinated. I stayed at the Hotel Bristol and saw several acquaintances, Russians and others, and they all seemed to think the news was exceedingly serious, but when I arrived in London the whole population appeared to be thoughtless and gay, and rumours of war were forgotten. Nevertheless, every now and then one was reminded of the small cloud which refused to dissipate on the horizon. One was vaguely conscious that it was there.

In London the first startling thing I recollect was the Austrian Ultimatum to Serbia; I forget on which day that was published in London, but I remember placards in the Strand bearing the ominous headline "To Hell with Serbia." and about the same time meeting a man in the street who said that somebody in the Foreign Office had told him that Austria did not mean business, and that there would be no war. I remember going to the Russian Embassy, where the impression was different.

My first idea was that the War might possibly be limited to the Balkan States. A Slav War, a War between Austria and the Balkan Principalities. It was difficult to see that Russia would not be dragged into this, but a Slav War of some kind seemed to be a certainty. Basing themselves on that hypothesis, or rather on what seemed to be that certainty, some friends of mine had the idea of organising a Red Cross Unit which should go to Serbia. We looked about for an available doctor to take charge of this Unit. On Tuesday, July 21st, I went to talk to a doctor who lived in Vincent Square, and proposed to him that he should take charge of this Unit. I have forgotten his name. He was not an Englishman. When I suggested to him that he should go to Serbia, he said he would gladly go to war on the Austrian side. "But," I objected, "in a week's time we shall be at war with Austria, because if Germany comes into the war Austria is bound to be on the same side as Germany."

"Perhaps," he said, "you have special information?" I said I had no special information, but it seemed to me purely a matter of common sense.

"Whether England is dragged into the War or not," he answered, "depends entirely on Russia."

The conversation lasted two hours, going round and round in a vicious circle, the doctor repeatedly saying he was willing to go to

Austria but not to Serbia, and therefore it came to nothing, as I was equally convinced that, should a war come about, there would be no question of being on the Austrian side.

The next thing that I remember was that I determined to go to Russia. The difficulty was how to get there. The Empress Marie was in England, and was going home to St. Petersburg. I obtained leave to travel in her train. Her train was to start finally, after the journey had been put off once or twice, on Saturday, August 1st. In the meantime the political situation was obscure. Was England coming into the War or was she not? In this week of turmoil two occasions stand out with startling vividness in my mind. One was a ball given at the Savoy Restaurant, and one was an evening at the Russian Opera at Drury Lane. I cannot remember the date of either of these occasions, but both of them could be placed if one took the trouble to refer to the newspapers of the time.

At the ball I had supper at the table at which, together with Lady Diana Manners and Claud Russell, there was a young German. I did not know then and I have never since ascertained his name. That evening in the newspapers there had been accounts of the excitement in Berlin of crowds shouting "Down with Serbia!" and "*Hoch*, England!" At our table Claud Russell asked the German (who seemed a pleasant young man) why the crowd in Berlin had shouted "*Hoch*, England!" The German said that he supposed the reason was that the people there thought that England would remain neutral during the war. I remember saying to him that the German people would have a rude shock of disappointment, as I felt certain that we should come in, but as a matter of fact I was being, from our point of view, a great deal too optimistic.

The night at the Russian Opera I imagine to have been Friday night July 24th, or possibly Monday July 20th. Chaliapin was singing. I went with some friends. We had a box. They had invited Mr. Lloyd George, who was anxious to hear this Russian music. Mr. Lloyd George arrived rather late, and a lady, who was sitting in the box next to ours, who was handsome and formidable and covered with jewels, made a demonstration of protest at the arrival of the Minister by standing up in the box, turning her chair round with her back to him and stamping it on the floor, and then sitting down with a stiff, forbidding cast-iron, inflexible, uncompromising back to him.

On Friday night, July 31st, I dined at the Russian Embassy. Count Benckendorff took me aside after dinner and advised me not to go in the Empress's train to Petrograd. I should arrive, he said, if we did not go into the war, at a moment of terrific disappointment and disillusion, and the situation might be unpleasant. He advised me not to risk this.

On Saturday morning (August 1st) there was, I remember, an atmosphere of great hopelessness about the situation. In the afternoon I went down to the North of England and remained there till Monday morning. On Monday morning I was much frightened by the tone of the press in the North of England. So far from there being any enthusiasm for the war, there seemed to be a strong and decided feeling against it. The question still seemed to be regarded as a lot of fuss about Serbia. Nobody seemed to realise the fundamental facts of the situation.

On the journey back there was a German woman in the restaurant car. She cried without stopping.

I arrived in London late on Monday evening. That afternoon Sir Edward Grey made his famous statement in the House of Commons which changed the whole situation. One began to breathe freely. England was not going to make, so one hoped, the great refusal.

The events of the next week are in my mind a crowded chaos, dark with the shadow of an intolerable nightmare.

I remember going to the House of Commons and hearing Mr. Asquith's statement, and late in the night in St. James' Street meeting someone who told me that we were at war with Germany.

He reminded me of Moltke saying, when the news of the final declaration of hostilities in 1870 was brought to him, "Also, *doch*."

I went to bed with those words ringing in my ears, "Also, *doch*." On Wednesday morning the news of the war was in the newspapers.

From that moment I was absorbed by the thought of how to get to the war. There were two possibilities, to go to Russia or to go out with the British Expeditionary Force; the second alternative, which was the more attractive was by far the more difficult.

I went to see Sir David Henderson at the War Office. He was then Director of Military Training, and a very old friend of mine. I had known him since 1897.

I told him I wanted to go to France as an interpreter. I said I knew seven modern languages, and he said he would send in my name officially stating that I knew four or five languages. He said he would do what he could, but he thought that if I were taken I would be employed in an office at home. I was convinced I could be of little use in an office, and I thought I could be of positive use at the front in France, as I could speak the language fluently, and knew the habits of the French.

General Henderson held out slender hopes, and he made me no empty promises, but he told me to hope for the best.

I remember walking past a post office one morning during this week in Southampton Street when somebody who was walking with me said: "They are putting up wire on the buildings against Zeppelins. The first night there is a south-east wind the Zeppelins will be over."

There was an oppressive feeling of nightmare abroad. Everybody was discussing whether the war would be long or short. "Are the Germans mad?" someone said, "or have they invented some new powerful explosive which will destroy the world? "Most people seemed to think the war would be a short one. Some people said: "We ought to send no troops to France, but only help with the Navy."

The question of Lord Kitchener's return was being discussed everywhere.

I went to the City. A rumour was about, which proved to be untrue, that Germany had declared war on Italy. A man in the City said to me: "It would be very curious if Germany had to fight the whole world and won. It is the sort of thing that does happen in history." This remark made me profoundly uneasy.

I remember an evening with the streets crowded with people, and a sullen roar that rose and fell every now and then from the crowds cheering the King out- side Buckingham Palace.

A man, slightly intoxicated, in evening clothes, waving a flag, made a speech on the top of a taxi in Trafalgar Square. I met a few friends in the crowd outside Buckingham Palace. The crowd was cheering the King, and all this was like a sultry, oppressive dream. As day succeeded day I grew more and more doubtful as to my prospects of getting to France with the British Expeditionary Force, and my hopes were finally dashed by getting a letter from Sir David Henderson saying my name had been put on the waiting list. I thought of the Russian alternative, and someone advised me to go and see Sir" Hanbury Williams, who was going to Russia.

I did this, and he said he was willing to take me to Russia. I told him I had already applied to Sir David Henderson, and that if Sir David were able and willing to take me I would go with him, otherwise I would gladly go to Russia.

And then, suddenly, on Saturday, August 8th, when I had given up all hopes of going to France, I got a note from General Henderson at 6 o'clock in the afternoon saying I was to go to France with him, and telling me to report at the War Office next morning.

It was too late to get any uniform, as the shops were shut; but I had already with some foresight ordered some khaki on which it was only necessary to put badges of rank in order to make it into a kind of uniform.

Early the next morning (Sunday, August 9th) I went to the War Office for orders. There I saw Major Salmond, Colonel MacDonough, and various other officers belonging to the Intelligence, and I signed a paper and was informed I was a Lieutenant in the Intelligence Corps attached to Headquarters R.F.C. They told me I must not communicate with the Press. I went to Downing Street to say goodbye. The news of a great battle in Alsace had been received, in which the casualties on either side were said to be between 13,000 and 15,000. The French were said to have gained the victory. This news was apparently believed.[1] Everybody was still discussing whether the war would be a long war or a short war. Most people seemed inclined to think it would be a short war.

My uniform was far from satisfactory. Six people endeavoured to put on my putties; none of them were entirely successful, except finally in the evening, Sir David Henderson. In the afternoon various people came to No. 32 Queen Anne's Gate, where I was living. Among others Conrad Russell. He was in the Yeomanry, and was mobilised but was not going to France. He said it was unfair that he and Bron Lucas, who had been in the British Army for over seven years, should not be going to France whereas I, who had not been in the Army at all, was going off at once. "We are now," he said, "both of us two little cog wheels in an enormous machine, and if scraps of dust get on to us we retard the working of the machine."

We talked of the Germans. "We must be careful of one thing," I said. "Not to be made prisoners, for in that case the Germans will kick us on the head."

"How can you," he answered, "you, who know the Germans well and have lived in Germany, talk such rubbish?"

Major Salmond came to fetch me after dinner at 9 o'clock at 32 Queen Anne's Gate, and we started in a motor to Farnborough. We slept in the Queen's Hotel, in a billiard room which was full of officers.

---

1. It was quite untrue.

# CHAPTER 2

# Farnborough to Maubeuge
## *via* "Port B"

*August*, 1914.

The next morning I got up at half-past five, and went into a remote and secluded part of the country to put on my putties at my leisure. This, although a long operation, was not entirely successful as, when it was finished, they were so tightly bound I could scarcely walk, but I did not dare undo them again.

We had breakfast, and after breakfast Captain Longcroft arrived, and we three started off as an advance party to make arrangements for the arrival of the Flying Corps in France. But at the time I knew nothing. I did not know where we were going nor what we were going to do. I only knew we were bound for Port B., but even this was not referred to. I did not exactly know who these officers were. I knew that we were connected with the Flying Corps, and that was all. I did not know what the Flying Corps was or that there was a Flying Corps. Colonel Sykes came to see us off at Farnborough Station.

Salmond's canvas bath was discarded from his kit at the last moment, and thrown on to the platform, as it was considered to constitute excessive weight. We went by train to Redhill. The conversation was Greek to me. Longcroft and Salmond talked the whole time of "bumps," "pancakes," "stalling," "taxiing," and I did not dare ask a question.

On the platform at Redhill I put a penny into the penny-in-the-slot Fortune Teller and the figure pointed at the following saying: "Do not trust appearances: keep up a stout heart." What appearances, I wondered? I went into the town and bought a pair of gaiters to use instead of putties, but Longcroft and Salmond said they would never do; they disapproved both of their cut and their colour, so I had to keep on my excruciating putties.

We arrived at Newhaven at 1 o'clock. We asked when the boat was to start for Port B——. The railway transport officer to whom we put this question seemed altogether weary of life. He had evidently been asked this same question many times already this same day.

In the afternoon I bought in a booth a pair of black naval gaiters, but again Longcroft and Salmond said these would not do either. We bathed in the dazzling sea, the last bathe and the last piece of real leisure for a long time. We dined outside the town at a place called Seaford, I think. The waiter was a German, and he took the gloomiest view of the war, looked at from the English side that is to say, and the most cheerful view looked at from the German; in fact he was bubbling with optimism.

We slept in the railway station attached to the R.F.C. in a railway carriage. A Daimler car arrived with its driver, whose name was Northcourt, from the Works. It was to go to France with us.

The next morning (August 11th) my uniform was fixed up. There was some discussion as to whether I was a lieutenant or a second lieutenant. It was settled that I was a lieutenant, and a tailor on the pier was told to sew on to my coat the necessary badges of rank, which he did.

We spent many hours at the pier watching trains and material being checked. Finally we were suddenly told we were to sail in a boat called "*The Canterbury*" at 3.30 p.m., which we did. A small party of mechanics went with us. In mid-channel we passed nine French men-of-war. As we neared Boulogne in the darkness a great deal of signalling and hallooing went on, and a small tug came to examine us. Ultimately we got into the harbour. It was low tide, and we had to climb up a slippery ladder on the face of a wall to go ashore. As soon as we got ashore we asked for news. "The French have retired from Mulhausen," was the answer. "It's of no military importance," said someone, a phrase we were destined to hear many times during the next four years. We slept on board the boat.

When we woke up the next morning (August 12th) in France early, between four and five, we all became aware of a startling new impression. All the nightmare cloud which had hung over the last few days in London seemed to have been blown away. Everybody was brisk, cheerful and optimistic. This was so throughout the war. Whenever one used to come back to London on leave one felt at once conscious of being plunged back into an atmosphere of gloom and depression, and whenever one came back to France from England one seemed to step from a dark room into a bright one.

We got up at five and started at seven for Amiens by train. The train was crowded, and every station was crowded, partly with soldiers being mobilised and partly by crowds of French people, who shouted "*Vive l'Angleterre*," and threw flowers and fruit at us.

In the railway carriage with us there was an elderly Frenchman, who explained to us, with the aid of a map, the German plan of campaign. He said he had gone into the matter carefully, and that the Germans would be beaten this time and quickly. They had made a miscalculation. It was not the same as in 1870.

The French, he said, had been doubtful as to whether the English were going into the war, but he, who knew the English, was convinced they would do so.

If we hadn't come in —— and he shook his fist and laughed. When he heard that Salmond and Longcroft belonged to the Flying Corps he said:

"*Ah! les aviateurs ils n'ont pas besoin d'aller a la guerre pour se faire casser la geule ceux là.*"

We arrived at Amiens at 12 o'clock and reported to the French authorities. Longcroft wanted to go up to the Aerodrome at once. This upset the French authorities, who said they had not yet had their *dejeuner*. Here for the first time we came into contact with one sacred, almost appalling fact that, whatever happens, the French nation must not be disturbed during the hour of their midday meal. Whatever happens they must have their *déjeuner* at the appointed hour, and the rite must not be disturbed nor curtailed.

It was said later that when General Foch was offered the supreme command of the Allied Armies, he only made two conditions; the first was that he should take over the command at once, and the second was that whatever happened he should never be disturbed during the hour of *déjeuner*. We learned this lesson on August 12th. Longcroft and Salmond, in spite of their impatience to get to work at once, were obliged to wait until the hour of *déjeuner* was over.

After luncheon we went up to the Aerodrome and found out what it was necessary for us to get. We had to arrange for many things. Water carts had to be obtained, pegs for the aeroplanes and many other things, also a certain consignment of B.B. Oil had to be found in the station. We spent that afternoon interviewing various people, who promised to get what we wanted, and various officials at the railway stations (there were two stations) on the subject of the B.B. Oil.

We slept in our valises on the grass on the Aerodrome. We awoke with the dawn and bathed in the dew. A small crowd watched the operations and cheered.

Amiens was bedecked with flags, and everywhere we were greeted by enthusiastic crowds. There was a man driving about in a motor car, which was covered with Union Jacks. He asked us if he could be of any help. We said we wanted some wood. He said he had a friend who had plenty of wood. He drove us to his friend's house in the car. He said he was an Englishman and came from Birmingham. I said I knew Birmingham, just for something to say. When we arrived at his friend's house he disappeared, and we never saw him nor his car again. I believe him to have been a German. The friend was an enormously tall and very big man. He said he was not able to serve as a soldier because he had sprained his ankle, which was bandaged. He had a large supply of petrol, wood and other necessaries, of which he was willing to sell us any amount. I afterwards ascertained that he belonged to a German business firm. He asked a lot of questions about English military matters.

I spent the next morning (August 13th) checking boxes of some kind of material which were being hauled out of a train by a company of French soldiers who were under my command. They pulled out the boxes from the train on to the platform, and an English corporal checked what was taken out in a small notebook. Never had I before the war thought I should spend a day at Amiens station checking goods with the help of a company of French soldiers and an English corporal.

The first three squadrons of the R.F.C. (which consisted only of four squadrons) flew over from England and landed at the Amiens Aerodrome early. The first pilot to land was Harvey-Kelly[1] in B.E.2 A. machine. Salmond and Longcroft on the journey out had both prophesied that he would be the first pilot to land. The second pilot to land was Burke.[2] who commanded No. 2 Squadron.

In the afternoon Prince Murat, the Liaison officer, reported for duty, and said he was attached to our Headquarters.

General Henderson, Colonel Sykes, Barrington-Kennett, and

---

1. Subsequently a Squadron Commander and killed fighting in the air.
2. Subsequently a Wing Commander, then Commander of the Central Flying School, and finally killed fighting gallantly in the Infantry.

Colonel Brooke-Popham, arrived from England. We moved from the Aerodrome into the Hôtel Belfort.

The whole of the rest of the day was spent between two stations chasing officials and looking for the B.B, oil cases.

Early, at 5.30, the next morning (August 14th) I went to Mass in Amiens Cathedral; I stood between two soldiers, a Frenchman and an Englishman. This is where Edward III heard Mass on the way to Crécy.

Later in the morning Sir John French came up to the Aerodrome to see the Squadrons.

I had luncheon with some French people at Amiens at the Hôtel du Rhin. They were intensely depressed and absent-minded. They appeared to be looking into the distance. They kept on repeating the war would be a very long business. They said that a million German soldiers were already in France. They said it would be long, very long. "Did I think the Russians would be able to help—to give a *coup de main?*" This was the first note, not of pessimism, but of uneasiness I heard expressed in France since the war began. They said little, but there was no doubt about their anxiety. They evidently thought matters were very serious, and that they were in for a long, long war.

Sitting at the same table was a young cavalry officer. He was expecting to go to the Front the next day. Halfway through luncheon he received a telegram saying that the commanding officer of his unit had been killed, and he was to go and take over the command at once. He started up, said goodbye, and went off then and there. The other Frenchmen kept on absent-mindedly looking into the distance. They appeared to see things I could not see; they kept on saying every now and then: "They have got a million men—*Cela sera dur, très dur,—long, très long.*"

The next day (August 15th) we were to start for our next destination. I did not know where we were going, but I started at 4.30 in a car with Brooke-Popham and Captain Buchanan, the signalling officer.[3]

It was a strange, uncanny drive. During the early part of the journey it poured with rain. Later it cleared up, and we drove along a straight road through acres of deserted country, rich cornfields all ready to be reaped, but nobody to reap them. Everything was silent and deserted. Women and children came out to look at us, to cheer us, but no men were to be seen anywhere. It was like driving through a country of

3. Afterwards killed.

the dead. At one place we were stopped, and a capable, but suspicious, woman, who spoke English perfectly, came out and cross-examined us narrowly in order to find out whether we were really Englishmen, as we said we were, or Germans in disguise. Several Germans, she said, had driven past already. However, we satisfied her. We arrived at 9 o'clock at Bussigny Station. There was no accommodation, but, after some talk, the lady who managed the Railway Restaurant allowed us to sleep on the floor in a room next to the buffet.

Early the next morning we went on to Maubeuge to get ready the aerodrome there. It was a long and busy day of incessant work from 5.30 a.m. to 8 p.m. We had to get billets and make everything ready. Brooke-Popham worked like a slave. He did everything himself.

He told me to draw a map of the aerodrome, but I didn't know what to mark on it. The result was picturesque rather than useful.

I dined in the town at the hotel. An immense crowd of officers, English and French, various billeting parties—one officer told me his life was spent in saying *Débarassez moi cette cour*, or pigsty or barn as the case might be. There was some excitement because a spy in French uniform had been arrested owing to the indiscretion of his remarks and the sharpness of the *demoiselle* behind the bar. It was a marvel how one got food, but one got it.

General Henderson and Colonel Sykes arrived at Maubeuge on August 17th.

Our complete staff consisted of General Henderson, Colonel Sykes, Chief of the Staff, Major Salmond, who looked after operations (G), Colonel Brooke-Popham, D.A.A. Q.M.G., who dealt with the transport, Captain Barrington-Kennett, the adjutant, who was responsible for personnel, discipline, etc., (A), and Major Cordner, the medical officer.

Besides these there was a wireless officer, Lieutenant Lywood, a signalling officer, Captain Buchanan, and myself; and a French liaison officer, Prince Murat.

Our office and mess consisted of a little tin shed at the Aerodrome, on one of the walls of which there was an enormous French map.[4] Near the aerodrome there was a large brick French airship shed, containing two airships.

The squadrons arrived, and I had my first experience of billeting—with Cogan.

---

4. We were foolish enough to leave it behind.

We measured rooms to see how many men could sleep on one floor. In the afternoon an officers' fatigue party was summoned. We took off our tunics and hurled boxes on to a lorry; what for I don't know. We dined in the mess for the first time. The menu consisted of warmed, or, rather, tepid bully beef and biscuits, whisky and sparklets. It was incredibly nasty.

I slept on the aerodrome in my valise.

On the edge of the aerodrome there was a small *estaminet*. Therein the early dawn I used to get a cup of French coffee as the mess coffee left a great deal to be desired.

I went to the French Staff Headquarters at Maubeuge to get various staff orders for the day, fodder for horses, billets, etc. I had a long conversation with one of the staff officers. He showed me the situation on the map. He said the war would be a very short war. I said that up to now wars had always got longer and longer, for instance, the South African War and the Manchurian War. He said that was because those wars were fought in countries where there were very few railways. But in a country of this kind where there was a network of railways a long war, he said, would be impossible. In spite of this, he was not particularly optimistic. The impression was that the Germans were coming on in heavy formation against the line of Namur, which was being very lightly held by the French owing to the extreme strength of the position. It was hoped that the Germans would come up against us and take a knock.

Someone suggested that we should get a piano for the mess, which shows that we expected to be a long time at Maubeuge.

On Wednesday, August 19th, I was woken up early by the sound of voices. A quarrel was going on—a quiet, slow, deliberate quarrel between the mess cook and one of the mess servants. It proceeded in slow waves till it almost reached a culminating crisis. Then it would subside and begin all over again. Every now and then the crisis, when it came to blows, seemed to be on the verge of being reached, especially when one of the quarrellers said: "In my regiment," and the other (who was an ex-Coldstream Guardsman) answered: "In *your* regiment!" in a tone which would have exasperated St. Simon Stylites; but the crisis never was reached.

Forage was wanted for horses. It was said that it was impossible to get it, and that we should have to scour the villages. I went to the French H.Q. in the town, and a man gave me a pink ticket which got us all that was necessary.

The weather was fine and hot. There was no excitement. Life was like a cheerful picnic. People talked of being in Germany soon. I met Basil Blackwood in the town of Maubeuge, and we dined together. He told me about the time he had had getting over from England to France in the Intelligence Corps. The manual labour was terrific, he said. Four or five of the other people who had been in the same situation as himself eventually struck, and complained to the officers. The officers asked them if they had any complaints. They said "yes," and detailed their grievances. They were at once sent home. Basil was asked also if he had any complaints. He said "None whatever," and he remained. He intended to exchange into the cavalry.

The days were spent so far as I was concerned in buying every sort of conceivable article: clothing, food, maps, wood, fodder, cloth for landing T's. In one of the shops a Frenchwoman alluded to B.K. to me as *Monsieur votre fils*. A girl in one of the shops gave me a little medal to wear round my neck.

A mechanic came from Renault's to look at the Renault engine. I interpreted. Something was wrong with a sparking plug. What is the French for a sparking plug? *Bougie*. I found this out before he came— as it is impossible to guess the French for sparking plug if you don't know it.

On Sunday, August 23rd, we heard guns firing in the morning and the afternoon.

Murat, who had driven to Namur, said it was being heavily shelled. Lywood showed me some of the intercepted German wireless. In the midst of a long cipher message there occurred a short poem:

*Immer leste*
*Ist es beste*
*Schlagen feste,*
*An die weste.*

Further on came the sentence, *Ich bin müde.*

In the afternoon I went out into the fields, and we heard the noise of guns distinctly—the pilots said that villages were on fire—Louvain is reported to be burning—somebody (not in the R.F.C.) is reported to have said it must have been a haystack.

CHAPTER 3

# The Retreat and the Advance

*August-September,* 1914.

On Monday, August 24th, early in the morning, between five and six, I woke up and heard somebody talking to Brooke-Popham about the fighting. The somebody said that *they* had gone back.

"Who—the Germans?" asked Brooke-Popham.

"No," said the other man, "*we* have gone back."

I went to the little *estaminet* and found the girl, who looked after it, in a great state of trepidation. "Were we going to leave them?" Yes. But we would come back? We hoped so. At 9 o'clock we got orders to leave. I went with Brooke-Popham to Birlaimont in the Daimler at the head of a great line of transport lorries and light tenders. The lorries were of all shapes and sizes—one came from Maple's. It was black, and had Maple painted on it in large gilt letters. Brooke-Popham chose an aerodrome, and the lorries came charging down the road into it: one went into the ditch. Scarcely had the arrangements begun to take shape when we got orders to leave and to go to Le Cateau. We arrived at Le Cateau about four in the afternoon, and established an Aerodrome there outside the town. I had had nothing to eat all day.

General Headquarters were at Le Cateau.

I went to see Guy Brooke, who was on Sir John French's Staff, and he gave me some poached eggs. He was busy ciphering a telegram. Later in the evening I went into the town. Everybody was gathered together at a café.

We slept, and when I say we, I mean dozens of pilots fully dressed, in a barn on the top of and underneath an enormous load of straw.

We spent an expectant morning at Le Cateau. Everybody was quite cheerful, especially the pilots.

On this day there was the first fight in the air. A German machine was brought down. There were two other fights beside this, and Harvey-Kelly brought down a German, who got out of his machine, chased him in the wood and shot him.

A German aeroplane flew over us quite low. Everybody fired at it. Nobody hit it.

Some French cavalry arrived. They bivouacked on the road and spent the whole morning there. We were standing by.

I went to the commander-in-chief's house to see Guy Brooke. He made me stay for luncheon. In spite of the disquieting symptoms of the situation, Sir John French seemed to be in good spirits. They were all packed up and ready to go.

In the afternoon we started for St. Quentin, and arrived there between 4 and 5. We occupied a small house with a garden, which was stocked with sunflowers, and we slept in the misty garden. There was nothing for dinner because the people who managed the mess forgot to buy the food. I went to G.H.Q. with David Henderson. He went inside and I waited at the door of the hall of the hotel which G.H.Q. had occupied. The door was guarded by a Scottish sentry in a kilt. Streams of people came in and out—with passes. It was raining. I had got on a Burberry. Presently a fat man with curly black hair came along in khaki without any badges of rank. The sentry stopped him and asked for his pass. The fat man got angry, and said he didn't need to show a pass. By his intonation, gesture, expression, diction and handling of the English language I perceived he was . . . not English. He didn't say who he was, but he gave us all to understand he was a man of immense importance. The Scottish sentry was quite inflexible, and wouldn't let him go in if he refused to show his pass.

He tried to force his way past. The sentry interposed his solid body. This made the fat man explode with rage. He said: "Do you know who I am?"

Then I—no doubt unwisely—intervened. I said: "The sentry is quite right to ask for your pass." His wrath was then diverted to me.

"Who was I butting in? Was I an officer?"

"Yes I was."

"He didn't believe it."

"Did I know who he was?" The sentry then tried to calm him, and patting him on the back said: "Don't take on so."

"How dare you touch me?" said the fat man. "You think I'm a private—I'm not a private."

I said (still unwisely): "There is not the slightest danger of your be-

24

ing mistaken for a British private."

This made him more angry than ever, and he said he would have me sent back to the base. But he did show his pass.

B.K. slept next to me. In the middle of the night somebody woke him up to do something. He woke up and stood up automatically and said: "I will do it."

The next morning (August 26th) General Henderson came back from Headquarters saying that everybody was intensely gloomy, unnecessarily so, he said.

One officer had come up to him with a very long face and said: "Cambrai has fallen." He answered: "What has it fallen on to? "He himself was absolutely calm, and kept everybody else calm. He never showed the slightest sign of anxiety for one single moment. Some of the pilots reported columns of Germans miles long, and said their maps were black with lines showing columns of German troops.

A great chase at the aerodrome took place after a woman spy, whose conduct was thought to be suspicious. She was not caught, however.

The afternoon was rainy, and we started for La Fère. We arrived there late in the evening. I drove with B.K. He was intensely depressed. He had heard, so he said, bad news. The news was not so bad as he thought it was. He thought the Guards had been defeated. "This has never happened in history," he said. "They have never been beaten," but what he had really heard was the news of the splendid fight at Landrecies, which reached us in the vague garbled form of a rumour of a big defeat.

The pilots landed all their machines in the rain without a crash. We were billeted in an hotel. As we arrived we met a party of French cavalry officers who were arriving also. They had had no news for weeks, and were rather astonished at our being where we were. I went to Burke's billet after dinner. When I got back, about 10.30, I found Brooke-Popham asleep on the stairs. I said: "Surely you have got a room?"

"Oh, it doesn't matter," he said. I went upstairs and found that his room had been appropriated by two of the drivers. I turned them out. They said they thought it was too good to last, and Brooke-Popham had a night's rest in a bed.

On Thursday (August 27th) we started at 6 o'clock in the morning and halted just outside La Fère along the road. Pilots landed with their maps showing long black lines of German troops on every road. The remains of a broken division was said to be arriving. It did arrive, and it was supplied with food by our transport officer, St. John. How he did this was a miracle. These men arrived in a state of the greatest exhaustion, but it was curious how quickly they recovered. One man, who seemed to be in a state of utter collapse, as soon as he had been given some food, produced a small hand looking-glass, which he put up on the lorry and began to shave. As soon as he had shaved he said he felt quite restored. I spent the day guarding a small new portmanteau which was full of gold, and which belonged to Brooke-Popham. A machine crashed in a turnip field.

A naval officer, who was attached to us, walked up and down the road saying we would sell our lives dearly.

That morning we realised the full seriousness of the situation. Rumours kept flying in that the whole of the British Army had been surrounded.

That morning, up to half-past ten, I expected to see German helmets coming over the edge of the turnip field every moment. Towards midday more reassuring news came, I know not where from.

At the end of the road there was a village and a *château*. The *château* was looked after by an old caretaker, who was most inhospitable. He consented, however, to let the general have some coffee early the next morning.

On Friday (August 28th) we started at four in the morning for Compiègne. I went in Murat's car. As soon as we arrived we went to see the Mayor, and Murat got us billets in a school: about the best billets in the town.

We had luncheon at the hotel, and went up to the aerodrome afterwards, which was on the top of the hill beyond the railway. This was inconvenient, because one was held up at the level crossing. In the evening Colonel Sykes told me to go and order dinner for him and the general at the hotel at 8. At 6.30 I asked for transport to do this. B.K. said he would take me. We started, but just as we were starting it was reported that some troops—some of the stragglers whom we had picked up at La Fère—had set their hut on fire. So we went down to the bottom of the ground, and B.K. harangued the men most effectively. But this all took time. Then we were held up at the level crossing. The result was by the time we got to the hotel we were late. It was crowded, and with great difficulty I got a table. We had a very late dinner. General Huguet, the head of the French mission, attached to G.H.Q., was sitting at one of the tables. It was said one could tell the state of affairs by whether his face was gloomy or not. I thought it was more cheerful. It was settled that I was to go to Paris the next day with Brooke-Popham. Our school was crowded with pilots, who were in tearing spirits.

The next day (August 29th) I went with Brooke-Popham to Paris. We went to Bleriot's firm and bought a machine, to the Gnome factory, and to the Embassy. We also went to Daimler's. Northcourt, the driver, wanted some "sleeves." What was the French for "sleeves "(the sleeves of a Daimler car)? Not *manches*. I didn't know and Northcourt didn't know, but the man in the factory understood by his gesture and expression that he wanted "sleeves," and produced them. (The word turned out to be *manchon*). Such is the free-masonry of craft. Language between two of the same craft is quite superfluous. We also bought some tyres and some car headlights, which Brooke-Popham paid for in gold, to the intense astonishment of the shopman. "*Les Anglais sont épatants*," he said. People in Paris were entirely without news. They had no idea where we were. They thought we were still at Mons. We went to the Magasin du Louvre to buy some things, and when I thanked the lady who was serving us for the trouble she had taken to get us what we wanted, she said: "*C'est nous au contraire, Monsieur, qui vous remercions*."

While we were away the Germans dropped the first bomb of the war on our aerodrome. It was a little tiny bomb, which did not do any damage at all. It fell quite close to my valise.

The next morning (August 30th) we started from Compiègne in the morning mist, and before starting we waited a long time at the roadside. A regiment of French Territorials was also waiting. One of them said it was absurd for the English to have sent troops to France. This started a vehement argument. I was very hungry and one of the French soldiers gave me some wine.

After a long and dreary wait in the cold mist, I started with Brooke-Popham in the Daimler car, and we halted about n o'clock at a tableland overlooking a small village called Sailly, which nestled below in the valley.

This tableland B.P. said would be the aerodrome, and we carried sheaves of corn about and made the necessary arrangements.

In the meantime the mist had lifted and the sun had come out. I walked down from the plateau in the valley to the village with a sergeant, who it appeared had been educated at Odessa and spoke Russian. Never have I seen a more lovely village, with its little white houses basking in the August sunshine. Was there any water? Yes, there was a beautiful spring. A labourer came from a cottage and invited me to his midday meal.

He gave me an omelette, some soup and some cider. It was delicious. I went back to the plateau, and we had just got the camp fires burning, ready to cook the men's dinners, when they arrived, and everything ready for the reception of the squadrons, when we were told to go off at once. We drove through beautiful woods, and the people threw flowers and fruit at us. This latter gift was of a dangerous kind, because an apple which hits you when you are driving in a fast Daimler is an unpleasant missile if it strikes your cheek.

We drove on and on till it grew dark. We were bound for Senlis. This was not easy to find, and we were heading the whole line of transport, and we had to shepherd it to its destination. B.P. had to go on ahead, and so as to ensure the transport not going astray, he took with him a small party of men, shedding one at a time at every crossroads, with instructions to tell the transport to go to the right or to the left as the case might be. In spite of this, at one crossroads the man told the transport to go to the right when he should have told it to go to the left, so we had to go back, catch it and get it on to the right road again.

It grew dark, and a large moon rose over the misty fields. The poplars looked spectral, and the landscape had the silver witchery of a Corot picture. During the day we had said several times:

"Fancy being at war on a day like this! "and now we said: "Fancy being at war on a night like this!"

We did not get to Senlis till 8.30.

I went into the town to get some food. In one of the small hotels, which was burnt two or three days later by the Germans, I found a lot of pilots having dinner, and among others Harvey-Kelly, Walrond, and Corballis.

I dined with Walrond and Corballis at a little table.

Harvey-Kelly wanted a glass, so he asked the lady in charge of the hotel for a *profonde assiette pour le vin,* pronounced to rhyme with bin. She understood.

He said he had great difficulty with the French language. He had wanted to buy a looking-glass, he said, and had been sent to a shop for stained glass windows, having used the word "*vitraille.*" A lady at the table said to a French officer: "Dis *donc, Hubert, as-tu eu des aventures en aeroplane?*' This tickled Corballis, who christened me "Hubert" on the spot.

I slept at the hotel at Chantilly.

The next morning (August 31st) I got up at 6 and went back to Senlis, in a squadron tender. I bought a bell for the mess at Senlis, a beautiful brass resounding bell.

In the afternoon we started with Colonel Burke and Captain Crosbie. I was given a map and told to direct the proceedings. I didn't know how to read a map. At the first crossroads I was appealed to. I looked wise and made a rapid decision. It was the wrong road, and after much parleying and going backwards and forwards, stopping and inquiring at many villages, we at last got to Damartin and thence on to Juilly, where we established ourselves in an ecclesiastical college, a large building in a large garden.

After a peaceful day at Juilly and a nice bathe in a great pond which was in the college grounds, in the evening (September 1st) there was a sudden panic. About half-past nine the whole of Headquarters, away at Damartin about two miles from where we were, got the alarm that they were cut off by the Germans, and started off at full speed with, as Harvey-Kelly put it, a motor cyclist looping the loop in front of their Rolls-Royce cars.

The panic began in the evening. I was sent down to the School to fetch the General's kit in his car. There I found his servant and Colonel Sykes' servant having a gorgeous tea. I told them we must go at once. The kit was put in the car, but Colonel Sykes' servant evidently had some more things he wanted to bring and said he must fetch them. I said I couldn't wait any longer. Colonel Sykes' servant said he supposed it didn't matter, but the things he wanted to fetch were important despatches. He went to fetch them and came back with them. The important despatches consisted (I noticed) of several tins of jam and some potted meat.

The question was what was to happen to the Flying Corps. The machines could not fly at night then. There was nobody to guard us. Finally a troop of North Irish Horse were sent to look after us, and some French Territorials. The aerodrome was in a field by some crossroads. Troops were disposed so as to defend it. On one road Murat's car was placed. He put on his helmet, which he only did on great occasions. The helmet was shorn of its splendour by having a cloth covering it. He stood next to it all night, armed to the teeth. We lay down by some stones in the road. We were armed to the teeth also. I had a revolver but no rifle, but B.K. said "I will defend you." Some of the North Irish Horse kept on champing up and down this road all night and disturbing us. One of them kept on treading on me. *Uhlans* were supposed to be about three miles off. In the middle of the night a lady arrived in the village with a large bag, which was flung down on the road. This, she said, was the post. "*La Poste*"—and she disappeared. No Germans appeared in the night. The German cavalry, as it turned out afterwards, were themselves cut off. When the dawn came we looked rather bedraggled, and Salmond's face was white as chalk from the dust which he had gathered sleeping on the road.

We started the next morning (September 2nd) as soon as it was daylight. We arrived at a place called Seres. General Henderson and myself had luncheon in a farmhouse with a prosperous family. Near the house was a beautiful, well-stocked garden, full of fruit and flowers. It was a pleasant hot September day. There was a smell of cider in the air. We had an excellent luncheon, omelettes and delicious Burgundy. A great discussion was going on between the different members of the family. A fat old man with a beard, with the assistance of his wife and cousin, was trying to persuade his mother-in-law, the old lady to whom the house belonged, to go away. The old lady said she had been through the 1870 War and that she considered one ought to stay in one's house till the end. Householders and priests should never, she said, desert their posts.

The son-in-law said this was ridiculous, and everything was packed up in a great hurry and a cart was harnessed. At the end they persuaded the old lady against her will that she must really go. It is not, they said, like in 1870. The Germans are much worse than they were then, and they are now five miles off. They will burn the village, everything. It would be madness to stay. "*Les Prussiens*," he said, "*déferlent comme une vague*" (are unfurling like a wave). The old lady gave in to their arguments, and when everything was packed and the cart was harnessed, she went out by herself and sat in the garden—the well-stocked, pleasant, prosperous garden in which the fruit trees were all laden with fruit—and she sat on a seat, and as she looked about she laughed bitterly, her face grim and scornful under her neat black bonnet.

In the afternoon I went for a very long drive with Brooke-Popham to look for a possible aerodrome. At one place where we stopped an old woman came out of the house and greeted us in German. "*Wie geht es?* she said. In the evening a Zeppelin was seen in the distance and chased, but in vain.

The next morning I drove with B.K. to Paris. We passed great entrenchments and masses of troops. I went to the Embassy and saw the ambassador, who told me he was thinking of burning the archives preparatory to leaving Paris. I also went to a bank, where everyone was intensely pessimistic. We got back late at night not to Seres, but to a place called Touquin. The aerodrome lay between two villages, Touquin and Pesarches. In the village of Touquin we occupied a little garden, a *jardin de curé* full of flowers. There we slept in our valises.

The next morning (September 4th) news came from the air of the south-eastward move of the German troops. General Henderson said to me, as we walked up and down the garden: "In twenty years' time people will be lecturing at the Staff College and instancing this move—that is to say, the moving of an army from one front across to the front of another—as one of the great mistakes of the war."

News also came that the Germans were preparing a raid on the Flying Corps in armed motor-cars. We packed up and left hastily and went to Melun. The population of the village were extremely alarmed at our departure. We tried to reassure them, but they said the Germans would be there and the place would be destroyed.

We slept in a field near the aerodrome, just outside the town. In the middle of the night it poured with rain. My valise proved to be quite rainproof, but B.K. and Salmond were soaked.

We established our headquarters in a little house at the end of the aerodrome. When I say house I am grossly exaggerating. It was a passage open to the four winds with a yard behind it and a road in front of it. It was full of flies, and dirty linen was being washed in the yard, making a terrible smell. There was no door. A small child in a field hard by kept on playing a tin trumpet until Murat could stand it no longer and went and took his trumpet away. He then started to scream, and continued to scream for the rest of the day.

The squadrons were billeted in an empty girls-school in the town. There I found a comfortable and quiet bedroom.

The next morning (Sunday, September 6th) was the day the battle of the Marne began.

General Henderson said that the tune of a *Te Deum* kept on ringing in his head.

Although the battle had begun, to us it was a day of waiting. At 6.30 in the evening we had a general parade, and Legions of Honour were distributed to the pilots and medals to the mechanics.

I slept again in the girls-school, where some of the squadrons were billeted. A pillow fight on a gigantic scale took place. The pilots dressed themselves up in the girls' night shirts, and one of the dormitories was invaded from the outside by a herd of pilots and, though valiantly defended, it was finally taken.

The next day we moved in the afternoon back to Touquin. Since our departure it had been occupied by the Germans. We had a new house. The shops had been looted, but no atrocity had been committed.

On September 8th I went to Paris with B.K. to get some maps from the French War Office. The French Government had gone: the Embassy also, except the Ambassador's coachman who refused to leave Paris. We had luncheon at a restaurant. Sitting next to us was a man in a French uniform who plied us with questions. He asked whether the English officers had suffered heavy casualties. He also asked whether we considered there was any truth in the rumour of the arrival of the Russian troops in Flanders. I said: "In war one must believe everything and—nothing." This rumour was at that moment current everywhere. Some colour seemed to be lent to it in Paris by the arrival of a great many Russian immigrants, and outside the War Office there was a large notice written in Russian telling Russians to go to the right or to the left.

The officer who sat next to us said that his mother was English, and came from Birmingham. He said Von Kluck's move was admirable, "*d'une audace énorme.*" He spoke French with an accent. He said he was employed at the Paris H.Q., but this, as we afterwards learnt, was not true. After the first few minutes' conversation I was convinced that this man, although wearing a tight-fitting, light-blue French tunic, was not a Frenchman. In the first place, a Frenchman whose mother vaguely comes from Birmingham is an oddity. In the second place, he was a gross feeder. He ate a cold *pâté* in hunks. In the third place, he protested too much, and his questions were not the kind of questions a French Staff officer would ask.

He asked us, for instance, if we knew Colonel Stewart, who had been imprisoned in Germany for espionage, and he supplemented the question by asking whether, when Colonel Stewart had been arrested he really was spying. We said no, it was only an in- stance of the crass stupidity of the German General Staff, which he must know was the stupidest in the world. (Colonel Stewart happened at that moment to be in Paris, and we had seen him that morning at the French H.Q.). After the conversation had lasted a few moments I conveyed my suspicions to B.K., who caught on without raising an eyelash, and then we had great fun. We both of us with one accord, and without consulting each other (which in the circumstances would have been, of course, impossible), set about to make him angry. This we did by talking about naval matters and the German fleet. We told him we were sincerely sorry for the German fleet, and that it must indeed be a bitter humiliation to every German sailor to think that the *Goeben* had been obliged to slink for shelter to the Turks. We said that the British fleet was not only superior to the German fleet in quantity but in quality. In fact, we said a string of things which were calculated to annoy a German, but which, if he were pretending to be French he would have to agree with.

He did not seem to like it at all. He got up presently and left. We then asked the proprietor of the cafe about him. He told us that the night before our friend had got very drunk and had expressed violent pro-German sympathies, and had abused everything French, and expressed the greatest contempt for the French nation. So that even if he was not a German he was certainly not a good citizen. We reported the matter to Headquarters, and found that no man of his name or use was employed where he had said he was employed at the H.Q. in Paris.

In the evening we arrived back at Touquin. All this time our mess had got nastier and nastier. That evening there was scarcely anything to eat, and General Henderson struck, and said he could bear it no longer. The Mess President was deposed, and B.K. was made Mess President in his stead.

The next morning (September 9th) we moved to Coulomniers. This was an exciting moment, as it was the first tangible step in the advance. We were arriving at a place which the Germans had left in a hurry, and which bore all the outward and visible marks of a German occupation.

There was no food in the place. A great number of the shops had been looted, and some of them were gutted. Inscriptions in German, written in white chalk, were on the shutters. We were billeted in a large empty school, and the Aerodrome was outside the town on the top of a hill.

While I was waiting on the steps of the G.H.Q. a soldier came up to me and said he wanted some butter for General Snow, who had had a fall from his horse. He said there wasn't any butter to be had in the whole town, and when I asked him whether he knew the French for butter he said he did not. I went with him to a shop and we bought some butter together.

With some difficulty I raised some dinner for the general in a little hotel, which was kept by an old lady, who told us a great many stories about the Germans. She dwelt a good deal on their dislike for the English. "*Ah! ils ne vous aiment pas*," she said.

During the Manchurian War I used to carry with me a pocket edition of Dante. I began to read it at the beginning when I arrived in Manchuria, and I finished it in 1905 when the war came to an end.

I had the same book with me now, and at Coulomniers, the first night we got there, before going to sleep, I began to read it again in bed, and I made a rule that whenever I should begin I would read a whole *Canto*. I also made a second rule that I should only read it when I had absolutely nothing else more readable at hand. And I registered the hope that by the time I got to the end of the *Paradiso* the war would be over. As it turned out, by keeping to my rule I reached the end of the last *Canto* of the *Paradiso* the night before the Germans asked for an armistice, or rather the night the news of the German request reached Paris in 1918.

Every time I read a *Canto* I marked it with the date and place. I made this plan on September 9th, but I fell asleep before I had read two lines. It was not till the night of September 10th that I read and finished *Canto* 1 of the Inferno. That evening there was a gorgeous sunset, and out of the golden clouds an aeroplane appeared and did a slow spiral. It was the first time I had witnessed this magical performance.

We only stayed one day longer at Coulomniers. Our stay there was quite uneventful. All I remember about it, is that one felt vaguely hungry the whole time; General Henderson certainly never had enough to eat. He used to arrive at luncheon rather late, and by the time he got there everything had been wolfed up. Even the little back room in the hotel which we had discovered was not very liberal in its food supply. The only other thing I remember is catching sight of a bound copy of *Monte Christo* in the *Mairie*, and being seized by an insane longing to steal it. I did not steal it, however.

We left Coulomniers on September 12th. The Maple lorry, which carried all our Headquarters *impedimenta*, stationery, typewriters, etc., was always overloaded, as all the Headquarters clerks used to get into it or on to the top of it. On this occasion one clerk too many got into it and it broke down irrevocably just as we were starting.

We started in the morning and arrived in the afternoon at Fère-en-Tardenois, the new G.H.Q. The Aerodrome was beside a road, outside a village called Saponay. We were billeted in two villas just outside Fère-en-Tardenois.

These two villas were elegant little houses, full of pretty china and neat furniture, the sort of villa in which I imagined Madame Bovary might have lived.

The Germans had left them in an indescribable state of filth. They had not broken much, but they had emptied all the drawers, scattered all the clothes on the floor, and broken the children's toys to bits. The caretaker who looked after these houses told us they had been occupied by officers who, after drinking heavily, had left in a great hurry.

The work of cleaning and tidying them up was long and onerous, but it was successfully accomplished before dark. Many of the shops in the little town had been looted, and some of them bore on their shutters the word "*schonen*" written in chalk.

Food was difficult to get, and we obtained with difficulty a piece of horse from the butcher.

# Chapter 4

# Fère-En-Tardenois

*September-October,* 1914.

Here were a lot of wounded men everywhere in the neighbourhood, more than the transport of the R.A.M.C. could then deal with; and one doctor sent in to us on Sunday (September 13th) to know whether we could lend him any cars or lorries to take the wounded from a village to the hospital at rail-head. We were able to provide a motor-ambulance and two other cars besides. I drove with them and with our doctor to the village, which was about seven miles from our headquarters.

We reached the place where our help was needed; a white village basking in the heat and the peculiar stillness of a hot autumnal Sunday afternoon, broken only by the crowing of cocks and the buzzing of flies. There we found a large crowd of children and old men and women gathered together in the street outside a farmhouse and pressing round what was apparently an object of interest. This turned out to be two stretchers, on which were two bodies: two German soldiers, each covered with a blanket, their waxen faces covered with pieces of pink gauze.

I thought they were dead; but the doctor who met us, and who was in charge there, said they were severely wounded. In the yard of the farm and round about the gateway were groups of wounded English soldiers. The doctor suggested sending the two Germans off in our ambulance at once, as they were the two worst cases; but as they were lying still, and the English soldiers were impatient to get away, these were packed into the ambulance and the cars, which were sent off to the hospital and told to come back again as soon as possible.

We carried the two Germans into the yard. The doctors went into the farm. I spoke to one of the Germans in German.

He said he was very cold. Indeed, underneath his thin blanket he had but little on, and his chest was bandaged. He had been wounded in three places. The doctors came out again, and between us we lifted the two Germans up and put warm blankets beneath them and over them; but they still said they felt cold, so we settled to carry them into the stable where the horses were.

We carried the men through a barrier of restive, kicking cart-horses into an empty stall which formed the corner of the building, and laid the stretchers down upon the straw. They said they felt warmer. I sat down on the straw between the two stretchers. One of the men was fair, with blue eyes and yellow white skin. He looked dead, but for an occasional flicker of the eyelids. The other had been wounded in the head, in the forehead over the eye, as well as in the body. One of his eyes was swollen like a dark plum, and he looked as if he had been stung by a wasp. His head was bandaged. He was the worse of the two, and could hardly speak.

The conversation which follows came in short, faint sentences, with long pauses between them. The fair man said he was glad of the warmth after the cold they had been through—the cold and the wind of long marches at night with nothing to eat. The weather had seemed to us tropically hot all the week, but he had not felt this. He kept on murmuring that the cold had been terrible (*furchtbar*), terrible . . . . the marching terrible . . . the wind terrible. . . . He spoke in short sentences, and after every sentence relapsed into silence and shut his eyes. He asked if he would be taken to England. When I said yes, he said: "Is that certain? "(*Ist dass bestimmt?*)

I went to the doctor's and asked if I might give the men some tea. They said yes. I brought them some tea in a china cup with a spout. The fair man said:

"Has the doctor allowed it?" (*Hat der doktor dass erlaubt?*)

I said yes. They both drank a little. I sat down again between them. After a long silence, the fair man said: "*Sie sind ein sehr netter Herr.*" (You are a very nice man).

The other man opened his one eye, smiled, and said "*sehr nett.*"

Then there was another long silence. They shut their eyes. The fair man suddenly asked me if I was a soldier by profession. I said no. He said he was not a soldier either, but a post-office *employé* at Düsseldorf.

I said Düsseldorf was a pretty place.

He said "Yes, but life there is very dear," and he sighed.

I, for something to say, said:

"Life is very dear everywhere now, but dearer than everywhere in America."

"America! "said the fair man, and he heaved a deep sigh and stopped and shut his eyes.

"In America," I went on, "a dollar which corresponds to four *marks* doesn't go further there than one *mark* does in Germany."

The fair man opened his eyes and murmured:

"*Eine mark fünf und zwanzig.*" (One *mark* twenty-five). Then he shut his eyes once more. The ambulance came back. Both men were lifted into it. Neither of them spoke another word.

The next morning I went to the clearing hospital. Neither of the wounded Germans was there.

The squadrons were now comfortably established at Saponay:

No. 2 commanded by Major Burke; No. 3 by Major J. Salmond; No. 4 by Major Rawleigh; No. 5 by Major Higgins.

Most of the pilots were billeted in the village. One Squadron (No. 3) was billeted on the Aerodrome itself, the messes being in kind of dugouts made in haystacks.

Headquarters were billeted in the two little villas I have referred to already. I shared a bedroom with B.K. Our office was in a little tin house. Our chairs consisted of boxes. Everything was still primitive. We still expected to be perpetually on the move. In the meantime the battle of the Aisne was proceeding.

Warfare in the air was still in the gentleman-like stage, and I have a note in my diary under September 15th that No. 5 Squadron call the anti-aircraft gun (there seemed to be only one which gave them trouble in those days) *Archibald*. This was the origin of the word *archie* which was soon to be adopted by the British Army and to pass into the language.

The Headquarters of the First Corps were at Bourg; those of the second at Muret; and those of the Third at Ecurie. To go to a Corps Headquarters seemed in those days like going to a promised land. To reach Bourg you passed our gun emplacements, which were in position on a high plateau. We also had some advanced machines there, and one even had the chance of being shelled on the roads between this plateau and Bourg.

This September was a beautiful still golden month, and I used to spend a great deal of time with the squadrons. There was nearly always something which they wanted done. The mayor of Saponay gave a good deal of trouble at one time. He complained of the men stealing his fruit. He made difficulties about the billets. In fact, he complained of everything. Finally Murat, who was wonderful at bringing mayors to reason, dealt with him, and threatened that he would be court-martialled and shot, a fate which he was careful to point out had already overtaken several recalcitrant mayors. After that this mayor gave no more trouble.

We spent a good deal of time in buying provisions. There was no canteen in those days, and cigarettes were scarce. Sometimes one bought a turkey, sometimes a sheep. We used to get these from the neighbouring farms. One of them had been occupied by the Germans, who had evidently been satisfied with the inhabitants there as they had written on the door "*Gute Leute.*"

On September 18th the first experiments with dropping bombs from the air were made by Major Musgrave. One bomb was dropped, and it exploded but not exactly where nor how it was expected to explode.

Newspapers used to arrive fairly regularly, but we were very much in the dark as regards the general situation. I had no idea, for instance, there had been a big battle at Tannenberg, although I knew the Russians had suffered a reverse. We used to see the accounts of great victories in the German wireless, but in those days one paid no attention to that source of news. It seemed so extremely biased. Yet I have no doubt the greater part of it was accurate. Our optimism was rosy. The impression was that the Germans had bitten off more than they could chew (which was a correct impression), and that the war would probably be over in May.

On September 19th we heard that Rheims cathedral was on fire.

On the 20th I went to Epernay with B.K. to buy some wine. When we got into the town we drew up in a side street, and a French officer asked us to let him have an India-rubber tyre, which we did. He then asked us where we came from, and many other questions; where our General Headquarters were, etc., etc., and went away. We suspected him afterwards of not being a Frenchman.

We went to the Champagne factories. Being a Sunday nearly everything was shut. We got in, however, to one of them and bought some wine. Epernay, they told us, had been occupied by the Germans, but there had not been much looting. They were only there three days, and left in a hurry, but, said the man who was showing us around, they knew exactly what to ask for—the best brands—and exactly where to find what they wanted. They would not look at the inferior wine, but they went straight up to the shelves where the good wine was and said "Give us that."

In the meantime the Flying Corps was growing. When it had flown to France it had left behind a nucleus consisting of an administrative Wing, which was to form a larger force. This administrative Wing was in charge of Major Trenchard, at Farnborough, and he afterwards told me that all the nucleus consisted of was one clerk and one typewriter, a confidential box with a pair of boots in it, and a lot of unpaid bills incurred by various officers in the Flying Corps during the rush to the front. Major Brancker was working at the War Office. Lord Kitchener was already planning and legislating for a force of fifty squadrons. It is impossible to make people understand now how fantastic that seemed then.

Lord Kitchener's Army seemed the most wild of dreams. "Where," people used to say, "are you going to get the officers from?" And the expansion of the Flying Corps seemed to the outsider the experiment of a lunatic.

Nevertheless, General Henderson had decided on a policy of expansion, and for that purpose, in order to form new Squadrons in England, some of our officers were sent to England. Longcroft, who was attached to No. 2 Squadron as an extra officer, left us I think, on the 23rd, and I remember his departure causing the greatest consternation in our small circle. Of course we knew nothing of what was going on at home, nor of the policy that was in the minds of the high authorities. Everyone was indignant. Some people said: "They are trying to start a rival show in England. They are taking away our best men."

But in small ways the expansion began to make itself felt. Two wireless officers came to us and photographs were taken from the air. Our mess soon became too big for the little villa where we had our meals, and B.K. decided to split it up into two messes and make an A Mess and a B Mess. The members of the prospective B Mess were disinclined to shift, and although the arrangements were made, and the orders given, the days passed, and nothing happened. At last, on September 23rd, B.K. told the Mess sergeant to lay dinner for B. Mess in the second villa which we occupied, and A. Mess were able to sit down to dinner eight instead of sixteen in one small room.

B. Mess, however, were at first a little bit sore.

On September 23rd masses of French troops streamed through the village, and passed the aerodrome. They had marched over sixty miles, and were in splendid form, although hungry for tobacco. Just about this time it was reported that two Germans were hiding in a forest in the neighbourhood. Murat organised an expedition to hunt them and round them up, but he came back without any Germans but with a brace of wild duck. He used to say that our G.H.Q. was not properly guarded, and that he would undertake to kidnap Sir John French and the whole of his staff with one armoured car.

There was a rumour one day—whether it was true I don't know— that someone had walked in to G.H.Q. one evening while the staff were at dinner and stolen all the papers he could lay hands on.

In those days, before the trench barrier stretched from Switzerland to the sea, it was not impossible for Germans to drive about behind our lines, and one day a party of Belgian officers, who had spent a little time near our Aerodrome, were discovered at the next place they halted, Villers-Cotterets, which was occupied by the French, by mere accident not to be Belgians at all but Germans, and were shot.

I remember a curious incident which happened at this time. A detachment of French Red Cross doctors visited the aerodrome one afternoon. We talked to them. They looked round, and one of them came across a copy of *The Daily Telegraph* which was lying about. *The Daily Telegraph* described the battle as going well for the English and badly for the Germans. One of the doctors took it up and read it. He flew then into a violent passion and said he had always thought English newspapers spoke the truth, and it was quite untrue to say that the Germans were in such a bad position as this. The whole thing was grossly exaggerated. The doctors then went away in a huff. There was no further explanation of this incident. It is unlikely that the whole of this detachment could have been Germans in disguise, but why they should have been indignant at anti-German literature I do not know.

During all this time we used to hear little of the German fliers, but one day (September 25th) a German machine flew over Fère-en-Tardenois, and was fired at without effect.

A tragic incident occurred I think about this time, but I have no definite record of the date. One of the pilots was practising signalling and dropping lights. He was flying quite low over our trenches backwards and forwards. The machine, as so often occurred later during the war, was thought to be behaving in a "suspicious manner" and was fired at by our troops, and before the men could be stopped firing it was brought down amid the cheers of the men. When the machine crashed they saw that the pilot was an Englishman and that he was dead.

On Monday (September 28th) there was great excitement in the camp. Georges Carpentier arrived in a car to get some petrol. The mechanics were extremely excited. I asked one of them if he knew Carpentier. He said: "No, but I have studied his career." He was invited to dinner by B. Mess.

B.K. had got news two days previously that his brother, in the Oxfordshire and Buckinghamshire Light Infantry, was missing and wounded, and wanted to go to an advance hospital to get news. He also wanted to find out something about some anti-aircraft guns. On the same day that Carpentier visited us I went with B.K. to Braine, Bourg, and beyond. On the way we passed Sir Douglas Haig on horseback with his escort. He stopped us and asked where we were going. B.K. satisfied him. After a long and very round-about drive we came to a small field hospital. B.K. went in and I waited outside.

As I was waiting a shrapnel shell burst in the middle of the road we had just left. After a short interval a second shell burst in the field beyond the hospital, and then a third somewhat shorter. B.K. came out. I said, laughing, "We are being shelled." Then I saw he had just received news that his brother had been killed. He had been buried in the little cemetery a few yards off. We went to look for the grave and found it. His grave, with some others, was just freshly dug; flowers on it and a neat wooden cross. B.K. saluted. I left him there alone two or three minutes by himself; then we drove away. A third shell burst on the road.

Looking back on those days at Fère-en-Tardenois, one remembers the time passing in a golden haze. Never was there a finer autumn. And the French landscape, and especially that region of France where we were then, seemed to bask in the richness and the tints of that fine September.

The little gardens were laden with fruit, and the reaped fields were bathed in a calm light. How, one used to wonder, were they reaped, and by whom? The country seemed deserted, save for an old woman here, a child there, and a stray white horse, and yet silently and surely the work was done. In the distance you saw brown ricks, and great long shadows played over the plain.

I remember the heat of the stubble on the Saponay Aerodrome: pilots lying about on the straw; some just back from a reconnaissance some just starting, some asleep, some talking of what they would do after the war; the blazing farmhouses where we used to buy eggs, and chickens, and once a goose. The smell of cider; the courtesy of an old farmer's wife, the proud scorn which lit her face when she said that whatever the Germans might destroy they were incapable by their nature of building a gable or an arch like those of her farm or carving a panel like those in her kitchen. "*Ils n'ont pas de goût!*"

There was a *château* quite close to Fère-en-Tardenois, where we went one day, one of the saddest and most beautiful places I have ever seen. In the garden there were great avenues of trees and a large Renaissance viaduct. Everything was buried in gold and crimson leaves; and Death seemed to be holding a quiet revel there, like a king who commands a private performance in a secluded retreat for a few friends, far away from the theatres of carnage where his public actors were performing daily with so much sound and fury.

In the church at Fère-en-Tardenois, Mass used to be said to a congregation huddled in the chancel, while the aisle was full of wounded and a faint smell of iodoform pervaded the place, and a hospital orderly made the Cure laugh by saying the place would be much better ventilated if the stained glass windows could be broken.

I remember the clicking of the typewriters in our little improvised office, and a soldier singing "Abide with me" at the top of his voice in the kitchen. And then the beauty of the Henry Farmans sailing through the clear evening, "the evening hush broken by homing wings," and the moonlight rising over the stubble of the aerodrome, and a few camp fires glowing in the mist and the noise of the men singing songs of home.

# CHAPTER 5

# The Move to the North and St. Omer

*October-November,* 1914.

The first time I had a rumour of a move northwards was on September 30th. A little French boy told me in a shop in the village that the British Army was about to move northwards and would probably go. He said he had heard this on the highest authority. During the next few days the news became more definite.

On October 2nd we knew the move to the coast had begun. On October 7th, a German left a card on us, *pour prendre conger,* from the air. He dropped a bomb on the aerodrome. It fell in the field, on the opposite side of the road to where No. 5 Squadron were established. Theoretically, it was a beautiful shot, practically it hit a turnip. And this was the case with many bombing efforts in the future

Our move took place on October 8th. We got up at cockcrow, and the work of packing began. Everything was hurled into lorries. I remained behind with B.K., who toiled like a slave to get everything off. B.K. had very strong principles about leaving a billet as you found it. Here it was a case of leaving it in a state very different indeed from that in which we found it. We had found the billets—our two little villas—like pigsties—we left them spotless and dustless, with newspapers neatly folded up on the table. We started at 9 a.m. in the Daimler, and motored through Senlis and Clermont, where we had luncheon at a small hotel.

As we were getting towards Abbeville the car broke down. We were held up for hours, B.K. slaving and toiling on his stomach under the car, and as it grew darker and darker the driver got keener and keener on pulling every bit of the engine to pieces. Finally we were towed into Abbeville by an ambulance, and arrived after 8 and went to the Hôtel de France, thoroughly exhausted and hungry. We found the hotel crammed with officers, who had just finished dinner. I ordered dinner for B.K. and myself, and we were just going to begin to eat it when someone told B.K. he was wanted. Someone or something had gone astray, and, leaving his untouched dinner, he went out in search of it. We were billeted in the town in delightful panelled rooms near the cathedral. The room had curtained beds, polished tables and no electric light. An ideal bedroom.

The next morning we moved outside the town to a *château* called Moyenneville. The squadrons were billeted in Moyenneville Village, and there was an aerodrome close by. Our billet was an oblong red brick rather dilapidated *château*, which stood in a faded, rustling park and a dishevelled garden.

The trees were not yet bare, but all of them were red and yellow, and the garden was full of dead leaves. Inside there were dignified grey-panelled rooms, covered with old English sporting prints of racehorses.

I spent a day of unremitting shopping in Abbeville, and I have noted that on October 10th I bought 500 kilograms of wood, one field of potatoes, one pound of butter, one pot of honey, one pound of biscuits, three cheeses, three chickens, 10 pears, one brass alarm bell.

On Monday, October 6th, we got orders to move again. We got up at 6. The *concièrge* of the *château* made a great deal of fuss about some petrol which he said had been stolen. He was given some more petrol. We didn't start till 1. I went with B.K. and three pilots. We stopped at Hesdin and had luncheon at the hotel.

We arrived at St. Omer at 8.30, and took up our residence in a small *château* on the hill between the town and the aerodrome. We didn't expect to stay there long, so no real steps were taken to make ourselves comfortable at the start. The *château* was a modern *stucco* building, red and white. Downstairs there were two drawing-rooms, a dining-room, and one bedroom, and a small sitting-room. The small sitting-room was Colonel Sykes' office. One of the drawing-rooms was made into an ante-room, the other into the office. The bedroom downstairs was Brooke-Popham's. Upstairs General Henderson had one big bedroom and a small office. Salmond, B.K. and I shared a second, Murat had a third, and the fourth was to be occupied by other members of the staff.

We sadly overcrowded this house. In the office B.K. used to sit at one table (a card table), Salmond at another very rickety piece of furniture. Brooke-Popham had a second small card table for his work, which soon became littered with papers. The sergeant-major sat on a box in front of other boxes. A bevy of clerks filled the room. Each clerk had a typewriter, and each clerk's box had about a dozen candles stuck on to it burning and guttering. The atmosphere was quite solid. We thought on arriving that we were going to stop here a few days. As it turned out this little *château* was the R.F.C. headquarters until 1916, and again in 1917, and until the end of war it was always occupied by an R.F.C. staff.

The morning of the day we arrived, the Germans dropped a bomb right in the middle of the school occupied by G.H.Q., but before G.H.Q. arrived. The bomb knocked down Murat's cousin and an old lady. This, which must have been a pure accident, was talked about as an instance of the miraculous divination of the German Secret Service, and their uncanny knowledge of the movements of the British Army. The squadrons were established on a fine aerodrome on the top of the hill, once a steeplechase course, where there was still a tin Tellier shed. The four squadrons were drawn up in line along the road: No. 5, No. 4, No. 3, No. 2.

The first thing to do was to get all the billeting arrangements made, and for this purpose we went to see the Mayor of Longuenesse, a village just outside St. Omer; and Murat had several interviews with the owners of the small villas and *châteaux* that cluster round St. Omer, in one of which the notorious Wainwright spent a few weeks planning his most successful murder.

Directly we arrived at St. Omer the weather became damp and raw, and when I think of St. Omer now it seems to me like a city of perpetual damp and incessant rain.

On October 15th, a cold, grey day, I made the first of very many visits to Hazebrouck with General Henderson and Colonel Sykes. I waited in the square while they went into Corps H.Q. While I was waiting some lorries full of German prisoners drove past on their way to the station. One of the lorries halted. It was soon surrounded by an angry crowd, which began to boo and hiss, and someone began throwing things.

I addressed the crowd. "*Le Grand Napoleon a dit,*" I said, "*qu'il n'y a rien de plus lâche que de maltraiter les prisonniers.*" He may have said so. I hope he did.

In any case the effect on the crowd was immediate. I talked to one of the prisoners, a bearded Bavarian. He said our men treated them very well, but that they had been stoned by the crowd. He complained of the bitter injustice of this. "The allied prisoners," he added, "when they get to Germany are given cakes and even chocolate (*sogar shoko-lade*), and we are stoned. *Das ist unmenschlich.*" Then the lorry drove on to the station.

At St. Omer quite a new kind of life began for us. The war began to settle, although we were unaware of the fact, for when we got there the race to the sea was not over, and the battle of the Yser had not yet been fought. But everything became more regular; books used to arrive. And a great quantity of guests used to stream through the house. In fact, someone said our *château* was exactly like a *Dak* Bungalow, whatever that may be. It was certainly like a damp bungalow. Pilots, observers, staff-officers, administrative officers, experts, etc., used to arrive from London, and sometimes from Paris, and sometimes from the sky, and stay the night. They used to sleep on the floor of our bedrooms in their valises. Sometimes there were as many as five officers in one bedroom. It was no place for those who like privacy. Personally I enjoyed this perpetual ebb and flow of guests.

I shared, as I have already said, a bedroom with B.K. and Salmond, and we often had a guest or two sleeping on the floor. After going to bed we used to brew tea in a small kettle, and we used to talk and talk till late in the night. We used to get up about seven, and we always sang songs while dressing.

An interminable series of billet troubles soon began. A Flight of one of the squadrons lived in a little cottage which belonged to a man who was once a soldier in the Foreign Legion. He was an admirable housekeeper and an excellent cook, and he said he liked having the officers living there. "*Mais Oh! les ordonnances*," he used to say with a sigh.

One of the first and most serious of the billet troubles happened like this.

Some mechanics belonging to one of the squadrons had been billeted in an outhouse belonging to a villa inhabited by a local lady. The lady had sent a message to say that the men had left the building in a filthy state. This aroused the anger of B.K., and we set off to strafe the squadron in question. Before doing this we went to the billet. There we were met by the gardener's wife. We told her our errand. She at once said the story was untrue. The men had left the billet perfectly clean. She took us to see the billet, which was just as it had been left, she said, and was, as she said, perfectly clean. The whole thing was a piece of spite on the part of her mistress, "whose husband," she said, "had been taken to the war forcibly between two *gendarmes*."

We then went to interview the lady of the house. She repeated the story and the allegations, and said the squadron had left the place in a filthy state. Then she sent for the gardener as a witness to corroborate the story. Now a dramatic incident occurred. The gardener flatly contradicted his mistress and denied the whole story. So she stood convicted of deliberate slander against the Allies. She stamped her feet with rage, and we departed in dignity.

A few days later we had further trouble with this angry lady. Murat went with B.K. and myself to see her. The word *politesse* being mentioned, Murat said: "*Ce n'est pas une question de politesse, Madame, c'est la guerre.*" She did not like people being billeted there. I was reminded of Bonaparte-Wyes's poem:

*Dear Nicolas, dear Marie, I am quite*
*A seeming fixture in your villa white.*

This lady thought the officers were becoming seeming fixtures in her villa, and she resented the fact.

During all these days the battle of Ypres was going on, or rather, those operations which Sir John French speaks of as the "Battle of Ypres-Armentieres," which he says opened on the fifteenth of October.

One heard the news in snippets.

One day at luncheon General Henderson told us that three Germans, with a machine gun, had held up in a little house a great quantity of our men a whole morning. Finally, two of the Germans were killed, but the third went on fighting after he was covered with wounds, and succeeded in holding our men up till he at last was killed himself.

"He deserved to live," someone said.

"He deserved to die," said the general.

I remember also his telling us of some German volunteers who marched into the Yser arm in arm singing the *Wacht am Rhein*, and that the whole of the first wave of these boys was mown down. But a second wave of boys came on singing the second verse of the song, and they, too, were mown down. I see in Sir John French's book that this must have happened on October 23rd. On October 25th, St. Crispin's day, the anniversary of the battle of Agincourt, I went to Mass in the cathedral at St. Omer. One could not help thinking that Henry V had heard those very same words spoken in the very same way just before the battle of Agincourt. That battlefield was not an hour's drive from St. Omer. Now, in the cathedral, French and English soldiers were praying for victory against a common foe.

That same afternoon I went to one of the stationary hospitals in the town, and had some talk with a German prisoner who was being treated. He was a young medical student. He told me Warsaw had been taken. I knew this to be untrue, and said so. "Ah, you have not been told that yet," he said. He spoke at great length, and with great frankness about the war. He admired the British troops and the British equipment and the horses, the saddles, etc. He spoke slightingly of the French for wearing red trousers. He said it was fortunate that there would be no more British troops in great numbers; fortunate that conscription would not come about in England. Nor would it affect the question if it did, he added, as any child could see it was much too late in the day to improvise the *cadres*, let alone the units of a great army.

I did not argue the point. I said something about the Belgians. "*Dass sind nicht Menschen*," he said. (They are not human beings), and he told me strings of stories of atrocities committed by the Belgians on German soldiers. He was serenely and completely confident in the final victory of the Germans. This was the first and last time I had any conversation with a German officer throughout the war.

On the 28th of October, just after the second phase of the battle of Ypres had begun, I went with General Henderson to Ypres itself. No. 2 Squadron was established just beyond the town. The headquarters of the first Army were at the *château* of Hooge, and thither the general went. I waited for him in the garden. While he was inside, a German machine flew over and dropped a bomb in a field just behind the *château*.

There was at once a great racket of machine guns. Shortly afterwards a Morane-Parasol belonging to the French flew over. This was a newfangled machine in those days, and it was plentifully shot at, but luckily without effect. When the general had finished his business we drove into the town, and I went to see the Cloth-Hall and the Cathedral, which were still both of them intact. We had luncheon at an hotel, and I remember the General saying: "It's lucky the Germans were just too late to get to Ypres."

The next day I went to Dunkirk for the first time with Brooke-Popham. We visited a naval squadron. Carpentier was attached to them, and all defaulters were made as a punishment to box five minutes with him. This punishment combined being a great honour and privilege and hurting very much indeed.

In the meanwhile the operations at Ypres were becoming momentous. Sir John French says in his book that he regards the fighting during the period between October 27th and October 31st as more momentous and fateful than any which he directed during the time he was commander-in-chief. Turning to my diary I find nothing more exciting than this:

*Friday, October 30th—St. Omer.*—Another billet-drama. In a house belonging to two old maids near the aerodrome, where two officers are billeted, a cupboard has been broken open. B.K. and I went to investigate, and were treated to an immensely long Sherlock-Holmes-like story about a lock. We didn't make head or tail of the matter. Nothing of any value nor of any possible use to any man or woman appears to have been stolen, and the lock is to be repaired by the squadron.

*Saturday, October 31st.* I spent the whole day in the aerodrome. Dinner with No. 2. Squadron, B Flight,

On Sunday night B.K. and I dined at the Hôtel du Commerce. It was the first—and last time—he dined out during the whole period he was with us. Colonel Seely joined us, and told us he had spent the day with the French troops at Wytshaete, and that the shelling had been appalling. But he thought the crisis was over. He offered to take me out with him the next day. On that Sunday, November 1st, we knew at Headquarters that the situation was critical, but we none of us mentioned it.

The next day was a perfect Autumn day. We started about 9. Colonel Seely drove. I held the map and refused to give any definite opinion as to what was the right and wrong way. We drove to Cassel. From Casselhill the whole landscape looked like a mellow Dutch picture: the straight trees, the villages and the blue fields and plains bathed in calm, luminous sunshine. Colonel Seely said he thought the war couldn't last very long, because the different nations would get tired of paying the gigantic bill not only in money—for money, he admitted, never stopped a war beginning nor made it end—but in men and loss of property the bill was too big. I said I thought nations in this respect were like boys at a private school who suddenly said: "We are going to strike; we are not going to do a stroke of work today," but when the master came into the room they went on and all talk of strike was forgotten.

We drove through Poperinghe to a place about three miles from Dixmude. Dixmude was being shelled by the Germans, and defended by the incomparably gallant French Marine Corps. We halted near a small field hospital, which was established in an *estaminet*. The people asked us to put our car out of the way. In front, beyond a low field, men (marines) were lying in the trenches. There was a dull intermittent noise of shelling—and over Dixmude a rather more lively series of bursts.

We walked across a field into a small tumble-down house and went upstairs; but there was nothing to see, only the dull misty distance and occasional muffled noises; sometimes the crack of a rifle. We walked back to the *estaminet*. A Belgian officer arrived in a car and walked into the *estaminet*. A motor then turned up, heaven knows where from, bearing a lady, two chauffeurs, two doctors (Red Cross, English), and a boy scout. One of the doctors said he knew nothing about the lady or the other people. There were no wounded in the village, and the French marines begged us to take the cars out of the way, as this cavalcade attracted fire, which we did. The doctor wanted to go to Dixmude.

Colonel Seely borrowed a Belgian officer's car and took him there, leaving me behind. Colonel Seely brought the doctor back about ten minutes later. We went on past the French guns through a village which was deserted and empty, and where the church steeple had been hit by a shell. We had luncheon in the village. Then we went through the deserted country till we came to a French headquarters, where we interviewed a French General. He went out with us and walked across two fields. The trenches were occupied by cavalry; and I recognised and spoke to an officer whom I had last seen at Le Cateau. Colonel Seely said he wanted to go to Langemark. The French advised him not to.

As we were walking back across the field to the H.Q. office, which was in a cottage, a large Black Maria burst at some distant from us. "*Grosse Marmite*," said the French general. We went on to Langemark. We got there just after sunset. The place was deserted but for a French battery, whose officers were occupying the shell of a *château* next to the church. There was nothing left of the church except a cross and a tower. The churchyard was pitted with Black Maria holes. We went into the *château* and talked to the officers. They were cheerful. They said the Germans had been shelling them day and night, but lately had confined themselves to shooting at noontide and just before sunset. They told us some astonishing stories about hecatombs of dead Germans who had been mown down in the recent fighting.

There was one pit hard by, they said, which was filled with hundreds and hundreds of dead. The French trenches were not far from the *château*. We left these officers. We started to drive back with a man to guide us to show us the holes, as the road was full of holes. We reached the road we had come by, which led from one village to another. When we had driven up it, it was quite quiet. Now it was moonlight, and as we started to drive down this road the Germans began to shell it. The shells burst in the field beyond the road. Presently the road came to an end and we reached a village where there was another French headquarters. There we were arrested. The French thought Colonel Seely was a spy. Presently a French Colonel arrived from his dinner. I got out and showed him our papers. I said that Colonel Seely had been Minister of War.

"Oh, yes," said the French Colonel, "*Ulstaire.*" Then all was settled and we drove to Ypres, where someone told me my brother Hugo had been wounded. Thence we proceeded through masses of troops, which were moving backwards and forwards, home to St. Omer.

The next day I went to Poperinghe to try and find my brother in one of the hospitals there. The search was fruitless. I went to three or four hospitals, all of them crammed with wounded, officers and men. It was an inferno of suffering. A dark inferno, too. One man was moaning for more morphia. He had had one dose, and he had just got to the stage when nature imperatively cries out for another.

There was now a slight lull in affairs: the final phase of the first battle of Ypres lasting from November 11th-November 21st. Referring to my diary I find the following entries:

*Saturday, November 7th, 1914*—St. Omer.—Our transport officer went to get some coal this morning. He drove down to the place where there was coal and filled his lorry with it. Just as he had finished doing this the man who looked after the coal—to whom it belonged— an officer, arrived on the scene. Our T.O. said to him: "Can I give you a lift?" and he drove him on the box of the lorry which was full of his own coal, where he wanted to go to.

*Sunday, November 8th, 1914*—St. Omer.—Went to mass in the cathedral. Further billet now at the Red Villa, inhabited by the difficult lady. We went to see her in the morning—B.K. and I. While we were discussing bedrooms a German aeroplane flew over, white in the azure sky. The Archies fired at it—aimed carefully but missed it—and the lady, in a state of great excitement, called out: "*Ils ne l'auront pas, ils ne l'auront pas!*" Why?

Rather a solemn dinner.

At the end of dinner, in a pause of tense silence, one of the guests said: "I was the last man to leave Maubeuge."

"I was the first," I said, and this was true, because Brooke-Popham and I headed the great retreat.

*Monday, November 9th, 1914—St. Omer.*—Went to see the Mayor about a billet in the village of Longuenesse. We had words. On the floor of his drawing-room I found a German ten-*pfennig* piece, which I held up triumphantly. As I walked away from the village a *gendarme* came galloping after me to assure me that the mayor of Longuenesse was not a German spy. Further billet trouble at the farm.

Just about this time an exciting incident happened on the aerodrome. In the long line of transport which was drawn up along the aerodrome on a road fringing the top of a wooded hill, there was a closed lorry, which was then used as a bomb store, and was full of bombs. Bombs in those days were not the formidable instruments they became later. They were comfortable pocket bombs. One night, I forget at what time, a miscreant threw a live bomb at the bomb- lorry and it went off. The whole lorry did not blow up, but an explosion was caused, wounding, I think, five men, one of whom died in hospital. A court of inquiry was held, but the matter was never explained and the miscreant was never found.

A few days later someone threw a bomb through the bedroom window of one of the squadron billets at Bailleul, but no harm was done. We all went to the funeral of the man who had been killed by the bomb on November 10th. He was buried in the cemetery half-way up the hill beyond our garden. It was a grey, damp day, the grave was muddy; an infinitely sad spectacle.

Lord Roberts arrived at St. Omer on the 11th, and I saw him as he walked round the aerodrome one bitterly cold afternoon. I am not certain which day he came to see us. On Friday he caught cold, and on Saturday evening he died. The Prince of Wales paid a visit to the aerodrome about this time.

Lord Roberts' funeral was on Tuesday, November 17th.

The Flying Corps was continuing to expand, and it was now settled that it was to be organised into Wings. There were to be two Wings and one Headquarters Wing.

On the 18th, at luncheon, I was told I was to go and fetch Colonel Trenchard, who was arriving from England, where he had been in charge of the administrative Wing at Farnborough since the war began. He was coming to take over the command of the First Wing. I had never seen Colonel Trenchard and I wondered how I should recognise him. I arrived at Boulogne. I went to the Fish Market and bought fish. Then I waited for the boat. The boat came in about half-past four. Standing quite by himself on the deck of the boat was a tall man, with a small head and a Scots Fusiliers cap on. That, I said to myself, must be Colonel Trenchard. It was.

He had brought a car with him but no petrol. We had to get petrol. Where from? A sailor volunteered information that petrol could be got from a particular spot. He went off with the driver and disappeared into the night. I thought they would never come back, but they did—with the petrol. We started for St. Omer; it was quite dark. In going out of the town we took the wrong turning, and sped on in the night towards Calais, the opposite direction to St. Omer. Colonel Trenchard asked me a great many pertinent questions, few of which I could answer. A certain intuition warned me after a time that we were going the wrong way, and when we came to a barrier where there were some French soldiers I got out and asked the way, and it turned out we were going swiftly and directly in the opposite direction to St. Omer. They put us right, and after a few more stops and looking at signposts and questioning of inhabitants, we got on the right road once more. But all this made us late, and we didn't arrive at H.Q. till eight o'clock. Colonel Trenchard slept on the floor of the guest room.

Our Headquarters had kept time with the expansion of the Flying Corps, and was growing apace in the way of clerks. Our office was fuller than ever, and the number of candles—for we still had neither lamps nor electric light—would have done honour to a cathedral.

In looking at the mess accounts for December, which were kept at that time by B-K, and which are now in my possession, I see that during the month of December twelve officers were sent a messing bill. But of these only seven officers belonged to our H.Q. permanently. The rest were visitors who stayed more than a week. I also note that our messing cost three *francs* a day, including wine, which was remarkably cheap.

My time at St. Omer was drawing to a temporary end. General Henderson told me he was going to take over the First Division, and asked me if I would like to go with him as Intelligence officer. I said I should like nothing better.

My main recollection of that first period of St. Omer is a stuffy office, full of clerks and candles and a deafening noise of typewriters. A constant stream of pilots arriving in the evening in Burberrys with maps talking over reconnaissances; a perpetual stream of guests and a crowd of people sleeping on the floor; a weekly struggle, sometimes successful and sometimes not, to get a bath in the town, where there was always a seething crowd of suppliants, and a charming, capable lady in charge who used to call one "*Mon très cher Monsieur*"; hours spent on the aerodrome, which were generally misty; and small dinners in the Flight messes in the various billets round Longuenesse and almost every day some inquiry or dispute, with regard to a billet.

Then a few expeditions along abominable roads to Bailleul, Poperinghe, and Hazebrouck; an occasional visit to Boulogne and Dunkirk, and a tense feeling the whole time that the situation was not satisfactory, but that it would somehow or other come all right in the end. At the same time, life was becoming more normal and more settled. One already felt that one had lived at St. Omer all one's life, and that one would be likely to spend the remainder of it there also. Books began to arrive. But the only books I find mentioned in my notes of this period are Cramb's the *Germany and England*, and a book by J. Allen called *Germany and Europe*. I remember that at this period I found it quite impossible to read any modern novel. The pilots, on the other hand, used to cry out for books.

At the end of my notes and diaries, which cover this first period at St. Omer, I find the following entry:

X (name unreadable) said: "German warfare is like Wagner's music. The Germans use every possible accessory . . . spies . . . . Zeppelins, flame-throwers . . . . smoke screens . . . . just as Wagner uses every accessory . . . . scenery . . . lights . . . . over and above the music to heighten the effect of the music."

To this remark I had added the comment that the result, as far as music is concerned, is less effective with all these adventitious aids than that achieved by men like Beethoven or Schubert by the use of simpler means, and I expressed the pious hope that the result would be the same as far as the war was concerned.

These remarks are followed by the entry:

*Bought a lobster.*

# Chapter 6

# With the First Division

*November—December,* 1914.

On Sunday, November 22nd in the afternoon Hilaire Belloc arrived at our headquarters on a visit, and the next morning we got up at six and went with Murat to Bailleul, and thence to one of the squadrons. I remember one of the pilots, one of the most gallant and brilliant of the pilots, who was afterwards killed, Lewis, later a Squadron and then a Wing Commander, asking Belloc why the newspapers abused the Germans in such a foolish manner. A machine went up from the snowy ground while we were there, and we then went on to Nieppe, where we saw the big gun, "Grandmother." Belloc left us after luncheon, and in the afternoon I left H.Q. R.F.C. for the headquarters of the First Division, whither General Henderson had already preceded me.

The headquarters of the First Division were billeted in a small village called Merris, between Hazebrouck and Bailleul. The office was situated in a large convent. The General had a room in a little house in the village; the rest of "A" Mess, to which I was attached, shared a second small house.

General Henderson was taking over from General Landon.

"A" Mess consisted of Colonel Jeudwine, Colonel Gordon, Major Lefroy, Major Webber, a French interpreter, and two A.D.C.'s., Mac-Cready and Rycroft. I lived in the house allotted to "A" Mess. It was quite small. There were two little rooms on the ground floor. One was used as an ante-room, the other as a dining-room. The house belonged to a crusty old man, who possessed an excellent cellar of wine.

Here a new epoch began for me and a totally different mode of life.

The first thing which struck one after living with the R.F.C. was the absence of transport. Instead of having either a light tender or a lorry or a Daimler at one's disposal, one had either to ride or to walk. And life with the R.F.C. spoils one for walking. The weather was disagreeable, a thaw following on a snowfall had made the roads into sticky stretches of mud. One had the usual feeling on arriving at a new place of being like a new boy at a private school; but the Staff were so exceedingly friendly that this feeling wore off almost immediately.

During my stay with the First Division I reflected a good deal on the nonsense talked about Staffs in general, both in this war and in other wars. Of course, if you accept this nonsense as a *convention* and talk of the idle brass hats and the drones and the pompous red tabs and the booted and spurred generals who do nothing, well and good, I am perfectly willing to join in; as long as it is understood that you know that it is a *convention*, and you know that I know that it is a convention, and you know that I know that you know that I know that it is a convention. Then we understand each other. But when other people who do not share this unexpressed understanding, Members of Parliament, for instance, talk in this way it makes me tired and angry. They have not the faintest, remotest idea of what a Staff does, nor of what Staff-work consists, nor what the men are like who do it, or how they do it.

And when they say glibly: "Of course the Staff-work was, as usual, very bad," it is just like hearing a totally unmusical person complaining of a composer's counterpoint. Half the army, I used to hear it said, do not know how the other half live. If this is true, much truer still is it that the outside public knows still less how that other half lives. In the first place, a Divisional Staff is engaged for the greater part of the time in incessant hard work of the most harassing and responsible nature. In the second place, the men who form such a Staff would nearly always be giving their eyes to be elsewhere: to be at the front. They are there because they have got to be there, and they are determined to do the best they can. The work has got to be done, and somebody has got to do it. But because they are on a Staff they don't change into supermen or into angels, and a pompous man will remain pompous on a Staff or become possibly more pompous, and an unpretentious man will remain unpretentious or become more unpretentious.

And if the man who is at the head of the Staff is a good man he will get rid of drones, but he will also make the best of the material available and not complain because every Staff officer is not a heaven-born genius. When people talk of other professions they are not so unreasonable. If they go to see a play acted, they will be satisfied if the acting is up to a good average level, and they will be surprised and delighted if in the company there is, say, one actor of outstanding talent. They will not expect a cast consisting entirely of stars of genius, because stars are necessarily rare. Yet in talking of the army, and especially of the new army, the army which was improvised and organised and created while the war was actually being fought, they used to be pained if every Staff officer was not a budding Napoleon.

What amused me throughout the war was the spectacle of men who had deservedly earned brilliant reputations in other walks of life handling a piece of ordinary Staff work. They often did it very well, but not so well—and they were the first to admit it—as the ordinary soldier who had no brilliant reputation to point to and fall back upon. This particular Staff consisted of a fine set of officers, all of whom had either previously, or did subsequently, distinguish themselves in the field, and of some who, alas, were killed later. Moreover, the actual routine of their life since they had been formed had been varied and adventurous and perilous in the highest degree, and one of the generals commanding them had already been killed by a shell which had fallen in his headquarters.

We had fallen on a period of calm.

On the 27th of November we received news that the Russians had surrounded the Germans, who were in the situation of the Boers at Paardeberg. This was true as it turned out. Unfortunately the situation did not last, and the Russians, by bringing up a division instead of a corps, were unable to keep the circle closed, and the Germans got away. But when the news came we were greatly elated, and the verdict of "A" Mess was that we ought to shove.

"Now is the time to shove like hell," was what everybody was saying. The news came from one of the Ambassadors. On the 28th the commander-in-chief, Sir John French, came to inspect the division. I saw him inspect the Guards' Second Battalion, and in speaking to the men he told them the Russian news. That same day I got a letter in which the writer spoke of the coming invasion of Germany and the destruction and violence which was likely would attend it. A story was also going about of a letter which came from Berlin with a message in it saying "look under the stamp." The receiver of the letter looked and found the words: "The Germans are in a panic."

So altogether prospects seemed cheerful. Yet I remember well, while we repeated to each other this news and discussed it from every point of view, we did not at the bottom of our hearts feel greatly exhilarated. We thought it was too good to be true. The French interpreter, who had been away for some days, came back with an amusing story.

He told us that the soldiers in the French trenches had put a top hat on the end of a stick and promenaded it up and down while a gramophone played the "*Marseillaise*," and the Germans, thinking it was the President of the Republic, had fired at it for all they were worth.

On November 30th the General told me he might possibly have to leave the First Division and go back to the R.F.C.; this would naturally be a most cruel disappointment for him. By December 1st the Russian news had already faded into the realm of "as you were." The Germans, we were told, had been surrounded, but some gap had occurred in the iron circle. Considering the way we were douched with alternate sprays of good and bad news, I think we were extremely patient.

On December 3rd the King paid us a visit. We were paraded in the village street, and the villagers were in a great state of excitement; but it rained and the cold was intense, and the ceremony was spoilt by the sleet, the cold and the mud.

The capacity for reading a book returned to me at Merris, although reading, except in bed, was difficult, as our ante-room was lit solely by a lamp, which worked by water, and made a whistling noise and emitted the most sickening, nauseating stench, but it was a choice between this lamp and semi-darkness.

I read nearly all Moliere's plays, which someone had kindly sent me from Paris in penny editions. But the only trace of this reading I find in my notes is one line from *Les Femmes Savantes*.

*Ce sont petits chemins tout parsemés de roses.*

I used frequently to walk or ride into Bailleul to see the squadrons which were there, and although I was very happy with the First Division, I suffered the whole time from R.F.C. sickness.

Colonel Burke, who commanded the Second Wing, had his headquarters at Bailleul, and I used often to go and see him. Sometimes he would drive me back in his car. He was training a new driver in map reading. This process consisted in telling the driver to go with the aid of a map to a place he didn't know. The driver then lost the way. Then you got out, looked at the signposts and asked the way of the first inhabitants you met. The favourite amusement of the A.D.C.'s in the

First Division was to go out shooting pheasants in the dark with two pistols and an electric torch. They shot no pheasants.

We were a very happy family, and Webber and Lefroy and the others used to tell us thrilling stories of the adventures of the First Division during the last months. I shared a servant called Prentice with Macready. The Mess was looked after by a sergeant, who was a great character. One morning, as I was looking out of my bedroom window, I saw him cleaning the boots in the little backyard. The girl who belonged to the house came up to him and, pointing to the field boot he was polishing, said; "Blacking, blacking, '*Oui, oui,*' he answers, '*Voulez vous* ——,' but I will leave to French scholars the pleasure of reconstituting the phrase with which he expressed his goodwill. On December 10th Macready and I accompanied the general on an inspection ride to the batteries, and my pony jumped a ditch without my falling off, which surprised me considerably. We went to see some experiments with arquebus shooting.

A large instrument which looked like the kind of thing the Romans and the Carthaginians are shown as using in picture books, shot a heavy missile into the air, which would be meant to fall in a German trench. It fell in this case on the foot of a friend.

On December 11th there was a Brigadiers' Conference. The Brigadiers came to our Mess and stayed for luncheon. Rumours of an impending attack were in the air. On the 12th we began to get excited: the attack appeared to be going to be a kind of large demonstration. On the 13th we heard that fighting had begun. I read the second *Canto* of Dante's *Inferno*. The next day, the 14th, we got orders to stand by to move at a moment's notice. Everything was packed up, but nothing happened. There was a shortage of boots in the division, and boots were not procurable, so I went into St. Omer with our Q. Officer to try and raise some boots. That evening, before going to sleep, I read *Canto* three of the *Inferno*; the last time I had read it was in the train, so my book told me, between Sofia and Bucharest, on March 31st, 1914.

On the 17th we had news of a bombardment. The lady who owned the general's billet wanted him to do something for her—I forget what—so she bribed him by giving him a bottle of 1870 Burgundy. This incident occurred on Saturday, December 19th. I note also that I had reached and finished *Canto* eight of the *Inferno*. So I was getting on. I noted the phrase:

*Vedi che son un che piango.*

I had dinner that night at the Guards' Mess, which was at Strazeele, in the house belonging to the *curé*. The *curé* made a speech about the colonel (Colonel, now General, John Ponsonby), in which he said that he was as good as gold.

On December 20th a German machine flew over Merris in the morning, and was attacked by a British machine. We witnessed the fight in the air. We heard shots, and the German machine went off. This was a day of great excitement. We got definite orders that the move was to take place. We were to move that night. The General also heard that he had to go back to the R.F.C.; General Hakin was to take over the First Division. This was a bitter disappointment. Everyone was miserable at General Henderson going. And it was particularly cruel for him to have to leave the division just as it was going into action.

All the H.Q. Staff moved off after tea. There was a great deal of scurrying, final packing and banging of doors, and bustle, but no confusion. We were left alone at six o'clock in our little house. The general told me I could stay with the division if I liked or go back with him. I had no hesitation in going back.

Before going to bed I read *Canto* nine of the *Inferno*, and came across this line, which was only too appropriate to a Flanders field:

*Simile qui con simile è sepolto.*

I dined that night with the *second echelon* Mess, who were not to start till the next day. The next morning I went back with the general and Macready to the R.F.C. Headquarters at St. Omer. The day after, the 26th of December, I started at six in the morning for London, on leave.

# PART 2
## 1915

CHAPTER 7

# St. Omer up to the First Push

*January—March,* 1915.

Arrived back at St. Omer with General Henderson on the 1st of January, 191 5. The Mess consisted of the same people as before, namely, Colonel Sykes, Major Salmond, Major Barrington-Kennett, Prince Murat, and Captain St. John. There was an addition in the person of Captain Hughes Hallet, a G.S.O., 2 or 3 (I am not certain when he arrived), and Evan Charteris, who was staying in the house on the way to taking up his duties with a Wing. There was also Macready, the A.D.C. who now took charge of the Mess. We still paid three francs a day for our food.

On the 2nd of January I went to Ypres, Furnes, Pervyse, and Dunkirk. The damage at Ypres was much greater than I expected to find, but the shops were still open. Pervyse was right on the edge of the inundated country, and we watched the grey floods from a rickety, shot-riddled little building. I never looked on a more desolate scene. It was pouring with rain, and the world seemed to have been first destroyed and then flooded. I still shared my same bedroom with Salmond and B.K., and we resumed the habit of making tea before we went to bed.

On January 9th I went to Paris with the general and Brooke-Popham. In Paris I saw and consulted Doctor Gosset, the celebrated surgeon, with regard to some trouble brought on owing to an old operation, and he prescribed a course which kept me in Paris until January 21st. I saw a certain amount of French people, and my impression, comparing the way they talked of the war with the way people talked of it in London, was this: the public in Paris, the man in the street, the people you met at dinner, although they often said and believed much more fantastic things than the English, understood a great deal better what war was and what in war was possible and impossible.

While I was in Paris we lost one of our best flying officers—Chinnery—in a tragic manner. He was flying a Voisin machine which he had come to Paris to fetch, and the machine crashed on the banks of the Seine, and he was killed.

On January 20th I met Doctor Dillon at luncheon. He told me he was surprised at the general optimism which seemed to prevail with regard to the bad economic plight of the Germans. He was convinced all their food precautions were dictated by prudence and were not a sign of want. Monsieur Flers, the playwright, and Monsieur Joseph Reinach, were at the same luncheon. They none of them appeared to me to be unduly optimistic, but rather confident and quite extraordinarily short of news. They had not the remotest idea what was going on at the Front.

I got back to St. Omer on the 21st of January. Salmond was going home to start a new squadron. We had a farewell feast the night before, with oysters. There were sixteen people at dinner: among others, Colonel Swinton, of tank and *Eye-Witness* fame.

Looking through my notes of this period they reveal nothing but a monotonous routine of life at St. Omer between the town and the Aerodrome, varied by occasional excursions to Dunkirk, Boulogne, and Amiens.

On the 2nd of February the first Voisin machine arrived, which caused a good deal of excitement. On the 5th of February I spent a night with No. 2 Squadron at Merville, then commanded by Major Dawes. We had a good deal of music after dinner, and the pilots sang a song called:

It's a long way to 8000.

Billet troubles continued; Archie batteries arrived; almost every evening we played chess after dinner, at which Murat was a great expert. He had a dashing Napoleonic touch in his play, and he very often opened the game by playing King's rook pawn to King's rook fourth. He sometimes won.

On February 7th B.K. caught influenza, and had to stay in bed, but he insisted on doing his work in bed, and continued working up till midnight. This illness was destined to have tragic consequences for him and for us. On the 8th he was moved into the hospital.

On the 10th we had experiments in bomb-dropping on the aerodrome. Longcroft went up and dropped a bomb; it fell in a slightly unexpected place, and went off as it was supposed to do with a bang. That evening a pilot, whose name I have not recorded, told me that he thought flying was a very soft job compared to what the infantry had to go through in the trenches, and that he felt he was not really in the war. Another pilot asked me to get him some books by Arnold Bennett or Compton Mackenzie.

B.-K.'s work was taken on by Major Reynolds. B.K. came out of the hospital on February 11th. The next day I drove into Boulogne with him to see him off on leave. He was still weak, but tried to carry his own bag. This, however, he was not allowed to do. The next day I went with Brooke-Popham to Strazeele to draw a pump from the R.E. Stores for draining the Aerodrome. There was a shortage of pumps, but we got one, and it seemed comic in later days to look back on the day when we went to get one pump.

On the 15th I went for my first flight in the air. Longcroft took me up in B.E. 2 C. I was so tightly packed into the machine that I could not move. We flew over St. Omer, but it was a grey day, and the country seen from the air looked like an uncoloured photograph. With Longcroft piloting one did not feel a single jerk or bump, and he made a beautiful landing.

On the 21st I went with General Henderson to Aire, to the Headquarters of the First Wing, where we had luncheon with Colonel Trenchard. The house was steam heated and like an oven. The billiard table was boarded over, and had maps on it. Every kind of newspaper seemed to be taken in. When we came away the general said to me: "It's extraordinary how happy they are in that Mess."

On the 25th we had a second visit from Hilaire Belloc. I went with Evan Charteris to fetch him at Boulogne, and we arrived back at midnight. The next morning we all three of us went to Hazebrouck, where we had luncheon with Colonel Burke at the Second Wing Headquarters. After luncheon we went to see the Squadrons at Poperinghe, on our way to Ypres.

We visited Ypres, but we got blocked on the way back, and had to go back by Cassel. Belloc and I had been invited to dine with Sir John French, and we only got back just in time.

On the way back from Ypres, Belloc sang a good many songs; some of them were about bishops. When we got home, and the car was waiting to take us to the commander-in-chief's house, while we were washing, someone asked the driver who he was waiting for. The driver said: "Two officers and a *clergyman*." The clergyman was Belloc.

I should mention he was wearing a broad wide-awake hat. We had dinner with Sir John, but I have no record of the conversation.

The next day Colonel Sykes took Belloc and myself to Plugstreet, where we saw the trenches, and to Neuve-Eglise, which was visited by a shell while we passed through it. Belloc went away at 5.30, having had a satisfactory experience of Flanders mud.

My first visit to the real trenches—the trenches which were like catacombs—was on March 3rd. For although Plugstreet was in the front line, the trenches there, being in a wood, were exceptional and not typical.

I went with Grant, who was at that time a liaison officer, by Aire and Bethune to Cuinchy. We walked through a labyrinth of catacomb-like trenches made of mud, and saw the brickfields. One of the trenches was called Kissing Lane, another Judy's Passage.

I looked through a periscope, but could see nothing at all except grass. A soldier in the trenches gave us an amusing lecture on the service rifle. All it was fit for, he said, was to be cleaned in the trenches.

In my diary there is an entry on March 4th to the effect that during the last two days 16 glasses, 10 tumblers, 12 coffee cups, 12 liqueur glasses, and 1 soup tureen had been broken in the Mess.

On March 6th Murat left us. He had to go to Paris to undergo a serious operation; indeed, what turned out to be a series of operations. He was a very great loss to us. All through the retreat he was suffering from internal troubles, which made this operation necessary (fortunately it cured him), but he never referred to them, nor ever let anything interfere with the unflagging zeal with which he served our interests. Nobody could deal with an obstinate mayor or a peevish householder as well as Murat.

He always got us the best billets, and he did everything promptly and efficiently. Besides this, everybody liked him, and whenever I went to a squadron later, the first person the pilots asked after was always Murat. Later on he came back to us for a short time, and, although General Trenchard made every effort with the French authorities then, to keep him, we were not allowed to do so.

On March 7th I saw Julian Grenfell at his billet in Belle Hotesse. He was in tearing spirits. Rumours of fighting were in the air.

On March 8th the Headquarters of the Third Wing, which was commanded by Brooke-Popham , and stationed in a small white *château* on the top of a hill near Longuenesse, decided to give a dinner party, and to invite the owner of the *château* and his wife, who were living in the town while their *château* was being occupied.

In the morning I went with Evan Charteris, who was attached to this Wing, to buy provisions for the feast. We bought some sweet and dry champagne and some lettuce for a salad, and various other delicacies.

The owner of the *château*, an extremely courteous gentleman, and his charming wife arrived punctually. But, unfortunately, the Mess Sergeant (an absolutely exemplary man) and the other servant in the house both got drunk from the excitement and strain of preparing the dinner. The Mess sergeant could not walk, and he stood stiffly leaning against the door like the Tower of Pisa. The soup fell down the lift with a crash. There was a long pause. Finally, after a certain amount of scurrying and discussion and "business without," we got some cold chicken. But the salad arrived *boiled* and steaming, and looking like a solid, spongy pulp of green seaweed.

The guests made a vain endeavour to get some of the dry champagne, which they evidently preferred to the sweet brand, but the hosts insisted on plying them with the sweet brand, which they politely, but, no doubt reluctantly, were obliged to accept. As dinner went on we realised that the cook was drunk too. Towards the end of the dinner one of the hosts, who was fearfully overworked, went to sleep, and we had to pinch him to wake him up. The guests appeared to be quite unruffled by the various catastrophes, and said they had enjoyed themselves very much. They said they thought the war would last a long time.

On March 10th we established an advanced Headquarters at Hazebrouck for the Neuve Chapelle push. We started early, and arrived about 8 in the morning. A terrific bombardment was going on at Neuve Chapelle, in which more shells were fired than during the whole of the South African War, but we did not hear a sound. Our Mess was at the Headquarters of the Second Wing, a brick Queen-Anne house with a moat round it. In the evening we got news of the prisoners taken. This was the first time during the war that aircraft co-operated with artillery in battle. Some of the pilots were up nearly all day sending wireless messages. The weather was bad. On the 11th I saw a pilot crash on the Bailleul Aerodrome on landing. Both the pilot and the observer were taken out unconscious and sent to the hospital.

On the 12th General Henderson was laid up, and had to stay in bed.

On the 14th one of the pilots I knew best, Barton, had a bad crash. He went out on a night bombing expedition, and apparently flew into a tree. He was found walking about a field. The bombs, luckily, did not go off.

On the 14th there was a terrific bombardment in the evening, which we heard this time. I suppose this must have been the German counter-attack at St. Eloi, which the Germans took, and which we re-took almost entirely.

On the 15th I went to Belle Hotesse again to search for Julian Grenfell. I found him. His regiment was all ready for a move, which had just been cancelled. He was lying asleep in a barn on a large sheaf with his greyhound. I woke him up gently. He said: "Shall I kill you?" Then he took me into the Mess and we had tea. He showed me a poem he had written (about an A.D.C.), and gave me a copy. He told me he had written lots of poems. This was the last time I ever saw him.

On March 17th we left Hazebrouck, and came back to St. Omer. The push was over. The general was up again, but the doctor said that he must go to the South of France.

On the 18th I went with General Henderson and his A.D.C., Captain Barrington-White, to Paris. They left Paris for Nice on the 20th. That night there was a Zeppelin raid (the first) over Paris, but not of any importance.

On the 22nd I dined with some Russians, and we drank to the victory of Przemysl. The news of the capture by the Russians of that puzzlingly named city had just been received. There was a Zeppelin alarm at nine o'clock, and the city was plunged into darkness, but no Zeppelins came. I walked home through dark and absolutely deserted streets.

On the 23rd I got back to St. Omer, and I note that I reached on that date *Canto* 22 of the *Inferno*, which seemed to show the war making a little progress.

The spring had come, and the evening of the 26th was full of delicate promise. In the twilight the dewy trees were soft against a green and lilac sky. In the East great snowy cold clouds were piled one on to another, faintly reflecting the glow in the West.

# CHAPTER 8

# Another Entr'acte at St. Omer and Another Push

*March—May,* 1915.

The first day on which the spring made itself felt that year was on March 24th, a lovely afternoon. The birds were singing and there was a soft spring rainbow in the feathery clouds.

Our life had entirely gone back into its normal ruts.

Murat had been succeeded by Lieutenant Philonneau, Captain Festing, from the Northumberland Fusiliers, arrived to take over Barrington-Kennett's duties (D.A.A. and Q.M.G.) Salmond had come out again with No. 1 Squadron, and in this squadron was Victor Barrington-Kennett, Basil Barrington-Kennett's younger brother.

I saw him shortly after his arrival, and he told me that he had given a lecture to the men, and at the end of it had asked them some questions. Among others: "Who commands the R.F.C.?" There was a silence, and then a man answered: "Colonel Seely." A flying school had been started at Le Crotoy on the coast.

I can find no further record of anything in the month of March except that, having complained to the mechanic in charge of the Mess that the accounts were rising higher and higher, stale bread was given to us at luncheon and no coffee for breakfast the next day, and when I asked the A.M. the reason he said: "It's too expensive."

One evening in April, just as we were finishing dinner, one of the motor cyclists flung open the dining-room door and said, in breathless, dramatic tones: "Sir, a Zeppelin has been reported flying towards St. Omer." We went up to the aerodrome, but save for a display of search-lights, nothing happened. Furse, a gunner who had been wounded as an observer early in the war, came to us as a Staff officer.

He understood the possibilities of aircraft and artillery from both sides, and what should be the nature of their co-operation. On April 7th I went with him to see various battery commanders. We found the gunners quite extraordinarily sticky with regard to the co-operation of aircraft with artillery. They seemed to have no belief in it at all. And all Furse 's arguments fell on deaf ears. It is intensely trying to have to deal in war-time with a new weapon.

On the 16th I went to Bethune to find B.K., who had gone back to his regiment, the Grenadier Guards. When he had recovered from his bad attack of influenza the doctor had told him that office work was bad for him. So he applied to go back to his regiment. He was offered the command of a squadron, but he was unwilling to accept this as he thought a squadron commander should fly himself.

B.K. had been one of the first pilots in the Flying Corps before the war. It is impossible to state too strongly what a loss his departure was to the whole corps. He had himself laid the foundation of a certain tone; he had always been keen about instilling a certain spirit, and although there was nobody less of a martinet, he had always insisted on the extreme importance of discipline. He had recruited from the guards a nucleus of excellent non-commissioned officers, and had thus established a solid frame-work of tradition and sound principles, which in a new Corps dealing with a new weapon, and a weapon such as the aeroplane and with all the qualities and defects which flying must necessarily entail, was, of course, of vital importance.

His influence was great, and time and again I heard pilots say: "B.K. says we ought to do this or that."

B.K. was out when we arrived at the billet. But we waited till seven o'clock, when he came in. We had a long talk. He wanted to know how to cook a cauliflower. This was the last time I was to see him.

On the 19th General Henderson came back from Nice, restored to health and looking quite a different man. On the 20th I went, with Festing, to Dickebush, and we climbed up a hill with a name which I have never managed to spell correctly, and watched Ypres being shelled. The counter-attack on St. Eloi was going on. On the 22nd I went to London with General Henderson, and stayed there till the 28th. The day after we came back was at St. Omer one of the loveliest days I can remember. The large beech-tree in the garden was on the point of coming out. There were no leaves on it, but the buds were on the point of bursting. Against the light blue sky the reddish branches looked pink and feathery. The magnolia tree in the garden was half out, and the cuckoo was calling. Far away there was a faint booming; perhaps a spring thunderstorm, perhaps guns. May was a beautiful month.

The day Hill 60 was taken and retaken (May 6th), the nightingales sang themselves hoarse and the cuckoo never stopped. In the evening, Gould, the finest Mauriçe-Farman pilot in existence, took me up in his machine. And neither coat nor cap nor goggles was necessary. Like all great artists, he seemed to do nothing at all, and to let the machine fly itself.

On the 8th I moved, with General Henderson and Barrington-White, to advanced Headquarters at Hazebrouck. This meant another push. We occupied a large white villa with a beautiful garden full of lilac and laburnum, near the station. We heard the news of the sinking of the *Lusitania*, and in *Canto* 26 of the *Inferno*, which I read that night, I marked this appropriate line:

*E per lo Inferno il nome tuo si spande.*

The next day (Sunday) was the feast of Joan of Arc. I went to Mass in the morning. The church was full of wounded soldiers, some of whom had been gassed. The church windows rattled from the noise of shelling in the distance, and the *curé* spoke of the *curé* of Bailleul, who had just been killed, *par un éclat d'obus.*

On the 10th I went into Bailleul and saw Edward Horner, who had been severely wounded, and was in the hospital there. The 11th was a gorgeous day, and I went in the morning to Cassel with General Henderson. He wanted to see General Plumer, who was living in a square white *château* in a wooded garden at the foot of Cassel Hill. Nightingales were singing in the garden, and while I was standing by an artificial pond, General Plumer strolled out and talked to me, and fed the ducks with some bread. I have no record of the fighting in the air which took place during this push.

I was told afterwards that the weather conditions were perfect. It was perhaps the only day on which a big battle was fought during the whole war that the conditions for the work of aircraft left nothing to be desired, and yet everything, so I am told, went wrong; that is to say, as far as results on the ground were concerned.

On the 13th we received news of the big French fight at Lens, and it was either on this day or one of these days that the French commander-in-chief came to Hazebrouck. I had some talk with one of the officers who was with him, who said to me—"*C'est le com-*

71

*mencement de la fin.*" He said that the Germans had dropped a bomb on the French G.H.Q. at Chantilly, which he described as the despairing bite of a mad dog.

The Italian situation was causing a good deal of anxiety at this moment. Otherwise there was a temporary wave of optimism; among the people I saw, at least.

On the 17th May, I went with General Henderson to General Trenchard's Headquarters at Merville, and there we had news of the Festubert fighting.

On the 19th I got news that Julian Grenfell had been wounded, and on the 20th General Henderson sent me into Boulogne to see if I could see him but he was too ill to see anybody.

That night, in the middle of dinner, Barrington-White said there was a rumour that B.K. had been killed. The next day the rumour was confirmed.

If ever a man deserved a soldier's death, to die leading his men and the men of his own regiment into battle, it was B.K. But of all the bitter losses one had to bear throughout the war, it was, with one exception, this particular loss I felt most, minded most, resented most, and found most difficult to accept.

He was not an old friend of mine. I had never seen him before the war. But he was bound up with every moment of my life during the first months of the war, and I had got to know him intimately and to admire him more than others and to delight in his company more than in that of others. He had left the Flying Corps, and I should probably not have seen much more of him, unless as would have perhaps been possible later, he had returned to it. But when this particular piece of news came I felt the taste of the war turn bitter indeed, and apart from any personal feelings, one rebelled against the waste which had deprived, first the Flying Corps and then the Army, of the services of so noble a character. He was the most completely unselfish man I have ever met: a compound of loyalty and generosity and a gay and keen interest in everything life has to offer.

Not long ago I heard a little boy of eight years old asked if he knew what the word gentleman meant. He said, "Yes, of course."

On being pressed for a definition he said:

"A gentleman is a man who loves God very much and has beautiful manners."

This definition exactly fitted B.K.

Here is the last letter but one I received from him which I kept.

His last letter I have lost. (It was about cooking cauliflower.) It was written before I went to see him at Bethune:

|  |  |
|---|---|
|  | N.B.— |
| 2nd Bn. Grenadier Guards, | Crack Brigade |
| 4th Guards Brigade, | "   Batt'n! |
| 2nd Division. | And don't forget it! |
| 13-4.15. |  |

My dear Maurice,

Your honesty is only equalled by your benevolence, for I feel convinced that the Mess debt to me did not amount to the sum you sent. If at a later date you find that your mathematics were at fault, mind apprise me, and I will refund the erring *francs*. Well-a-day I find this life most pleasant and full of incident. One's days pass in a rich succession of interludes—eating, sleeping, designing entrenchments, drainage-improvements, dugouts, etc., spying, sniping, night-patrolling, and last but by no means least, constant *gingering*.

Our pastimes consist of reading, writing and (when counting up dead Germans) arithmetic—chess, bridge, patience, and the discussion of a nice point or two. Altogether life is quite pleasant if only one could eliminate the constant stream of rifle-bullets, Jack Johnsons, bombs, whizz-bangs, and the like. So far I have not even been struck by a bullet, much less by one of the more clumsy missiles. I hope to keep all such at a distance, as I should hate to forego the opportunity of quaffing a nice glass of wine with you when our foes have been reduced to a state similar to that I once reduced Brewster[1]—my request was he should make an omelette.

Don't fail to pay me a visit and that right early. Enquire my whereabouts (2nd Bn. G.G.) from 2nd Division H.Q. at Bethune, and if you can, bring some literature. By the way, I left one or two of my books behind. *Jorrocks, Lamb's Essays* and *Macaulay's Essays* amongst them. Also, when you come bring some cigarettes for the men if there are any surplus at R.F.C. H.Q. There used to be as a rule. My brother Victor was over here yesterday for an hour or so. He seems fit and enjoying himself. Is the H.Q. pretty lively these days, plenty of quibs and digs in the ribs?

Bring your latest spy-spotting monocle when you come, as the

---

1. The original cook at H.Q.

folk here are not above suspicion. Greetings to all, including the H.Q. Staff. I can hear the tic-a-tic interspersed with an occasional ping.—Yours, B.K.

That day I went with General Henderson and saw his son, Ian Henderson, who had joined his father's old regiment, the Argyll and Sutherlands. That night I read Dante's *Inferno*, *Canto* 33, and noted this line .

> *E se non piangi, di che pianger suoli?"*

Belloc had been invited to visit us again, and it was suggested that he should lecture to the R.F.C. I went into St. Omer to arrange about a lecture hall for him. In the meantime, no better news of Julian Grenfell arrived, and all those I saw who knew him seemed intensely anxious about him. Belloc arrived at St. Omer on the 26th, and the next day I drove with him to the battlefield of Agincourt, near Hesdin, and he explained the battle and the battlefield to our driver. He lectured in the afternoon on the Russian front, and it was a most interesting and lucid lecture.

That evening an unfortunate incident happened at dinner. I had, knowing there was mutton for dinner and that Belloc hated mutton, bought some *écrevisses* in the afternoon, and explained carefully to the cook, who was now a Frenchman (whom we had obtained from the French Army, as a great favour), how they were to be cooked, namely, *à la Bordelaise*. They were to be served to Belloc when we ate the mutton. Everything seemed to be clear. But when the mutton was brought in the Mess corporal brought in the *écrevisses* in a separate dish and handed them round as a *vegetable*, and, in spite of my protests, every one took one. So there were only two left for our extremely hungry lecturer.

Late after dinner that night a man brought me a letter from Boulogne telling me that Julian Grenfell had died of his wounds in the hospital on the afternoon of the 26th. That night I read the *Purgatorio*, *Canto* three, and was struck by this line, which is extraordinarily appropriate to Julian:

> *Biondo era e bello e di gentile aspetto.*

whom I had known ever since he was a little boy with golden curls and little green knickerbockers before he went to school. The next day our advanced Headquarters moved back to St. Omer. The push was over.

# CHAPTER 9

# St. Omer Once More, and Italy

*May—August,* 1915.

On May 20th I went to No. 1 Squadron at Bailleul, commanded by Geoffrey Salmond. I had a long talk with Victor Barrington-Kennett.

The last push and its failure had had a depressing effect on the pilots and everyone else, especially on those who had lost those whom they most cared for.

On May 31st I spent the night with No. 4 Squadron at Bailleul, commanded by Longcroft. They were living in tents in the aerodrome on the side of the Nieppe road.

Dinner was ready in a large tent, and we had scarcely sat down when a Zeppelin was reported on the horizon. Longcroft jumped into a scout, flung a handful of bombs into it, and in a moment was soaring into the sunset. We walked up on to the hill, and we could see the Zeppelin a thin, black mark on the low horizon. Longcroft was not away long, because directly he got up into the air he said it was impossible to see anything for the mist. In the meantime the sun had thoroughly set, and it grew dark. Flares were lit on the aerodrome, and soon we heard Longcroft's machine buzzing in the air. He flew in through two trees, and made a perfect landing in the dark.

Then we sat down to dinner, which turned out to be one of the gayest feasts I have ever attended. Speeches were made and songs were sung, and all the glass was broken. Then we went quietly to sleep in our respective tents.

On June 2nd, which was a lovely day, I was sitting in the office at St. Omer censoring letters, when Simpson, a gunner who had stayed with us, walked in and asked me to go with him to Félix Potin and help to buy some whisky. He wanted to take some out to a battery, and they would not let him have any. We went to Félix Potin and bought the whisky successfully. He asked me whether I would like to go with him to the batteries, and I said I would. So we started for Ypres.

We went first to one battery and then to another, and doled out whisky. Then we thought it would be interesting to drive into Ypres. When we got beyond a certain point on the Ypres road, there was a sudden silence: that peculiar hush which falls when you get beyond the line where, instead of the ordinary business of life men are carrying on the silent business of fighting.

Presently we met some troops clattering down the road at a sharp trot. I felt that something a little unusual was going on. We turned off to a side-road on the left. We met a sergeant, and we stopped and spoke to him. "It's very warm up there, sir," he said. We felt we would have done better to stick to the main road, as there were a good many shrapnel shells bursting about the place, and, after we had passed, some high explosive. We went on, however, and we got into Ypres, which was quite deserted. After we had looked round a little, we went to a battery on the Dickebush road and doled out more whisky, and thence *via* Neuve-Eglise and Plugstreet to Armentieres, which was also deserted. There we found another battery, and gave the officers what remained of the whisky. Then we drove home at a tearing rate.

The day after this I went to Bailleul and stayed the night with Geoffrey Salmond at No. 1 Squadron. The director of the lunatic asylum had dinner with us.

At this period there were great discussions going on as to the organisation of the co-operation of aircraft with wireless with artillery, the system of signalling, etc., and the next day I went to General Trenchard's Headquarters at Choques, where an immensely long conference took place on this subject.

On Sunday I spent an afternoon in the trenches. I went with Reynolds to see his brother, who was with the Canadian Brigade commanded by Colonel Seely at Beuvry, a village near Bethune. We found his brother and we walked to the trenches. While we were walking across the field a large Black Maria went off at the end of the communication trench; we were well out of reach. We walked up to the front line trench and stayed there till eight. I had a long talk with a soldier. He talked a great deal about two snipers, whom he said gave trouble regularly. They were called Hans and Fritz. We looked through a periscope, but saw nothing.

As soon as it grew dark star shells began to go off. It was a beautiful sight, like fireworks on the fourth of June at Eton. Reynolds went down into a mine. I did not. We walked back to Reynolds' brother 's billet and had dinner in the yard of a cottage. We drove home in the mist.

On June 9th I received a telegram saying that a great friend of mine, Pierre Benckendorff, the second son of Count Benckendorff, who was Ambassador in London, had been killed in action.

I had seen him off at Moscow station when he started for the Manchurian War. And I had found him in Manchuria when I arrived there. Shortly afterwards he had disappeared in a reconnaissance and had been reported missing. The news of his death was even officially confirmed to me. But somehow or other I did not believe then that he had been killed. This time I had no doubts. A soldier, who was with him, said he had just time to smile and then he fell back.

When I got this news I felt what, alas, one was so often called upon to feel during the war, that the death of a particular person meant the end of a whole chapter of one's life, which was different from other chapters, and could never be repeated.

"All that is ended." That is what I felt when I heard the news of Pierre's death, and I should like in these pages to pay a small tribute to his memory. He was connected more nearly than anyone else with the happiest days I had spent in Russia. He was one of the most naturally intelligent human beings I have ever met. Completely unambitious, devoted to outdoor life, and shooting, and every kind of outdoor expedition and adventure.

He refused to speak English, although he understood it quite well, and could pronounce it perfectly, and he successfully concealed the fact that he knew French till he was nineteen. He was fond of reading Gogol's stories, Russian translations of *Sherlock Holmes,* and German translations of *Mark Twain*. He used to make me read *Mark Twain* (in German) aloud to him for hours, and laugh uncontrollably, partly at the stories and partly at my un-teutonic rendering, delivery and accent. He had the most satisfactory of all senses of humour, that kind of sense of humour for which nothing is too silly and too foolish. He would riot in the silliest games and occupations. One could spend hours drawing pictures with him that meant nothing, or inventing tunes on the piano. But he was happiest out of doors; shooting duck in the early morning, or waiting for wolves in the snow. The year before the war he was sent to Italy, after a severe illness, and there he no longer concealed his flair and his appreciation for the works of art of antiquity, and all epochs.

The only time he ever went to London I asked him what sights or public buildings or Museums he would like to see, and he said Sherlock Holmes' house. So we drove to Baker Street, and we agreed that Sherlock Holmes' house (according to the story of Colonel Moran in the *Return of Sherlock Holmes*), must be on the right hand side of the street as you drive towards Regent's Park. This is the sort of thing you could discuss with Pierre for hours. We once collaborated in a story I published called *Sherlock Holmes in Russia*, in which most of the subject matter was due to him.

He was a good officer, and once when he asked one of his men why he hadn't cleaned a rifle which was dirty, and the man said he *had* cleaned it, Pierre answered: "Then you deserve double punishment for cleaning it badly." He had the eye that sees everything at once, and the mind that understands without any explanation, and need not bother to learn.

In an article on foreign politics, which appeared in a provincial Russian review, discussing the European situation, the writer, a well-known professor, with reference to one of the many Balkan crises before 1914, said: "The reason why we escaped having to go to war was because we had as ambassador in London the first gentleman in Europe." Pierre was not unworthy to be the son of a father about whom such a thing could be said from so (as all who know Russia will understand) disinterested a quarter. And he had something also entirely his own, which I have already tried to indicate: a God-gifted naturalness by reason of which it was impossible for him not to understand anything or to strike a wrong note in thought, word or deed, or to be anything other than what he was.

He was more completely devoid of any kind of *pose* than anyone I have ever met. I remember his rollicking amusement when a young lady told him at Nice one day that he was "*beau comme un Dieu.*" I was at St. Petersburg just before the Japanese declared war on Russia in 1904, and I often saw a troop of his regiment, the *Chevalier Gardes*, riding by over the hard snow; their breastplates and helmets and golden eagles and white tunics glinting in the sunshine under a blue sky, all the brighter for the snow on the ground.

One day, a lady told me she was watching this sight, which was as common as seeing the Life Guards ride up St. James's Street, and as she was looking at the dazzling troop she noticed one officer younger than the rest and different; and, although she knew Pierre quite well, and was, in fact, his first cousin, she did not at once recognise him "with his beaver on," but she asked herself who is this apparition? and she told me she thought at once of Shakespeare's description of Prince Harry:

*All furnished, all in arms,*
*All plum'd like estridges that wing the wind,*
*As full of spirit as the month of May,*
*And gorgeous as the sun at Midsummer. . . .*

I never saw Pierre with his beaver on; but when he started for the Manchurian War it was difficult to believe that he would ever come back. He seemed to be of those on whom the gods have set their fatal seal. But a nobler fate was reserved to him than to fall in an adventurous war brought about by bungling and intrigue, and alien to the hearts of his fellow-country-men. He was *felix opportunitate mortis,* not only because the circumstances of his death were fitting, but also because, as subsequent events proved, his grief would have, must have, lain onward; his joy behind.

On the 11th I was ill with malaria, and I stayed with No. 16 Squadron, who were living in a large *château* at Choques, with a moat round it. We had a great pillow fight in the middle of the night, and all my bed clothes were thrown out of the window. I came back the next day to St. Omer entirely cured.

On the 14th a happy afternoon was spent destroying useless bombs on the aerodrome at St. Omer. You threw them from the edge of the aerodrome into a gravel pit, where they went off and fizzed harmlessly. But before throwing them you had to knock the pin. One of them went off prematurely, and set fire to the heather, and to our horror a wave of flame rolled towards the shed where the bombs were stored. And the wind was fanning the flame. We summoned a whole army of mechanics, and the fire was put out.

On the 13th I went with General Henderson to a whole series of squadrons, and on the 19th I started with him for London, stopping two nights in Paris on the way.

I was due in London to start back on July 1st, but while motoring back from the country my driver ran me in the mist into a hedge, and I was projected through the windscreen, and cut my head. The result of this mishap was that I stayed in London till the 21st of July, when I arrived back at St. Omer.

When I got back General Henderson told me I should very likely have to go to Italy in the immediate future as someone who could speak Italian was wanted to go there on business connected with aircraft with Captain Valentine, our representative in Paris.

On July 28th the Germans dropped three bombs on St. Omer town at midnight.

They also dropped a message to say that they were going to bomb the town daily throughout the next week until it was destroyed. An idle threat. The damage done was slight. One baker's shop was wrecked and one other house damaged.

On July 30th the Germans again dropped three bombs on St. Omer, this time at 5.45. The slight thud in the air woke me up.

I went to Ypres again with Victor Barrington-Kennett, and had a real leisurely exploration of the place. I spent some time in the ruined cathedral. The organ was still intact, but the staircase leading up to it was destroyed. Our batteries stationed just on the fringe of the town barked all the while. The town itself was deserted and silent. In the sacristy of the cathedral there were a lot of books and missals quite intact. A harvest of souvenirs for those who wanted such things. I had no inclination to take even a chip of a brick away. I dined with No. 1 Squadron that night at Bailleul, and stayed the night.

It was now definitely settled that I was to go to Italy and to start at once. I started after dinner the next evening, and broke the journey at the First Aircraft Depot at Candas, a village which is on the way to Amiens.

The next morning I resumed the journey, and halted at Vert Galant, on the Amiens road, where we had some Squadrons. I arrived in Paris in the evening. The next morning I saw the ambassador, and had a long talk with him, but I kept no record of it. The next day I spent walking about Paris, and on the evening of the 4th I started with Valentine by the night express for Turin.

We arrived at Turin on August 5th about two o'clock in the afternoon, and proceeded at once to the Aviation Headquarters, which were in a barracks. Thence we went at once with a Captain de la Polla to see piston and propeller shops. The object of our mission was to see the Caproni machine; to find out whether it could carry the Beardmore engine; and if it was advisable to order one for the R.F.C. Before starting I learnt all the Italian technical terms I could.

The next day we went in a military motor, driven at an incredible speed, to the Fiat motor works , and after luncheon by train to Milan, where we were met by one of the Gaetani family. We dined in a cafe in the big arcade, and one of the guests was a distinguished actress belonging to the *Comédie Française*. The next day we went to Malpensa, the Italian flying school, and there we saw the Caproni machine. We had luncheon at Gallerata, and drove from thence to the Isotto-Fraschini works. A great deal of conversation was poured through me, but I have no recollection of what it was all about. The net result was that a Caproni machine was ordered. The next day we visited the Dion works, and in the evening we started for Rome, as it was at Rome that our business had to be settled.

We went to the War Office, and saw General Morris, who was in charge of the Italian aviation. He said one thing which stuck in my mind, and which made me laugh a good deal internally, although I kept an absolutely grave countenance. He said: "What I am going to say to you will be absolutely unintelligible and unthinkable to you as Englishmen, but I regret to say that here, in Italy, it is a fact that there exists a certain want of harmony, a certain, occasional, shall I say, friction? between the military and naval branches of our Flying Service." We murmured "impossible."

That night we drove to St. Peter's and to the Coliseum. They both looked singularly beautiful in the velvet darkness. The city was dimly lit for fear of air-raids, but there were numbers of blue lights which heightened the majesty and the mystery of the stately Roman buildings.

The next morning I went to the Palatine. While I was there, basking in the gorgeous colours and the blazing sunshine, a small boy drove by in a large cart with two mules. I was smoking. Catching sight of me, he leapt from his cart, lit a cigarette at mine, and then drove on in silence with a lordly swagger, like a Prince.

In the evening we started back for Turin. At Turin we had more business at the Aviation Office and at the Francia Works. We started for Paris in the afternoon, and a man met us at the station with a parcel of steel obdurator rings.

On the 13th Valentine drove me back from Paris in his racing Panhard. We left Paris at 4.15, and we arrived at St. Omer at 7.20. Valentine drove at a terrific speed, but with consummate skill. He would calculate accurately what a man in a cart about three-quarters of a mile ahead would be likely to want to do . . . and not give him time to do it.

When we arrived we found that General Henderson had gone to London for good, and General Trenchard was commanding the R.F.C. in the field. I was filled with consternation at finding General

Henderson gone. Having been with him since the beginning of the war, I looked upon his presence as a matter of course, apart from all such questions as old acquaintance, friendship, and my appreciation of what he had been and done, and of his indescribable kindness to me personally, and of all the qualities which everyone who came into close contact with him felt and knew.

Apart from all that, I felt adrift, like a stranded bondsman face to face with a new Pharaoh, and a bondsman who felt he had no qualifications.

# CHAPTER 10

# St. Omer and Another Offensive

*August—December,* 1915.

The day after I arrived in Italy, Valentine told me I would be most useful to him in his Paris office, so I gathered this move had been suggested. The last thing I wanted was to go to Paris.

General Trenchard sent for me, and told me he was willing to keep me for a month. He would see by that time whether I would be of any use to him, and if I was of no use I should have to go. He told me whatever I might have heard to the contrary, he was not so bad a person to serve under.

He then asked me if I should like to stay on. I said I should like to go to London and talk things over with General Henderson. I also said that I should hate to go to Paris. He told me I might go at once, and I started that afternoon. I saw General Henderson, and he told me I had much better stop with the R.F.C. There was nothing I could do at the War Office. So I went back, and, stopping on the way in Paris, I reached St. Omer on the 20th.

When General Trenchard took over, the R.F.C. consisted of three Wings and a Headquarters. The first thing he wanted me to do was to make notes for him. The general's system of note-making was like this. He visited squadrons or depots or aircraft parks as the case might be and took someone with him who made notes (for the next four years the someone was myself) of anything they wanted. In the evening the notes used to be put on his table typed, and then he would send for the various staff officers who dealt with the matters referred to in the notes, and discuss them.

The first thing he would ascertain was if the matter mentioned in the note had a real foundation; for instance, whether a Squadron which complained that they were short of propellers had not in fact received a double dose the day before. If the need or the complaint or the request was found to be justified and reasonable he would proceed to hasten its execution and see that the necessary steps were taken. If the requests were found to be idle or baseless the squadron or the petitioner in question would be informed at once. But where the general differed from many capable men was in this: he was never satisfied with investigating a request or a grievance or a need or a suggestion.

After having dealt with it he never let the matter rest, but in a day or two's time he would insist on hearing the sequel. He would find out whether Squadron B had received its split pin or what Mr. A. had answered from England when asked for it. This did not conduce to our repose, but it did further the efficiency of the R.F.C.

The first long expedition I went with him was on August 22nd to the Third Army, where we visited No. 8, No. 4 and No. 12 Squadrons. But the first notes that I can read were made the day after, when we visited the first Wing. I have down in my note-book for that day that the general wants some Oxford marmalade for breakfast, that the road near No. 3 Squadron is too dusty, and steps must be taken to remedy this. That the first Wing are not to press at present to send home observers to learn to fly. That Christie wants some more double clips for the elevator control. There is also something not quite legible with reference to R.A.F. wires and Crossley spare axles. The general never referred again—that year at least—to his initial talk with me as to whether I should be of use to him or not, but when on the 24th of August, the day after he said he liked Oxford marmalade, there was Oxford marmalade for tea, he said to me, looking at it: "I see you have got a memory; I shall use it."

We all missed General Henderson very much, and the general told me he missed his influence with the armies. The Coldstream Guards were billeted quite close to us on the road to Boulogne at this time. And one night my nephew, Dermot Browne,[1] who was in that regiment, came to dinner with us, with John Ponsonby, who almost immediately after this became a Brigadier, and one night I had dinner at his Headquarters.

On September 2nd I went with the general to Paris. I was furnished with a note that we must bring back some paper felt washers for the induction pipes of the Le Rhone engine. We went to the Paris Aviation Office and afterwards to Darracq's Works. The next day the General had an interview with General Hirshauer, who commanded

---

1. He was killed at Loos on September 29.

the French aviation then, but he went with Colonel Leroy-Lewis, our military *attaché*, and I was not present. We also went to the Morane factory. We got back to St. Omer on the 5th, stopping at one of the Squadrons on the way.

In those days we only had one aircraft park to supply the needs of the squadrons. It was scattered about in various places at St. Omer. The general's idea, which he carried into effect shortly after this, was to have one aircraft park for the squadrons serving each army—what were afterwards the brigades. We went over the aircraft park on the 8th. I have it on record that the Banjo clearances were wrongly adjusted when they came out.

The next day the two Wing Commanders, Colonel Ashmore and Colonel Brancker, came to luncheon, and we went to the aircraft park with them.

On the 5th I went for my first long fly with Major Beatty in a B.E.2.C. We meant to go to Dunkirk, but we went somewhere near Calais and back. It was a lovely day. We went up to about 5,000 feet. There were no clouds, and we stayed up about an hour and a half.

Our staff now consisted of Brooke-Popham as G.S.O. 1, Festing as D.A.A. and Q.M.G., Major Beatty, who managed the Q. side, and Major Pope-Hennessy, G.S.O. 2.

Another push was coming on, and on the 18th a Wing Conference took place in a little school at Hinges, when the flying arrangements for the coming battle were discussed.

At this conference the three Wing Commanders (Colonel Ashmore commanding the first Wing, Colonel Salmond commanding the second, and Colonel Brancker commanding the third) were present, and their staff officers, Brooke-Popham, Pope-Hennessy, and myself.

The main points discussed were the number of gallons of petrol to be kept at rail-heads in case of an advance, the landing of agents behind German lines, the question of bombing trains, the supply of machines, etc.

On the 21st the bombardment began. I went with the general to all the squadrons in the first Wing. We visited seven squadrons, two Wing Headquarters, and one Aircraft Park. It was an exhausting day, and produced a harvest of notes. Here a few out of the multitude: No. 3 Squadron wants Ball-race No. 25 x 55 x 21½ for false nose. No. 2 have no V-typed under-carriages in the squadron. No. 10 leave their machines out in the sun. One machine, which was shot, is hung up for a cross-tube, under the fuselage, holding the sockets of the bottom-plane. No. 16 want fish-tail clips, and hot air-pipes for the Zenith carburettor. No. 1 want a Le Rhone false nose-plate, complete, with pinion and ball-bearing. No. 6 want oval tubing-steel, 3/4—3/8, and a front left-hand top-centre section of Fish-plate for a F.E. 2.A.

On the 22nd arrangements were made about wireless, dealing more especially with valve-prefixes, short-wave-tuners, the tactical call, the sterling-set transmitter, the short-wave tuner, etc. On the 23rd there was a heavy bombardment going on, and very heavy firing during the night of the 24th; and on the morning of the 25th, we sat in the office and waited for news. Rumours came of good news about the French offensive in Champagne. It rained all the afternoon. At sunset, about 5.45, a large rainbow appeared in the East. I saw the light suddenly in the office window. I walked down through the garden on to the road and a little way up the hill towards the aerodrome.

The sun had set. The west was all a blaze of watery gold, but it was still raining, and the rain drops pattered on the leaves of the trees. The fields on the right of the road were burnished by the sunset. Two white horses were ploughing, but it was too dark to see the plough-man. In the East, against great soft cottonwool-like masses of white and dull cloud (faintly tinged by the sunset) the little grey town with its red roofs stood out in clear outline, and the cathedral which domi-nates it, looked like a bird protecting her young.

A man in khaki went up the road, whistling. And near the church-yard, on the left of the road, a woman dressed in black was holding a wreath of everlasting flowers. It seemed to me more like sunrise in a dream than like sunset; no, not like a sunset or a sunrise, neither Autumn nor Spring, but the unearthly dawn of a new, strange season. I thought it was perhaps the presage of victory, but victory mingled with tears.

All this last page I have transcribed from my Diary word for word, but what I also remember happening and what is not in my diary, so that I don't know whether it happened that morning or the morning after, is a breathless period of excitement after we received the first favourable news of that battle.

Someone rushed into the office and said we would be off to Bet-hune in a few hours' time, and I drove down to the town and bought whole stacks of tinned meat to be ready for all emergencies. Then time went on; the news began to seem a little less good, and nobody said anything, but one realised that there was no need for extra rations of bully beef, and one felt that one would soon be settling down to the old routine—and that we were only going through what had happened already before.

The next morning everyone was in a state of alarm owing to the news in the German wireless which had been mistranslated and misunderstood. I went to the second Wing to get news, and heard that 8 guns, 1,200 officers and 10,000 men had been taken. When I got back I found everyone rather depressed. Things did not appear to be going so well. After luncheon I went to Hinges, to the first Wing. There the news seemed better. I climbed up a tower, from which Messines is visible, to see the battle, but I could see nothing.

On the 29th we got news that the French had broken through the German third line. This turned out afterwards, if true, to have been unavailing.

On October 3rd, 1915, life resumed its normal course. During a push our life was not normal. In the first place, in the office there was a table on which all the telegrams from the different Wings and Armies were arranged in order, and everyone was standing by in case of a move.

On the 4th I went with the general to look for his old regiment, the Royal Scots Fusiliers. They were supposed to be near Poperinghe, but we could not find a trace of it. We stopped just outside Ypres, and walked into the town. Every house by this time was smashed. A German machine came over while we were there, only one, but constant whistling for people to take cover went on the whole time we were there, when there were no German machines in sight.

On the 8th of October, 1915, General Henderson came out and stayed till the 11th. We went the round of the squadrons with him.

On the 9th of October, in the afternoon, we had a glorious exhibition of machines. Each squadron sent a machine fitted up with its pet gun, mountings, and gadgets—and one got the prize. The following questions were dealt with:—

Bomb sights.
Camera.
Incendiary bomb-tubes.
Wireless reel.
Bomb-barrier fittings (standard position close to fuselage).
Release gear (cam gear for releasing bombs).
Gun mountings.
Ammunition.
Wireless accumulators.

Wireless instruments.

Signalling keys (they must be inside).

Heating of carburettor.

Holes in planes.

Colour of cowl.

And, if *extra tanks are carried*, petrol, oil, pump, instruments, control pillar.

Map case.

On the 21st of October I went on leave, and stayed in London till the 28th, when I got back to St. Omer again. Just at this time the Fokker scourge was at its height. The Germans had made an exact copy of a French machine, namely, the Morane monoplane, and were using it with deadly effect against our B.E.'s, which were continuing to do the work of the army. The Germans were not continuing to do the work of their army on our side of the line.

By this time our Flying Corps was so used to doing what it wanted in the air without serious opposition that not enough attention was paid to this menace, and the monoplane, in the hands of a pilot like Immelmann, was a serious, and for us a disastrous, factor.

But the point is that our work never stopped in spite of this. The work of the armies was done, Fokker scourge or no Fokker scourge. It may be asked why we had not got the equivalent of Fokkers[2] in great quantity by this time, and the answer is that in aviation during the war everything was a compromise between progress and supply. As it took more than nine months for anything new in the shape of a machine or an engine to be available in any quantity, it generally happened that by the time a machine or an engine or the spare parts of both were available in sufficient quantities the engine or machine or spare parts in question by that time were out of date.

In spite of this difficulty, in spite of all the disadvantages we suffered from, which were caused initially and fundamentally by the broad fact that when we went to war we had only a partially ready Flying Corps and that a great deal of the most important mechanical factors of the Flying Corps had been made in Belgium or in Germany—in spite of this neither then nor at any time later did the work which the armies asked the Flying Corps to do for them relax whenever flying was possible.

You often hear it said that had the authorities in England been

---

2. For offensive purposes; as a defence against Fokkers they would have been useless.

more prompt and judicious and enterprising in their choice of the machines they ordered we should, at the outset of the war, have had an overwhelming mechanical preponderance over the Germans in the air. It is said, for instance, that we might have had the Vickers fighter in 1914 instead of in the summer of 1915, in which case our pilots could have shot down the Germans like sparrows. I remember hearing a friend of mine, who was himself an excellent pilot, exposing this fact. It was true we might have had the Vickers machine in 1914, so I ascertained; but what the pilot omitted to say, because he did not know it, was this: that the Gnome monosoupape engine, which was the engine of the Vickers fighter, was not in 1914 a reliable engine. It was only by the spring of 191 5 that it could be used safely.

Another thing few people realise is that till the outbreak of the war we had got all our magnetos from Germany. We not only had to make magnetos when the war broke out, but to learn how to make them. The French were in the same predicament as ourselves.

In London people were beginning to become alarmed at our air casualties. Up till this moment there had been very few casualties in the air, less than in peace time. Also the name of Immelmann captivated the public. Everyone one met said: "When are they going to get Immelmann?" In France, too, people began to say it was nonsense to talk of our supremacy in the air, when German machines were seen to be doing what they liked over our lines. And just at this period a senior infantry officer complained of a shoal of German machines that bothered him every evening near Poperinghe. Somebody was sent to see this shoal, and they turned out to be Maurice Farmans quietly going home to roost.

On the 30th of October, 1915, a startling incident happened, of which the General, Colonel Ashmore, and myself were witnesses. The king was in France, and machines were forbidden to fly in the area over his billet. I was driving with the general to Aire, and we passed quite close to the king's billet, when suddenly we saw a Henry-Farman machine flying low without marks, right over the king's billet. We had no Henry-Farman machines at that moment. Telegrams and messages were sent all over France to trace the machine without avail. The French knew nothing of it, neither did the Belgians. The explanation was that it was the French liaison officer who used to fly backwards and forwards from France to England.

On November 2nd the general had to go to London for a day. I note that we passed a wet stable, in which a lot of men were billeted.

They put a placard outside their billet, on which were written the words:

*Château Rue Matique.*

The problem of how to fire through the propeller was engaging everyone's attention at this time. The question was solved for the moment by having a deflector on the propeller, off which the bullet ricocheted, when it would, without a deflector, have hit the propeller. This system was invented by Garros, the French pilot, and copied by the Germans. They then adopted a gun which fired through the propeller, by virtue of an interrupter gear, a system which was definitely proposed by the Royal Aircraft Factory before the war, although it did not then get as far as the drawing stage. Our synchronising gear first came into existence in 1916.

On November 7th, 1915, the first Morane biplane arrived at St. Omer, and was flown against a Bristol scout. The General watched the two machines go up. It was rather cloudy, and after they had been up about half an hour he began to grow uneasy. Like all people who have an intimate experience of aircraft, he hated watching flying, and hated still more waiting for people to return. However, both the machines returned safely.

On the 8th I went with the General to London. We returned on the 15th. Nothing particular happened during the next few days, except that the first Wing was made to disgorge a clerk from their surplus, and arrangements for Christmas were made.

On the 22nd of November, 1915, I went with the general to watch experiments of bombing from the air in the Third Army, which General Allenby was commanding. We watched bombs being dropped from a machine, which went off satisfactorily and at a reasonable distance from the target. When we got back the following letter was written to the Third Wing, which I quote as an example of the kind of work which used to be done.

H.Q., 3rd Wing.

With reference to the questions raised by various officers in your Wing during my visit today, herewith the following remarks:

| Questions. | Answers |
|---|---|
| *No. 3 Squadron.* | |
| *V-type landing gear* | |
| 2 End sockets for strut tube | Ordered. Further |

| | |
|---|---|
| rear 5408-ii wanted. | information later |
| Machine 4793 sent from St. O. with bomb release handle outside. | Being inquired into. |
| *No. 13 Squadron.* Flexible petrol tubing for extra tank. | Telegraphed for. |
| No spare V. under carriages. | Being hastened from England. |
| P's. promotion. | Col. Brancker written to. |
| *No 11 Squadron.* 10 cwt. cable. | Ordered and hastened. |
| *Wing H. Q.* Copy of letter sent by G.H.Q. to Armies *re* A.P. | Herewith. |
| Reserve petrol. How much supplied per flight per H.Q. | An order will be issued later. |

On the 24th there was a concert on the aerodrome, given by the mechanics of No. 12 Squadron. A sergeant in the Artists' Rifles sang "I want to go back to Michigan" in a way which showed he was an artist indeed. He sang without emphasis or exaggeration, and his song was thoroughly appreciated. Mr. Kennerley Rumford also sang. It was a most amusing concert. News came that Furse, who had been on our Staff, and wounded in the head during the battle of Loos, when he was out on some wireless expedition, was seriously ill at a hospital. His servant was with us and desperately miserable. He received from his wife accounts so minute that they covered every moment of the day, of the course of Furse 's illness. He was sent home on leave. Furse got well this time, but only, alas, to be killed later.

On the 27th of November, 191 5, I went with Brooke-Popham to the Headquarters of the French Aviation Staff beyond Amiens. It was the first time I had luncheon with a French mess. Speeches were made, and I had to reply.

On December 2nd Sir William Robertson came up to look at the aerodrome and the Aircraft repairing section. We were told beforehand he would be sure to ask one question which the person asked would not be able to answer. This did occur. He asked someone what a particular propeller was made of, and the man didn't know, but had to refer to someone else.

So with almost daily visits to the squadrons we reached Christmas.

The Mess servants had their Christmas dinner at three. The drivers of the transport, the cyclists, etc., had theirs at six, in the stables. They had decorated the place magnificently. I went to see the decorations, and was given a huge glass of whisky. Our dinner took place at eight. Hugh Cecil dined with us. He now belonged to our Staff, but messed with B. Mess at Longuenesse. We had a long discussion about the war and the political situation. Hugh Cecil said if the war were to stop to-morrow England would not be worse off than she was before the war. The general said: "What about Antwerp?"

The next day a Vickers scout was flown over from England and made a forced landing in a ploughed field. The General had it rescued and flown off at once.

I was told I had to go to Italy again with a pilot called Cooper, who was our flying liaison officer with the French, the object of the visit being to get the Caproni machine we had ordered in the summer and to make arrangements for its being flown or sent back.

I started the next day with Cooper, and we arrived at Paris in the evening and at Turin on the following day about two. We went straight to the Aviation Headquarters, and found that no arrangements had been made about the Caproni machine. It was settled we should go to Milan.

*January 1st,* 1916.—From a letter:

. . . I returned from Italy last night. It was one of the most exhausting journeys I have ever done. We motored all day to Paris, then we rushed to the Gare de Lyons, and thence rushed to Turin. Then the next morning we got up at five and went by train, changing five or six times, to Vezzola, with two Italian officers, who discussed a point of higher mathematics during the journey. We got out at Adine, hired a motor, drove across the Ticino, and for all I know the Rubicon, and the Tiber, and Lake Maggiore, through Lombarda, and Novara and Arona, to Gallerata, where the Italians learn to fly. There we inspected the Caproni machine in a shed, and saw Pinsuti, the stunt Caproni pilot, and thence we drove to Malpensa, where Dante was born and Virgil died, and there we were introduced to 45 flying officers, who each one said his name and use and clicked his heels.

Then we had luncheon with the Flying School, which was commanded by Captain Falchi. At the end of luncheon the Captain made a speech about delicious England and the adorable English people, and I made a speech about divine Italians, quoting Browning, Dante, and D'Annunzio. Then an Italian pilot called Pellegrini, Cooper and myself went up into the sky. Into the grey, misty, sunless, lampless, sullen, unpeopled sky. And, as the machine climbed, the curtains of heaven were rent asunder, and through and over oceans of mist and rolling clouds, naked, majestic, white, shining and glorious, rose the Alps, like a barrier; and at our feet, dark as a raven's wing, loomed the waves of Lake Maggiore, fringed with foaming breakers; and the earth was outspread beneath us like a brown and purple carpet.

And we climbed and banked, and banked and climbed, and far beneath us a little Maurice Farman fluttered like a white dove. Then suddenly the three engines stopped buzzing, and we turned and banked and turned and banked and turned and banked and dived and turned sheer and steep till we gently rolled on to the ground.

Then we spent a few hours in technical conversation, and then we went by train to Milan and dined. After dinner we nearly missed the train, and finally got back to Turin at midnight. The next day we started for Paris. A Frenchman sitting next to us in the train whom I knew said: '*Il y a seulement quatorze personnes qui voyagent en temps de guerre et on est sûr de les rencontrer. Vous êtes l'une des quatorze.*' General de Castelnau was also one of the *quatorze*.

We reached Paris the next morning, and thence hither in the fastest motor in the world.

PART 3
1916

CHAPTER 11

# London and Back Again

*January—July, 1916.*

As the prospects of receiving the Caproni machine, should it ever be dismantled, seemed remote, it was settled that the machine should be flown over from Italy by Valentine. It was flown in the course of several months as far as Dijon, where, after many vicissitudes, it finally crashed.

On January 3rd, while the general and I were out Squadron visiting, the bomb store on the aerodrome, which was crammed with explosives, caught fire; Newall, who commanded the squadron on the St. Omer aerodrome (No. 12), saw the smoke, and with one corporal, broke into the shed from the outside and put out the fire. Some of the small incendiary bombs were already alight. Their boots were burnt. We went up to the aerodrome at once, and found the bomb store still smouldering. Newall received the Albert Medal for this action.

On the 4th, General Henderson came over from England, and on the 5th an S.E. propeller was found in an F.E. box. We did some wing and squadron visiting. General Henderson left us on the 9th. On the 5th we had an exhaustive and exhausting field day with the third Wing, and spent the night there. I reached *Canto* 22 of Dante's *Purgatorio*. The next day we started for Paris, stopping on the way at Chantilly, where we had luncheon. We went to Villa Coublay in the afternoon to see machines fly.

The next morning we went to Darracq's factory. While we were having luncheon the general got a telegram saying I was to go to London at once and report to the Foreign Office for duty. He was a good deal upset, because we had more business to do with the French, and he was without an interpreter. He said: "Of course if they really want you at once it would be criminal not to let you go." A wire was then sent asking if the duty I was required for was permanent or not. In the afternoon we went to Puteaux and Issy. That night we dined out. I sat next to X——. The general was on the other side of the table.

My neighbour asked me in French whether the general wasn't very young to be a general and what his name was. I said I would write it down presently on the menu, as, although he was supposed not to understand French, he would be certain to hear. Then we talked of other things. Later on during the dinner I wrote the general's name down on the menu. He leant across the table and said: "I hope they will be able to read my name in your handwriting."

We got back to St. Omer on the 13th of January. A telegram came from London saying the duty I was wanted for was permanent.

The next day I started after luncheon for Boulogne, and only just caught the boat after the fastest drive to Boulogne I ever had (49 minutes). I arrived in London at 7, and went straight to the War Office to report.

The directorate of military aeronautics was at that time occupying a loft right at the top of the War Office called Zeppelin Terrace. Of course I should have known better than go at that time of the evening, and expect to find someone. I tramped up empty resounding corridors and echoing and equally empty staircases till at last I did find an officer, and asked what it was for that I had been sent for so urgently. "Oh!" he said, "they want you to run some movies in Russia." That night I met at dinner an old friend and colleague of mine, O'Beirne, who had been for years at the Embassy at St. Petersburg, and was afterwards drowned with Lord Kitchener.

He asked me if I was going to Russia, and he said: "All I ask of you is not to say 'no' before you have thought about it at all." Mr. Balfour was at the same dinner, and he told me they wanted to send someone to Russia to organise propaganda. He was immensely kind, and said he thought I must be more useful there than where I was now. The great misfortune of the war, he said, was that there were so many square pegs in round holes. He was sure that was the case now with me. "At any rate," he said, "think over it."

The next morning, directly after breakfast, I went to see General Henderson. The first thing he said to me was: "You need not go to Russia if you don't want to." They couldn't make me go unless he ordered it. We discussed the question fully. He said he thought I was right in wanting to stick to my present job. Then I went to the Foreign Office. First I saw one of the Secretaries. He said: "Well, we hope you are going to Russia." I told him I didn't want to. Then I was shown into Lord Robert Cecil's room, and he made me a forcible appeal. The gist of his argument was that it stood to reason I must be more useful in Russia than I could be in the Flying Corps. "Do you expect anybody," he said, "to believe that you are of more use in the Flying Corps than you could be in Russia?"

I said I didn't expect anyone to believe it, but I believed it nevertheless to be the case, that I was far more useful in the R.F.C. than I should be organising propaganda work in Russia. I confined myself to one point. That we had a great deal of important work to do with the French, the French aviation Staff and French manufacturers and directors of supply. That General Trenchard could not speak French, and that it was highly desirable for him to have someone as an interpreter who had some idea of what was being discussed, and who knew exactly what he meant. He was not convinced, nor was I. And so the interview ended. But I should like to say, with regard to this latter point that what I said was truer even than I knew at the time.

Later on I listened to conversations at conferences at Versailles and elsewhere on the subject of aviation, when a fluent interpreter who understood English perfectly would nevertheless translate a phrase relative to aviation in such a way that it meant the exact opposite of what was being said, simply from ignorance of the subjects that were being discussed. Luckily there was always someone else present, who pointed these slips out to the general and the misunderstandings were rectified, but it showed one how fatally easy it was for a conversation of this kind to go wrong when the interpreter knew French and English but did not know aviation.

On the 22nd I had a final interview at the War Office. General Henderson said he was not going to order me to go to Russia, and I said I wouldn't go unless I was ordered. So the incident was closed, and I started back with General Henderson on the 23rd for France.

We stopped on the way at Dover and saw a squadron, and had luncheon with it. Just as we were sitting down the alarm was given, and a German machine was reported. A machine went up, and there was a good deal of firing but no results. The next day we crossed to France, met General Trenchard at Boulogne, and went by train all together to Amiens, where General Trenchard and I got out. General Henderson went on to Paris. In the train the two generals had a long discussion about the future of the R.F.C. The idea was that General Trenchard should go home as Director of Military Aeronautics and that General Henderson should go out to France and take command there.

On the 25th a new French liaison officer arrived *vice* Philonneau, called Lieutenant Duclos. The next two days we spent in going round squadrons. At one squadron one of the pilots showed us an elaborate gun-mounting of the Christmas tree kind, distractingly ingenious but a definite hindrance and handicap to the fighting efficiency of the machine, as a surprise. When the general saw it he said: "I never saw such ridiculous nonsense."

On the 28th Raymond Asquith came to dinner with us. He asked the general what the truth was about some air incident about which there had been a question in the House of Commons. The general told him that in the answer given in the House the facts of the case had been stated.

"Oh," said Raymond, "it was true! I thought as it was stated in the House of Commons it couldn't possibly be true."

The general, on his birthday (February 3), spent a happy day visiting the squadrons in what was now the Third Brigade.

The R.F.C. had now expanded from Squadrons to Wings and from Wings to Brigades. A Brigade had two Wings: a Wing of Fighting Squadrons and a Wing of Artillery Squadrons. A Wing was to be elastic, and had a smaller or a greater number of squadrons according to circumstances. But every corps was to have an artillery squadron to serve it. We started at 8.30 a.m., and for an hour and a half neither of us spoke one syllable. We were now expecting to go to London, and on the 4th the general gave a farewell dinner. Hervey-Kelly, Pretyman, Thompson, Webb-Bowen, Birch, and Lawrence came to dinner. The following lines were written on the menu:

*A was the Albatross caught in the lurch,*
*B was the Bullet and in it was Birch.*
*C was the Curtiss that went for the Zep,*
*D was the Delicate dangerous Dep:*
*E was for Essen the home of the guns.*
*F was the Fokker, the pride of the Huns.*
*G was for Garros, interned by the Spree,*
*H was for Hawker, who got the V.C.*
*I was for Immelmann somewhere in Heaven,*
*J was the Joyride from Dover to Devon.*
*K was the Kamshaft (if spelt with a K),*
*L was the Lorry that got in the way.*

*M was the Martinsyde merry and bright,*
*N was the Neutral too haughty to fight.*
*O was the Oleo supple and strong,*
*P was the Pilot who thought it all wrong.*
*Q was the Question denoting the Square,*
*R was the Rouget which sent it to Aire.*
*S was the Sopwith that fell on the floor,*
*T was for Thompson, who sent it to store.*
*U was the U boat employed by the Hun,*
*V was the Voison that carried some gun.*
*W's Webb, that is Bowen I mean.*
*X[1]*
*Y was the Yokel preparing to sup,*
*Z was the Zooming that made him sit up.*

On the 6th we had a visit from Lord Curzon, who went up in a machine, and on the 8th a party of Russian pilots visited us. We showed them round, and the General arranged for them to be given some Lewis guns.

On the 9th we started for London. As we were getting near Folkestone the boat stopped. A trawler had been blown up by a mine. Lord Curzon was on board, and talked of the necessity of having an Air Ministry and an Air Minister. A man, as he said, on whose broad back the slings and arrows of outrageous criticism would fall harmlessly. As we were leaving Boulogne the General got a telegram saying the French Air Minister had resigned. The next day I went to the War Office, and that night we dined with General Henderson, who gave a farewell dinner at the Naval and Military Club to Commodore Paine, General Trenchard, Longcroft, Webb-Bowen, etc. But in spite of this, all plans seemed likely to be changed, and General Henderson would probably remain in England.

We went back to France the next day, and the plan of General Trenchard being Director of Military Aeronautics and General Henderson going out to France did not take effect.

On the 20th of February, 1916, Commandant Du Peuty, of the French aviation, came to see us, and brought with him a French officer, who was to be henceforth our liaison officer with the French aviation. La Ferrière came from the French Flying Corps. His services to us proved invaluable, as he not only understood English but the

---

1. I forget X.

English, as well as aviation, and pilots, both English and French, and he did almost more than anyone to bring about the good feeling between the French and English services.

Commandant Du Peuty was originally a cavalry officer. He learnt to fly after the war began, and he soon proved himself to be one of the most daring of pilots and the soundest of flying officers and organisers. Our debt to him was incalculable, as I shall try to show later on.

Commandant Du Peuty left La Ferrière with us. The latter spoke English like a native. The next day the general and I went to Paris. We resolved this time to drive to Amiens and to go from Amiens by train. This part of the journey was not a success. In the first place, the train was half an hour late, and crammed to overflowing when it did arrive. An extra second-class carriage was added to it, and into this we squeezed ourselves. It was full of chattering women, and a small dog barked intermittently from the rack. The general was miserable. We were more than 35 minutes late, and the car got to Paris before us.

The next day we went to see Colonel Regnier at the French Aviation Office, and had a long talk. Afterwards we went to Villa Coublay and Puteaux.

The next day we drove back home through blinding snowstorms, and when we arrived at St. Omer we were greeted with the news of the Verdun fighting. Another piece of news was that a pilot, who had had his leg hit by an archie after bringing his observer safely down, had his leg cut off with a pair of scissors.

A Zeppelin was announced to be arriving at 9.30, but it was shot down on the way.

There was thick snow on the ground now, and every day news arrived from Verdun, which kept us anxious.

I went to see Ian Henderson, who was in a hospital at Lillers and was recovering after a slight attack of pleurisy. In the same hospital I saw a small child, who had been wounded by a bomb, being bandaged. She was holding a wooden sheep, and was very brave.

Here are some entries from my Diary and from letters during March:

*March 1st.*—From a letter: "A British pilot shot down a German Albatross today with his cross-bow. The German was so sure of being shot down that he brought his luggage with him, which consisted of a *Schnurbartbinde* and a small doll's portmanteau." The new type propeller should have its nose painted green. Three of them were not so painted in No. 10 Squadron.

*March 2nd.*—Went to 15, 5, and 6 Squadrons. Wypers Bluff taken and counter-attacked. There appears to be a lull at Verdun. A Morane biplane has arrived. F., in talking about General de Castelnau, said everyone had attacked him throughout his career. "*Mais on n'a jamais pu trouver rien contre lui sauf que c'était un homme tres remarquable.*"

No. 6 has no gun-mounting on the top plane of the Bristol.

*March 3rd.*—The news from Verdun is less good. The Germans have retaken Douaumont. Verdun is expected to fall. No. 21 has only three sheds.

*March 4th.*—The news is better. Distilled water is being issued for compasses and accumulators. Nine Lewis guns are to go to the French.

*March 5th.*—*Giboulées de Mars.* Went to Mass. A French bomb expert came to luncheon. Zeppelins reported to be about. No. 3 Squadron said a Morane pilot was lurking in 20 or 25 flying an F.E. He is to be given to No. 3 at once.

*March 6th.*—We have got a new machine. It did its trials and climbed 6,000 feet in two minutes.

*March 7th.*—Conference at Aire at first Wing H.Q. It snowed all the afternoon. Heavy fighting still going on.

Raymond Asquith came to dinner. My typewriter wrote this:

> *Blighty.*
> I want to go to Blighty, for I do
> Love Blighty more than any foreign land;
> I want to see the shingle and the sand,
> And Battersea, Vauxhall and Waterloo.
> I want to hear the noises of the Strand;
> Through the red fog I want to see a barge
> Move slowly down the river looming large;
> I want to hear the music of the band.
> I want to see the children at their play,
> Feeding the ducks upon the Serpentine;
> I want to hear the barrel-organs bray,
> When the wet sunset in a narrow mews,
> Reflected, makes the pavement puddles shine;
> And ragamuffins yell the football news.

*March 8th,* 1916.—In the afternoon we went up to the aerodrome to see experiments made with tracer bullets. The aerodrome was covered with snow. The sun sank an enormous ball of fire; the sky was dyed with a soft blush. Higher up it was blue; but very cold-looking and pure.

In that frozen space an R.E.7 suddenly appeared, and the sunlight caught it, and it glowed and glistened like a fire opal. It looked like a gigantic magical bird.

*March 9th.*—A terrible domestic crisis. One of the men told the French cook he was a robber. The sergeant said the cook was filthy. The cook was told we could get dozens of other cooks. The sergeant was told he was there to prevent rows.

*March 11th,* 1916.—Lord Derby came to see the General. In the afternoon we went to the Aircraft Park at Hazebrouck. We went in by the back way through a bicycle shed. This had a roof of green Willesden canvas, worth, the general said, its weight in gold. Scandal.

As we were driving back from Hazebrouck we passed a lot of lorries parked along the road. The general said if the war is still going on this time next year, put a note on my table in a year's time, *but not before*, that these reserve lorries must be cut down.

"*Puis se reprenant avec sa lucidité ordinaire,*" as Taine said about Napoleon, he added: "No, not next year, but at the end of next November, but not before."

*March 12th,* 1916.—The general showed the depot and the stores to General Butler, and after luncheon the aerodrome.

From a letter:

The *Hispano-Suiza* did 90 on the pitot tube. It is hoped the Le Vasseur Nieuport propeller will arrive tomorrow.

They say the engine with the silencer is faster. This is difficult to believe, but I do believe it.

She missed badly as Bettington was flying across, so he had to shut off.

The fan in the acetone dope room is out of order, so the men were told to knock off work there. In future no R.A.F. signalling lamps are to be kept at the 2nd A.P. The doping room there was not satisfactory. They were repairing a plane there, which is against orders, as it was laid down that *only doping* is to be done there. In the motor transport they were making water trailers for the Wings. Unnecessary!

Received from the London Library the complete works of Barry Pain.

*March 13th*, 1916.—The spring has arrived. A lovely day. A machine was reported to be down near Aire. I went there with the General and then to Brouay.

The uncovered wings of the De Haviland scout are straight as far as the outside strut, and then swept back.

Reading the *Octave of Claudius*, by Barry Pain.

*March 14th*, 1916.—News that Victor Barrington- Kennett is missing. The third brother in this war.

*March 15th*, 1916.—From a letter:

Today the Hispano got the legs of the Martinsyde with the Lang propeller.

The *le Vasseur* propeller absorbs the power, but not the efficiency, and with it the Hispano on the B.E. beat the Bristol on the climb, but not on speed.

The pitot-tube not having been calibrated, it was not reliable.

An LVG, an Aviatik, and an Albatross have all found a happy home in our lines.

*March 16th*, 1916.—Went to Bailleul, No. 1 Squadron.

From a letter:

In the back gun-mounting of the Morane biplane in A. Flight of No. 1 the taper-peg of the gas-regulator had no packing. A sergeant is to go and put it right.

Also the shock-absorber on the drum of the Lewis gun, which is round, is being changed for a flat and weak one; if this turns out to be reasonable the change must be adopted generally.

No. 7 still paint their tail planes, which is unnecessary, and makes the machine heavier.'

*March 17th*, 1916 (St. Patrick's Day).—One bicycle from the 3rd Aircraft Park, was found in the Motor Transport sheds in a filthy condition.

*March 18th*, 1916.—Some Russian newspaper correspondents came to see the Aerodrome at St. Omer. They went up in two F.E.'s. Some new parts arrived from Dunkirk. Had dinner at the Correspondents' billets with the Russians. Wilton, formerly *Times* Correspondent in Petrograd, was there. After dinner they all went to see some show, except Joukovsky, who stopped to talk with me. He quoted Swinburne by the yard. He said he did not much care for the Georgian poets: they seemed to him no different from minor Victorians.

*March 19th*, 1916 (St. Omer).—Game arrived. He is to be G. S.O.1. He comes from a Divisional Staff, and is furious at being sent to the R.F.C.

On March 22nd, 1916 we went to Paris *via* the Fourth Army.

The next morning, at 9.30, we went to the Air Ministry. Then to Nieuport's works, and after luncheon back to Nieuport's again to see the Acland deflector propeller device tried on a machine. It was hours before the engine started. As soon as it started, it jammed owing to the mechanic being too nervous, and the cartridges came out intact the wrong end. The general said the device would be dangerous in the air owing to the chain.[2] We then went to Villa Coublay, where we saw Morane and Saulnier.

We started back on the morning of the 24th of March. The roads were covered with snow. We stopped at Bertangles *château*, where the owner, M. de Clermont Tonnere, let one of our Wings have a lodging. It is a beautiful house at the end of a large, long avenue. The walls are covered with faded tapestry, and there is a fine stone staircase with a wrought-iron banister. We got home about five; it was appallingly cold.

It has now been settled that we should move into another Headquarters further south.

*March 25th,* 1916.—From a letter:

It froze hard in the night, and I was woken up three times by the cold and once by a mouse. When I came down into the cold, frosty and yet stuffy dining-room, someone, who was eating a fried egg, said: 'It does one good to feel alive.' These sentiments happened to be the opposite to mine.

I went to see our new *château* with Festing. It is called St. André, and is about three miles beyond Hesdin. It is a fine, massive *château*, with a long row of lime trees in front of it. It stands in the middle, and although by itself and separate from any other buildings, forms one side of an immense stable yard, in which there are trees. The stable buildings form the other three sides of the huge square. They are built in the purest Louis XIII style: low pink brick buildings, with stonework let into the walls, and grey slate roofs, beyond which there are hornbeams.

Up to now it has been used as a hospital for French soldiers, and looks dirty at present. The walls are immensely thick. There are two

2. Which it proved to be.

stories. The house is not very wide, so the rooms are narrow and high. Upstairs the bedrooms, most of which will be turned into offices, are small, and paved with bricks.

On the other side of the house there is a large garden and a kitchen garden, also an orchard. In the garden there are some fine trees. Some of the rooms have been used for diphtheria patients. There is an aerodrome not far from the *château*. You go in under a fine archway, where a coat of arms had been mutilated in the revolution. Under the house there is a deep vaulted crypt.

On leaving our present abode we are going to present the owner with a silver goblet. Read *To Ruheleben and Back,* by Pyke. A thrilling tale, beautifully written.

*March 28th*, 1916.—The cold is indescribable. It is windy, cutting, gusty, cloudy, and raw.

A French doctor (but not an unmixed Frenchman) from the hospital came to dinner. He said he wanted to see an English Mess. He evidently thought the English were strange animals. As the dishes were cooked by a Frenchman there was from his point of view nothing of interest. At the end of dinner he said with relief: "*Mais les cigares sont tout-à-fait bons.*"

All the following days were taken up with arrangements for the great move. The household thoroughly enjoyed these preparations. The general, not satisfied with our reports, visited the *château* himself, and went into every room. Every now and then someone would rush in and say: "What about extra sheets, and a leaf for the dining-room table? "

March 30th was the day of the great move to St. André. The whole house was upside down. All the clerks were busy flinging maps into cases, hammering boxes, ripping, tearing, rending canvas and other stuffs, and hurling packing cases into a lorry. Bates, the general's shorthand-clerk, went to him with a screwdriver instead of a pencil. The general, in order to escape the turmoil and confusion of the move, wisely settled to spend the day out. But before starting, we bought two stoves and two carpets for St. André in the town.

Then we went a tour of Squadrons, and arrived at St. André at six, where we found everyone buzzing like bees, and the house quite comfortable. An immense stove had been put in the hall, with a pipe which went right through the house. The general's office was upstairs with an *escalier dérobé* leading from it to the ground floor. You could also reach it by the main staircase. I finished Racine's *Iphigénie*. Noted these lines:

> *Songez, Seigneur, songez à ces moissons de gloire,*
> *Qu'à vos vaillantes mains présente la victoire.*
>
> (Act 5., 2.)

# CHAPTER 12

# Preparations for the Somme Battle

*St. André, April*—July, 1916.

About this time one of the periodical air agitations was going on among the politicians. The worst of these agitations was that they were too late to be of any use. It is no use making an agitation for obtaining in a few days time what it takes a year or more to make. The net result as far as we were concerned I tabulated as follows in my diary on April 8th:

Results of Air agitation:

A. Positive. Not the hastening of one bolt, turn-buckle, or split-pin.

B. Negative. 1. General hindering of operations in France.

2. Danger of spread of alarm and despondency among the younger personnel of the R.F.C.

This last factor was one which never seemed to occur to anyone in England.

G.H.Q. were now at Montreuil, and Sir Douglas Haig lived in a little *château* on the road to Montreuil, not far from the town. We used to drive in to G.H.Q. nearly every morning except when we were going for some long expedition. Raymond Asquith was employed at that time in the Intelligence, and while the general was interviewing the higher authorities, I used to sit in his office.

On the 8th of April there was great excitement because a Fokker was reported to have made a forced landing at Renescure. The Fokker was brought to St. Omer the next day. The general went there by air, and I met him in the car. He inspected the Fokker, which turned out to be an exact facsimile of the Morane monoplane. One of our best wing commanders was killed in the air just at this time, namely, Lewis.

He was taking up someone to show him the line, and was brought down by a direct hit from an archie just on the other side of the line. Lewis was one of the pioneers of wireless in the R.F.C., and one of the most gallant of pilots, besides being an excellent organiser and leader. He was a very great loss.

Only the day before he had asked the general whether he minded him going up. With the Fokker which had made the forced landing there was a German pilot. In the course of time he was brought to St. André and interrogated by Brooke-Popham. The pilot said he supposed we should copy the Fokker, in which case he would be shot as soon as the war was over. In the course of a conversation I had with him after his interrogation was over, he said that of course British pilots were paid for going up, and he seemed surprised and a little bit incredulous when I told him this was not so. He said the Germans had never used a Fokker with a stationary engine during the war. This was interesting, and, no doubt, true. And yet a great many pilots were convinced that they had flown past a Fokker with a stationary engine, which shows how deceptive appearances are in the air. This man was a native of Berlin, a clerk in ordinary life. He had mistaken the junction of a road and a canal, lost his way, and run short of petrol.

From a German machine captured shortly afterwards by the French we copied and adopted the disintegrating link for machine guns. One of the great difficulties experienced with the machine guns in the air was disposing of the empty canvas ammunition belts. When the gun was firing in the air the empty portion of the belt was liable to get blown about and thus affect the unused portion of the belt, and so stop the firing.

This difficulty was ingeniously overcome by building up a belt of separate metal links, which were only held together by the cartridges. As each cartridge was withdrawn from the belt by the action of the gun, the link in front of it, having nothing to hold it to the rest of the belt, simply fell off, and whether it was caught by the wind or not, could have no effect on the working of the unused portion of the belt. Such was the device invented by the Germans which we copied. This is the only device we ever copied from the Germans in aircraft throughout the war. The Fokker machine had a parabellum gun which fired through the propeller, but already in February of this year our synchronising gear known as the Scarf-Debowsky gear was in existence.

*April 13th,* 1916.—Navarre, the French pilot, has brought down four Huns in one day—the record so far. He is a genius. He makes rings round everyone else, and spirals down nose-diving. But he has the defects of genius in an alarming degree. That is to say, from a disciplinary point of view he is difficult to deal with in the extreme.

*April 14th*, 1916 (St. André).—We went twice to G.H.Q. in the morning. I saw Raymond Asquith. He lent me the *Spoon-River Anthology*. He said he thought the *New Statesman* was about the only readable newspaper left. He said one of the reasons people became agitated and hysterical about politics and the war in England was that the only thing which kept people quiet was a torrent of rhetoric, and that the ministers were now too busy to stump the country and dispense that necessary torrent.

*April 15th*, 1916.—We went on a long expedition to the Third Army, which was not without untoward incidents. At the first Squadron we arrived at there was a galaxy of Brigade Staff Officers. This the general cannot endure when he goes to see a squadron. He likes getting straight at the people without any barriers. Then we lost the way, or rather, we thought we were on the wrong way when it was really the right way. Reading the *Spoon-River Anthology*.

*April 16th,* 1916.—The Fokker machine has been flown to the Second Aircraft Depot at Candas, and Commandant Fort and other French officers of the French aviation were invited to come and look at it. The general and I went to Candas by air in two R.E.7S.; the R.E. 7. is a nice comfortable, roomy machine. It was a lovely day and the flight was enjoyable. Patrick flew over, and ran into the general's machine on landing. He had had the most amazing adventures in the Fokker, being chased by one of our machines in the mist, and having to land in the French lines.

*April 18th*, 1916.—The general has got an A.D.C. called Pelham who has arrived. This means that in future I shall not have to keep the Mess Accounts. Pelham proved one of the most valuable members of the Staff we ever had, and the most devoted, untiring and thoughtful A.D.C.

*April 19th*, 1916.—Le Prieur, a French naval officer, a genius, has arrived. He brought with him an extraordinarily ingenious gun-sight, which we are going to adopt. I translated a German brochure on how to erect the Fokker, and wrote three long letters about bomb sights in French. Here is one of them:

Head Quarters,
Royal Flying Corps.                    April 19th, 1916.

*Mon Cher Colonel,*

*Le Capitaine le Prieur a eu la bonté de venir nous trouver à notre Quartier General pour nous montrer son viseur. Nous en sommes enchantés et nous désirons vivement en procurer 300.*

*Nous sera-t-il permis d'en faire une commande pour ce nombre? Nous ne comptons naturellement pas les recevoir tout de suite mais le plus tôt possible.*

*J'ai envoyé au Capitaine Innes-Ker des renseignements précis sur le modèle qui nous est nécéssaire, afin qu'il puisse faire la commande aussitôt que vous nous en donnerez la permission.*

*Nous voudrions en même temps obtenir un ou deux des nouveaux Bi-plans Blériot avec moteur Hispano. Pouvez vous nous accorder la permission d'en commander trois? et pouvez vous nous livrer encore deux nouveaux moteurs Hispano, afin que nous puissions les monter vers le milieu du mo is de Mai?*

*Nous avons bien les trois quevous nous avez donnés, mais on est en train de les utiliser à des essais en Angleterre que nous ne voudrions pas entraver à moins que ce ne soit absolument nécéssaire.*

*Agréez, Mon Cher Colonel, l'assurance de mes sentiments bien dévoués,*

*Le Colonel Regnier,*
*Directeur de l'Aéronautique Française.*
*Boulevard St. Germain,*
*Paris.*

*April 20th*, 1916.—The road past the Aerodrome at St. André has not been tarred. Lorry No. 21542 was seen to be driving furiously.

*April 21st*, 1916.—I bet Hoare 10 shillings that someone would occupy Bagdad before two months elapsed.

*April 23rd*, 1916.—The window of the general's car was broken by my shutting the door of the car too vehemently. Tonight there was one of the most wonderful sunsets and twilights I have ever seen. The sky was green and luminous. Over the roofs of the farmhouses across the wide yard you could see from my window the tall, bare trees (hornbeams). One star in the sky turned the grey slate roofs to silver, so that they looked like the wing of a mysterious bird.

*April 25th*, 1916.—We had a fine exhibition of flying at Candas. Sir Douglas came to see it. Also Morane and Saulnier from Paris. Morane flew to Candas from Paris, and made a terrifically fast landing in a Morane-Parasol. A lot of hair-raising flying was done, notably by Patrick.

*April 26th*, 1916.—Patrick brought down an Albatross on our side of the line from 14,000 feet.

*April 27th*, 1916.—The apple tree in the yard is green, but the elms are still bare. Read *The Sinews of War*, also *La Jeune Fille Violaine* and *L'Echange,* by Claudel. The French have driven the Germans out of the air at Verdun.

*April 29th*, 1916.—The road at the St. André Aerodrome is still not yet tarred. There is too much denting in the Morane cowl. The archies must be warned that the Morane bullet is going to be flown home. It is indistinguishable from the Fokker in the air.

*April 30th*, 1916.—In No. 12 Squadron the cowls on the R.A.F. engines break at the tip.

*May 1st*, 1916.—The wind-screen on the Morane bullet is not satisfactory.

*May 2nd*, 1916.—Expedition to the Fourth Army. We took luncheon with us. Experiments were meant to come off in the afternoon with aeroplanes and flares on the ground, but the rain prevented them. La Ferrière has got the Military Cross. The unsatisfactory windscreen in the Morane bullet must be mentioned to Morane when we go to Paris.

On the 6th we started for Paris; we went *via* Pont de l'Arche, which is just outside Rouen. Nothing can describe the beauty of the drive through Normandy. At Pont de l'Arche we had a large engine repair shop which was one of the most efficient, well-organised, smoothly running and hard-working establishments of the whole war. We arrived there at 11, and spent the rest of the morning going over it. In the afternoon we went on to Paris along the Seine. In Paris we did business, and on the way back we stopped at Clermont, where the general gave Du Peuty his D.S.O.

On the 7th we went to London. It was arranged when I was in London before that I should be attached to the Russian Parliamentary Mission when it should come over to London on a visit. The mission had now arrived, and was being entertained in London. Among the Russian representatives was the notorious Protopopoff, who did a good deal of mischief later, and was largely instrumental in bringing the revolution to a head. I met him several times, and on one occasion I asked him if the ban on vodka would continue in Russia after the war. "God forbid," he said. "We have suffered enough from it already." One night a large banquet was given to the Russians at Lancaster House. Lord Kitchener was there. It was just before his departure on his last fatal journey. I got back to France with the general on the 14th of May.

*May 16th*, 1916.—I dined at the Hotel de France, Montreuil, with Raymond Asquith. It was a lovely evening. A full moon and a pink sunset, over which there were melting belts, gently fading one into the other, of light green, purple, blue, green, blue-grey, lilac and blue. Finished *Purgatorio, Canto* 28.

*Un, aura dolce, senza mutamento.* Appropriate for this evening.

The next day we made a strenuous visit to the First Aircraft Depot at St. Omer, and to a number of squadrons. We had now two large stationary Depots where stores were kept and aeroplanes repaired. One, which fed the northern armies, was at St. Omer; the other, which fed the Southern Armies, was at Candas, on the way to Amiens. Besides these, each army had an Aircraft Park, which was a mobile unit and was capable of moving at two hours' notice and dealing out supplies on the way to wherever it was going. All its stores were kept in portable, moveable boxes, which could be packed and put on lorries or a train at a moment's notice. To give a kind of idea of the work we did during a full day's inspection, I will transcribe the account of our expedition on May 17th in full.

*May 17th*, 1916 (St. André).—We started for St. Omer at 9 for the First Aircraft Depot. We arrived about an hour later. One Bristol is now ready, and will be sent with overhead top gun-mounting to No. 11. Squadron. This news was wired from the First A.D. Another wire was sent asking whether they can send us from home one of the Sopwith interrupters. The Nieuport seat is to be altered—for an eccentric one. The wireless transmitter is to go at the back of the observer's seat if the lip can be cut away. There were many other notes made at the depot, and still more at the squadrons.

No. 29 Squadron. The squadron had been mixing French and English gear in the Monosoupape engine Not having all English gear they put in all French gear. This practice is to cease. But how and why did they get French gear? That is the question. The squadron didn't know whether the parts were English or French. No French spares are to be used unless they have no English ones, and then the G.O.C. is to be informed. All French gear is to be returned. Sparking plugs are giving trouble. The First A.D. was wired to for English cam-gear. French spares, which had not been indented for, had been sent. Satellite-wheels which were really English were sent out as French. Bronze obdurator rings were wanted instead of brass ones. An endurance test for the tankage of the De Hav. is to be done at once.

At No. 6 Squadron the Le Rhone engine, No. 531 1, was not working well. R.A.F. wires were reported almost invariably bent when new.

At No. 1 the question of putting fabric over the hinges of the planes (as in the Morane biplane) was discussed. They have only one Le Prieur sight. What has happened to the 19 others?

No. 7 Squadron were one machine short. Other points that cropped up were the throttling of the no Le Rhone; Lorry 12,508, which arrived at 11 a.m., without a shelter. The lack of aerial winches in 13 and 12; parachute flares that failed to go off; split pins that were not supplied when asked for; and the lamentable case of a Bristol that was sent to No. 13 Squadron and put every bullet into its propeller with the Vickers gun, lit not having been fired at the Depot, and another sad case of a machine which was received from the Depot yesterday, rigged completely wrong, and in which the engine vibrated badly; but this is not nearly all.

We had luncheon in the car. Then to Abeele to No. 29 Squadron and No. 6. At Bailleul (No. 1 and No. 7) Longcroft met us. We went back by Merville and Aire. A tyre burst on the way back, and a second one burst just outside Hesdin. We had to walk back. We met a motor cyclist on the way. The general told him to go and order a car to fetch us. He said he had orders to go on and demurred; but the general sent him flying. It was a lovely evening: the young corn very green, and partridges running about in couples (one doesn't say couples but what? Clutches, braces?) The sky all lilac: the sun a blazing red ball, and the moon a tawny round shield; and cockchafers buzzing like small aeroplanes.

*May 18th*, 1916.—A domestic crisis has occurred. The Mess Sergeant has had a fearful row with the French cook, who has a fiery temper. I have no doubt it was the cook's fault. On the other hand, the rest of the household are determined to get rid of the cook. If they do so they will be foolish, as he is a good cook, and they will probably quarrel with any cook, at least they always have done so up to now, and the General will think it is the Mess Sergeant's fault. The blue on the rings of the Morane have been painted too light.

*May 19th*, 1916.—Today's great thought: Two acetyline welders are wanted for the Motor-transport.

*May 20th*, 1916.—The parachute flares have again failed to give satisfaction in No. 10 Squadron.

*May 23rd*, 1916.—I have been made a Staff Officer.

*May 24th*, 1916.—There are only four full tubes of hydrogen in the balloon store. The terminal of the electric accumulator is being painted.

*May 26th*, 1916:

*I killed a beetle in the night*
*That soared in spirals round my bed.*
*Do you agree that I did right?*
*I killed a beetle in the night.*
*It would persist with all its might*
*In soaring round and round my head,*
*I killed a beetle in the night*
*That soared in spirals round my bed.*

It was a cockchafer but beetle scans better.

*May 27th*, 1916.—The general sent me on a special mission to Paris. I came back the next day.

*May 29th*, 1916.—Light tender No. 24,133 was seen driving furiously.

*May 30th*, 1916.—We all went to Muret-Plage to see experiments with phosphorous bombs. We stood on the top of a small house and a machine went up and dropped the bombs, aiming at a disused piece of railway line. The bombs went off with *éclat*. Never have I seen such a firework display. After this was over I bathed in the sea. The sea, as usual, was boiling hot.

*June 1st*, 1916.—The First Aircraft Park report a shortage of potassium metabi sulphite.

*June 2nd*, 1916.—When we got to G.H.Q. we heard the news of the battle of Jutland. I had not noticed it in the official German wireless which I translate every day. When I got home I found it described at length in the Nauen Press, which used generally to be full of nonsense. Cowls are coming out painted like canaries, and the grass on the

Fienvillers Aerodrome is to be cut.

On June 7th, 1916, the general and I went to London. We stayed there till the 9th. The day after we came back experiments were carried out in dropping phosphorous bombs on a balloon. Nobody hit a balloon.

*June 14th*, 1916.—Wrote the following poem while waiting for the general in Intelligence G.H.Q.:

*Zeppelin, Zeppelin, burning bright*
*Over Dover in the night;*
*Sometimes over Folkestone too,*
*What is there 'twixt me and you?*

*Zeppelin, Zeppelin, how I wish*
*You were but a silver fish;*
*Swimming like a submarine,*
*Underneath the ocean green.*

*Zeppelin, Zeppelin, your delight*
*Is in dropping bombs at night;*
*How I wish that you and I*
*Were dropping bombs on Germany!*

*June 15th*, 1916.—Several 5000 round-Webb-ammunition-belts are wanted at once. 1 F.E. 2D arrived. The Rolls-Royce radiator is too large and can't keep the engine warm enough. The Rolls-Royce expert who is here says the service tank can't feed the carburettor properly.

*June 16th*, 1916.—I heard the following conversation today between a pilot who was waiting in the ante-room and a young sailor who is going to pilot a Blimp, and who looks like a cherub:

The Pilot: "You are going up in a gas-bag?"

The Sailor: "Yes."

The Pilot: "You will go a pop when they hit you. I should like to be there."

*June, 18th*, 1916. *Anniversary of the Battle of Waterloo (Sunday).*—Went to High Mass at Montreuil. The priest in his sermon said: "*On a dit qu'on peut être bon patriote sans être catholique; on ne peut pas être bon catholique sans être patriote.*"

Reading La Fontaine's *Fables*.

*Flore aux regards riants, aux charmantes manières.*

The rubber rings on the induction pipe cylinder head in the new

R.A.F. engine are *too hard.*

*June 19th*, 1916.—My new flannel shirt, which is made of good flannel, not shrinkable *an sich*, and which has never shrunk before after being washed several times, has today come back from the wash *all lumpy with tiny sleeves.* Will it ever recover? A medium nose-piece is necessary for all Clerget engines.

*June 20th*, 1916.—Colonel Barrès, commanding the French aviation, and Commandant Pugo, General Barrès' Staff Officer, came to luncheon. We had a conference with the General on future operations, La Ferrière and I interpreting. No. 27 are short of batmen.

*Il ne régnera plus sur l'herbe des prairies.* (La Fontaine.)

*June 22nd,* 1916.—A lovely and really hot day. We went for a long tour. The birds sang and the poppies flared in the wine-coloured clover, and tethered cows made a sleepy noise munching. Clips are wanted for the clock-mounting on the F.E.2B. Longcroft was shot at while he was in a kite balloon by a Lewis gun, and I suppose someone must have let off the gun.

*June 23rd*, 1916.—Visited some squadrons with Sir Walter Lawrence, who is staying with us.

*Le long d'un clair ruisseau buvoit une colombe,*
*Quand sur l'eau se penchant une fourmis y tombe;*
                    (La Fontaine.)

Everything is ready for the new push.

*June 25th*, 1916.—We went to Fienvillers, which is going to be our advanced H.Q. There we met Pugo and La Ferrière. A simultaneous attack was made on all the German kite balloons by the French and English. This was the general's idea, and it was settled when Pugo and Barrès came the other day. The general bet Pugo a *franc* we would bring down more than the French. We heard news of the bag at 4.30.; 15 Kite balloons were attacked and six were brought down.

*June 26th*, 1916 (St. André.)—News of three more kite balloons brought down yesterday. The Third Army have received a telephone message saying that the wire-cutting is going on satisfactorily on the Gommecourt salient.

# CHAPTER 13

# Fienvillers—The Battle of the Somme

*July*, 1916.

On the 27th of June we had moved to a little village called Fienvillers. This was our advanced Headquarters. The main bulk of our H.Q. remained behind at St. André. Fienvillers is a small village not far from Candas on the road to Amiens. Our Headquarters were in a little square house which stood at the meeting of five cross roads, with three rooms and a kitchen downstairs and six bedrooms upstairs, four of which were turned into offices. The advance Staff consisted of Game, Gordon, Corballis, myself, Pelham, and the wireless officer, Major Smith. I was billeted in the village in a Notaire's house just opposite our Headquarters. Beyond the village was the Second Aircraft Depot and Aeroplane Repair Section, which had now assumed gigantic proportions. There was also another aerodrome, on which two Squadrons were stationed, Nos. 27 and 21. These formed the H.Q. Wing, commanded at this time by Major Dowding. G.H.Q. was in a village called Beauquesne, about half an hour's drive in a car. Sir Douglas Haig lived in a *château* just outside that village.

On the evening of the 20th the R.E.'s. started on a long bombing raid. And the next morning at dawn the raid was repeated. I heard the machines starting at four in the morning, and went up to look at them. The assault took place early that morning, and all the morning telegrams came pouring in. The general sent me to Vert Galant to see No. 60 Squadron; to wait there and bring back their news in the evening. No. 60 was commanded by Ferdy Walrond, one of the pilots who came out in 1914, and were flying Morane bullets.

The Morane Bullet was a beautiful machine to fly, a monoplane, and very fast. It was the machine of which the German Fokker was an exact copy. And the general had ordered a squadron of these machines against his better judgment because the pilots had implored him to. He proved right and they proved wrong, because although the machine was a beautifully fast flying instrument, it suffered from the defect of all monoplanes: you could not see out of it except by banking, and a pilot cannot be banking the whole time. This machine proved to be the most expensive in pilots and cost us more in casualties than any other during the whole war. And the squadron which had these machines was the only squadron which had to be taken out of the line for a prolonged period.

I spent all that first afternoon at Vert Galant. I had luncheon with one of the Flights, and after luncheon, with Walrond and Smith-Barry, I saw the pilots start and then one waited, and waited. . . . Who would come back? Who would not come back? At 4.30 Ferdy Walrond came back with his machine riddled with bullets. I went home at 4.30 and reported to the general, and then went back again at six, and stayed till 6.30. This time I saw a lot of pilots hot from the fighting and in a high state of exhilaration as they had had a grand day. Here are some of the stories transcribed as they told them me in their own words:

*July 1st*, 1916.—Scott, in No. 5, said: "I saw a train about four miles from Cambrai on the Cambrai-Douai line, going towards Douai. I opened from 7,000 feet at it. When it saw me coming it pulled up and started going backwards to Cambrai; when I was at 1,000 feet I released my bombs. The train pulled up. Suddenly one of my bombs fell 30 yards in front of rear-coach, destroying the line, and preventing the train going back to Cambrai. Another bomb fell on the embankment. When about 300 feet from the train I came under heavy machine-gun fire. Flying wires, longeron, petrol-tank were shot, and several holes in the machine."

Gordon-Kidd, in No. 7, dived on a train. He saw it at 3,000 feet, side-slipped so as to save time, to 2,800 feet, and then came down to 700 feet and dropped his two bombs. One hit the cutting; the second one got the train plumb, and, as it was full of ammunition, it went off with a pop. All the other machines saw the train ablaze. Another bomb was dropped on the tail of the train.

Smith saw 9 L.V.Gs. going in formation to Bapaume. A lot of trains were seen between Cambrai and Bapaume.

It was a great strain waiting for Smith-Barry to come back; but he turned up all right, late.

The excitement about the fighting in the air during these first days of the battle was intense. St. Quentin Station had been bombed by four machines, all of which failed to return. The pilots, however, came down safely. But the damage they did was beyond all hopes, as they happened to hit an ammunition train in the station and a Brigade was entraining at the moment. All these men were scattered to the four winds. An indescribable panic ensued. It took the Germans hours to collect the scattered remnants, and then they could no longer be sent to the front. We knew nothing of this at the time, but heard it much later, first from German prisoners, then from refugees, and lastly, from the pilots themselves who did the deed, and who were prisoners.

Here is an account by a German prisoner of this raid:

At the end of the month of June the 22nd Reserve Division was at rest in the neighbourhood of St. Quentin. On the 1st July the Division was warned to proceed to the Somme front. About 3.30 p.m. the first battalion of the 71st Reserve Regiment, and the 11th Reserve Jaeger battalion were at St. Quentin Station ready to entrain, arms were piled, and the regimental transport was being loaded on to the train.

At this moment English aeroplanes appeared overhead and threw bombs. One bomb fell on a shed which was filled with ammunition, and caused a big explosion. There were 200 wagons of ammunition in the station at the time; 60 of them caught fire and exploded, the remainder were saved with difficulty. The train allotted to the transport of troops and all the equipment which they had placed on the platform were destroyed by fire. The men were panic-stricken and fled in every direction. One hundred and eighty men were either killed or wounded. It was not till several hours later that it was possible to collect the men of the 71st Regiment. It was then sent back to billets.

Gordon-Kidd, on the 3rd, dived on a train which was leaving the station half a mile S.W. of Abancourt, and proceeding to Cambrai from Douai. Both bombs were released together at 700 feet, and both exploded. They fell short of the track. The second bomb was released by accident simultaneously with the first. It would undoubtedly have hit the train. Recrossed the line under heavy machine-gun and anti-aircraft fire.

All the fighting during these days and throughout the whole battle of the Somme took place far beyond the German lines, and a German machine scarcely could put its nose this side of the line. Here is an extract from the Diary of a German infantry soldier written about this date (or probably a little later):

*Tagesüber kann man sich kaum in Graben sehen lassen wegen der englischen Flieger. Dass sie einen nicht aus den Graben ziehen ist ein Wunder, so tief gehen Sie. Von unseren deutchen Helden-Flieger ist keiner zusehen. Und doch das glanzende Verhaltniss 81: 29. Dass die Engländer tausendmal wagemutiger sind war nicht erwähnt.*

Every day one can scarcely show oneself in the trenches owing to the English airmen. It is a wonder that they don't come and pull one out of the trenches so low do they fly. Not one of our German air heroes is to be seen. And yet we are told of the brilliant proportion 81: 29. The fact of the Englishman being a thousand times bolder was not mentioned.

The man was being, without knowing it, extremely unfair to his Flying Corps, because if his German air heroes were doing their duty, they ought not to be seen by their infantry; they ought to be seen by us. And although not now, but not much later, this was the kind of thing our infantry in all sincerity would say about our Flying Corps, sometimes at the very time when their work was being most arduous and most successful.

On the 3rd of July I went to Vert Galant again, and again I saw Ferdy Walrond go up. But this time he did not come back.

Smith-Barry took over his squadron. Every morning I used to go into Beauquesne with the general. During the first days of the battle we had an extra office in that village, which consisted of a room with a telephone and nothing else: not even a Bradshaw to read. But later on I used to wait at G.H.Q. in the Operations office, which was supplied with a plentiful library of detective stories and novels. The entries in my Diary of this period are scanty in the extreme. Here are a few:

*June 28th*, 1916.—In the orchard where No. 27 Squadron live in tents, three small boys were found stealing lace handkerchiefs with Ypres lace on them, cigarette cases, tobacco and cigarettes from officers and mechanics. They were arrested by the sentry and marched into a tent, where they howled for hours, each saying and proving categorically that the other had done it. Finally gendarmes arrived, and they were condemned to spend the night in the tent and to be whipped the next morning by their parents.

*July 5th*, 1916.—Beauquesne in the morning, and Beauquesne

again in the evening.

*Dans le cristal d'une fontaine*
*Un cerf se mirant autrefois.*    (La Fontaine.)

Read Dante's *Paradiso* (waiting at Beauquesne in the office,) *Cantos* 1 and 2.

*July 10th*, 1916.—Luncheon at Beauquesne with General Charteris, General Walters, and some Russian officers. I went with General Belaieff to No. 60 Squadron. Smith-Barry showed him round. Read *Great Snakes*.

*Ce monde d'alliés vivant sur notre bien.*    (La Fontaine.)

*July 11th*, 1916.—The Germans in the trenches put up a notice the other day saying: "Tell your —— Flying Corps to leave us alone. We are *Saxons*."

As it happened, they were Bavarians.

*July 12th*, 1916:

*I went into a provincial town today*
*To buy a box of matches.*
*The air was sweet with smell of new-mown hay;*
*I went into a provincial town today,*
*And on the road I thought of how Edna May*
*Wore on her chin two patches;*
*I went into a provincial town today*
*To buy a box of matches.*

On the 13th July, 1916, I had an exciting experience. This is how I described it at the time in a letter written in error, half to one person and half to another. Both halves, however, were returned to me ultimately:

*July 14th*, 1916.—Yesterday I had the first whole holiday I have had since last August. How did I employ it? I employed it thus: In the morning I went to No. 27 Squadron and spent the time in gossip. I must mention that the weather made all serious flying impossible. Then I went home. But on the way I met on the road Smith-Barry, who commands No. 60 Squadron. He took me in his swift car to luncheon with one of the Flights (of his squadron). Then we had luncheon with Jimmy Tower. What did we have for luncheon? We had tongue for luncheon, and potatoes, and salad, and a salad made of fruit.

Then Smith-Barry said: "As it's a dud day and flying is out of the question, let us go and visit a French Squadron." I assented. First of all it was necessary to go and see the mayor of the village to arrange with him to cut the laurels in his field. And when I say laurels I mean *certaines herbes*, which were in the way. So we went to see the mayor. He was at home, and took us into his parlour. He was not at all like the mayor of Sheffield, nor was he like the mayor of L——, who was shot for being a German, which he was, nor was he like the mayor of Saponay, who was a disagreeable old man, but he was like a farmer, and like the kind of farmer you read about in the tales of Maupassant.

After a conversation the matter of the *certaines herbes* was settled satisfactorily. Then Smith-Barry put on his field-boots and his flying jacket. Then he ordered the Morane biplane. Then it began to rain. Then we walked to the aerodrome. As it was raining the machine was put back in her shed. And we waited and looked at the map, and Jimmy Tower showed us on the map where the nearest French Aerodrome was. Then the rain stopped, but it was still cloudy, grey and gloomy. Then I put on a leather coat and flying cap and climbed into the Morane biplane. Then the engine was started, and at once began missing because there was too much oil somewhere.

Then Smith-Barry turned round and said to me: "I am afraid we must give it up." However, some mechanics came and Addled, and presently the engine began to bizz and buzz and off we went. We had not flown very far, and were scarcely off the ground, before the machine tilted sharply left wing down. But of that more later. Then we zoomed up with a terrific yank and jerk. After a few bumps we got into a more or less calm area, and we flew right on till we got immersed in a great white, wreathy woollen cloud, and we dived out of it. Presently we saw the river (the Somme). Not long after we saw sheds beautifully *camouflés*, but beautifully visible also, and we dived down and landed (fairly well).

A lot of Frenchmen swarmed round us. We got out. It began to rain again, and the machine was put in a shed. I had a long talk with an Observer. Then the squadron commander, Commandant Villemain, came and took us to the Popote, where we drank tea and ate a *tarte aux fraises*, which was delicious. During tea, Smith-Barry told us that at the start, in getting off the ground, we had as nearly as possible crashed, because his left wing was an inch off the ground . He had never flown a Morane biplane before, and he was not used, he said, to its lateral control, or rather, to its want of lateral control (he said it had none, otherwise it was a charming machine); nor to the effect of a passenger being in it.

As soon as it stopped raining we flew home. And for a little time we—that is Smith-Barry—lost the way (no maps), and we suddenly found ourselves over the trenches. We made a demi-tour and soon returned safe to our landing-ground, on which we steeply swooped. The people who met us—Sommers, Portal, etc.—said that our start had been the most terrifying thing they had ever witnessed. The weight of one pencil on the plane and we should have crashed, which shows how lucky it is not to know and not to understand too much; as I had noticed nothing, or rather, *I had* noticed but thought that was the *star* way to fly. What would have happened if that machine had crashed, or if anything had happened to Smith-Barry, who is a star pilot? Jimmy Tower told me he had learnt German at Hildesheim, at Professor Timme's, the same family where I had learnt German.

On the 14th of July there was a further advance, and the next day more news and more bombing. I saw the machines come back.

*July 16th,* 1916.—Finished Dante; *Paradiso, Canto* 4.

*Come desiri, ti farò contento.*

*July 17th,* 1916.—Bron Lucas has got a squadron in England. The French cook has gone. This is what happened. The general said there was a smell of cooking, which there was. Gordon's servant repeated this to the cook. The cook hit Gordon's servant on the nose and made it bleed. Gordon spoke to the cook. The cook was rude. The cook was sent away. So now we have got a new cook.

*July 18th,* 1916.—Du Peuty came to see us. The R.E. 8. is at the A.D. It's camera needs a larger case. The machine is to be kept a fortnight so that the gun mounting and camera can be altered to what we want.

*July 21st,* 1916.—The general sent the following telegram to No. 24 Squadron:

Well done, 24 Squadron, in fight last night. Keep it going; we have the Hun cold.

Cooper, in 21 Squadron, was killed by a direct hit from an archie.

*July 23rd,* 1916.—Lord Northcliffe came to luncheon.

*July 24th,* 1916.—I went with the General and Toc Smith to Fricourt, where the fighting has been, to see the ground wireless stations and mechanics. We drove along the Albert road to Fricourt. The country at the back of the line looks like Hampstead Heath on Bank

Holiday, a mass of horse traffic and men.

*July 24th*, 1916.—From a letter:

I have been all day on the battlefield through the German trenches, which we took the other day. It is like a moonscape sprinkled with poppies and dead Germans' great coats, and here and there a gas mask. Shells were bursting in the distance, and our guns were firing, and there was a scream of whistling metal in the air everywhere. Troops swarming, aeroplanes flying about; the sky quite grey, so that one wondered if one were awake or not. I think on the whole not. The village of Fricourt is entirely destroyed, and that of Mametz is annihilated, and there is nothing left of it but crumbling stones.

*July 25th*, 1916.—From a letter:

The sight of the battlefield is amazing. It is one of destruction on a larger and more systematic scale than has ever occurred before. It is difficult to see in the villages where the houses were. The ground looks as though it had had streams of lava pouring over it for days out of a red-hot volcano. It is pitted with countless craters; some of them are bright yellow, with picric acid. And the noise goes on without stopping. In the further distance you see a column of shell smoke stationary in the air like a permanent geyser, only black. Was ever a battle like this fought in the world before? The answer is in the negative.

*July 26th*, 1916.—Sopwith No. 5721 is to be struck off strength and made into spares. The Second Brigade are not using the pannel for signalling with the gunners.

*July 28th*, 1916.—Finished *La Famille Valadier* and *L'autre aventure d'un joyeux garçon*, by Abel Hermant.

*July 31st,* 1916.—As we were coming back from the chief's house, the steering-gear of the car broke and we alighted in the ditch. Later in the morning the general made a speech to the Air Mechanics in the depot, who have been working like slaves ever since the battle began. They were all paraded in front of the shed, hundreds of them, and they marched and wheeled and formed different things so well that the general, when he began his speech, told them he thought they were the Guards. That pleased them. Then he told them how well he knew how "fed up "they must be with the work they were doing at such high pressure, how disheartening it must be sometimes owing to the way aviation had of letting you down. But they were keeping the squadrons up to strength and beating the Germans. They enjoyed the speech immensely, and I nearly cried.

*August 1st,* 1916.—The general sent me to the 2 A.D. to find out answers to the following conundrums. I saw Meade, who is in charge of Aircraft Repair Section:

| These were the Questions: | and these were the Answers: |
|---|---|
| 1. How did the test of the 160 do yesterday? | All right |
| 2. How many hours has it done now? | It had to come down yesterday because of the air-pump ball-race. It did about 2½ hours yesterday. Probably 18 altogether and 2 this morning. |
| 3. Strengthening the carriage of the 110 Morane-Scout. Just above the wheels. (a) Put down your suggestions. (b) Gun ought to have swan-necked feed so as not to flap about. | Machine ran into a hangar, Will send in report.  Noted |
| 4. How is the Sopwith getting on? | Still a lot of work to be done. |
| 5. When will there be any Nieuport Scouts ready for use, and how many? | 2 *can* be ready for issue. 1 certainly. 2 by midday tomorrow. |
| 6. Morane-Parasol. Have they taken off the Alcan device. | Yes. |
| This will also need a swan-neck feed. | Noted. |

*August 2nd*, 1916.—The Zeppelin sheds at Brussels were bombed by No. 27 Squadron. Two electric power houses were bombed at 800 feet. People were seen scurrying. Smoke was seen coming out of the engine sheds, and a bright red flame. Three trains were seen and any amount of rolling stock. Four trucks were blown up. Boyd dropped one bomb on to a train in the shunting yard. The trains were full of coal. No actual fire was observed. The second bomb fell in a field just south of the road. Four cows were killed. Smith dropped one bomb on the electric power house, Y., and one on sheds, X. The engine-sheds were sending up smoke and flame. Forbes dropped one bomb on the yard between two trains and blew up four trucks. The first bomb hit the main line and flattened a house on one side of it. There were no Archies.

*August 2nd*, 1916: From a letter:

Three or four nights ago a Highland regiment was billeted in our village. Its colonel lodged in my billet. Their mess was in the dining-room or parlour which was next to my bedroom. They had to leave for the front before dawn. About two in the morning I was awakened by the noise of boxes being nailed and valises being strapped and by various hammerings, knocks, and by general bustle. Presently I heard sounds of conversation. The officers of the regiment's H.Q. were having some cacao before starting. They didn't talk much. The voices stopped.

I thought they had all gone, but I all at once heard the voice of the lady of the house, a grey-haired *Ménagère*, who had got up to say goodbye to them. She was talking to the colonel. He was an oldish and mild grey-haired man. I had just caught sight of him the day before. He spoke French with great difficulty, not with a very bad accent, but he evidently didn't know many words. He was thanking her. He said: "*Beaucoup amusé ici.*" And she told him that she had been delighted, and that his men had behaved so well, especially the cook. He understood that and said:

"*Oui 17 ans soldat.*" Then she said something simple, I think about the weather, which he didn't understand, and he repeated the word several times and the conversation got into a tangle. She asked him if he was married, and he said "*Pas famille* "and something else which I didn't hear.

Then he added: "*Terrible guerre.*"

And she said "*oui c'est une terrible guerre.*"

And he repeated "*Terrible Guerre.*"

Then I heard nothing more and fell asleep, but I awoke again al-most immediately because the regiment was passing the house, the whole brigade . . . there wasn't a glimmer of light . . . and horses, guns, carts, ambulances, men . . . men and men . . . went by for hours on their way to the Somme, to go into the line.

*August 4th,* 1916.—I went with La Ferrière to see Du Peuty at

Moreuil, beyond Amiens. We had luncheon at his mess. After luncheon we went to two of the French squadrons. One of them was at Cachi, where the sheds are beautifully hidden in a forest of trees.

*August 5th*, 19 1 6.—I heard that Bron Lucas had flown over from England to St. André. So I asked the general for leave to go and have dinner there, which was given. I found Bron at St. André, and we sat in the garden after dinner and tired the moon with talking.

*August 6th*, 1916.—No. 70 Squadron arrived at Fienvillers. They have Sopwith two-seaters, commonly called "one and a half strutters."

*August 7th*, 1916.—The Martinsydes want cellon for their lower planes.

*August 8th*, 1916.—A French journalist came to luncheon. Finished reading La Guerre, Madame: the best war book I have read so far.

*August 10th*, 1916.—A wonderful night. The clouds looked like furrows of pearl in the moonrise. The sky was like a sea of delicate skeins of foam being softly unravelled by some unseen magician.

*August 11th*, 1916.—General Henderson arrived to stay with us for a few days. We had a lot of people to luncheon. He stayed two or three days, and one day we went for tour of squadrons together.

*August 17th,* 1916.—Visited the Fourth Aircraft Park with the general, and found some scandals, notably that the bootmakers were mending and making boots. This, although it sounds reasonable, is really a waste of labour, as the boots can and should be sent in to the place where boots are mended by the score, and the bootmakers can do something more useful in an aircraft park.

*August 18th*, 1916.—A happy day at the Depot and Repair Section. The Parasol gun-mounting: had they got it higher, had it been flown? The answer was the rear gun-mounting was completed late yesterday. The 110 Le Rhone was flown by Busby, and was found to be very fast: to run along after landing and to want space. Another big attack has come off. It is going well.

*August 20th*, 1916.—A new R.E. 7. arrived: a huge machine with a 200 Rolls-Royce engine carrying a crew of three.

*August 21st*, 1916.—Du Peuty came to luncheon. In the morning he watched the trial flights of the new R.E. Du Peuty flew away home afterwards, and shortly after he had started, G.H.Q. rang up and said a German was flying so low over their offices that they could not hear to work. This was Du Peuty, who was greeting them from the air. Someone else met him on the road, and he did a spinning nose-dive, which made the car driver lose his head and run into a ditch.

*August 23rd,* 1916.—We went to the depot at St. Omer. There was found to be no swivel gun-mounting on the F.E. and none in reserve.

*August 24th*, 1916.—Mons was bombed.

*August 26th*, 1916.—Finished reading Behind Bolted Doors, by Arthur Macfarlane.

*August 27th,* 1916.—Colonel Barrès came to luncheon and Commandant Pugo. Pugo gave the general a beautiful silver *franc* for losing his bet about the kite balloons. They have renewed the bet for next time.

*August 28th*, 1916.—Dined with Cruikshank at No. 70 Squadron. There was a Zeppelin alarm before dinner, and all the lights were put out, but it proved to be a false alarm. Finished *The Blind Eyes*, an exciting book.

*August 29th*, 1916.—Had my eye-glass mended by a skilled mechanic.

*August 30th*, 1916.—Received news that Mr. Cornish, the Vice-Provost of Eton, had died. This will sadden those in the Army who were his old pupils. I was not his pupil, but I owe him more than any pupil ever owed to any master. He pulled some of the weeds, or did his best to, out of my mind and taught me the things which were worth knowing and liking. He had the widest and most catholic mind I have ever come across; the gentlest irony, the serenest wit: there was nothing he did not understand and appreciate and enjoy; the northern counties of England, sunsets in Egypt, German storks, French cathedrals, Devonshire lanes, and Indian vistas evoked by Mr. Kipling; a football match; a meet of foxhounds; a picnic on the Thames; a pencil game, a charade; and, as for literature, his taste was unerring and his field of appreciation apparently unlimited. No one carried learning so lightly. He would enjoy himself and feel at home equally with Walter Scott or the Russian novelists, with Heine or Trollope; with Crabbe or Baudelaire; with Miss Austen or Villon. One never had the feeling: "It is no use talking of that, it is too new—or too this or too that":

*What is best*

*He firmly lights on, as birds on sprays.*

He was just the same about music and the other sister arts, and the most enduring picture of him that remains with me is his sitting at the piano and playing the serenade in the *Seraglio* of Mozart with absolute distinction. That night I read Dante . . . and who knew Dante as well as the V.P.? . . . and came across this line:

*Voi mi date a parlar tutta baldezza;*
*Voi mi levate sì, ch'io son più ch'io.*[1]
(*You give me full courage to speak;*
*You uplift me until I am more than myself.*)

He used indeed to make us all do and be better than our best.

*August 31st, 1916.*—We went to see the first experiments with the Tanks. A machine was sent up to see what a tank looked like from the air. One of the tanks walked calmly through a wood, knocking trees down right and left. I am reading O. Henry, and came across this:

*I will do anything but I won't kill and I won't wear pink pants at a cotillon.*

*September 2nd, 1916.*—Several people came to luncheon. They talked about Bron Lucas, who had been given a squadron in England, but who had applied to go back to be Flight Commander, because he wouldn't have a squadron in France (although he had been flying in Egypt) without being a Flight Commander first in France. The general said he knew very few people who would do that.

---

1. *Paradiso Canto* 16

128

CHAPTER 14

# Further Operations on the Somme

*September*, 1916.

During all the operations which had hitherto taken place our supremacy in the air had been undisputed, and the general used to say that if the war were to come to an end now we should go down to history in a blaze of glory. He was none the less uneasy as to the future, for he felt certain that the Germans would not accept this situation lying down. It was highly probable they would change their present policy for a more aggressive one, or at least strain every nerve to achieve this result. And in order to achieve this result the first thing they would do would obviously be to aim at an improvement in machines.

This gave rise to two disquieting thoughts: Firstly, should the Germans improve in moral and material should we be able to keep pace with them in improved machines? Secondly, if the Germans were to follow our example and adopt a more aggressive policy, the first thing which would happen would be a clamour for defensive measures from the whole army. Now, the general was convinced that a defensive policy in the air could only spell ruin.

I think it was during the month of August, possibly before, that Du Peuty sent us a long and beautifully written memorandum in which he summed up the result of his experiences at Verdun. The result of his experience coincided with the General's ideas, which were also based on his past experience, and which he had more than once stated in black and white. But the question was, would the R.F.C. be strong enough to resist the pressure of other arms which was certain to be exercised in asking for defensive measures? Such were the thoughts suggested by the trend of events happening in the air. And as each stage of the operations succeeded the other these ideas were confirmed, notably after the fighting that took place on September 15th.

But before I say more about this I will gather up the thread of the minor matters that happened before that date. During the first days of September we had several visitors, among others, Lord Derby, Mr. Asquith, and Mr. H. G. Wells. I took Mr. Wells to see the Aircraft Repair Section, but I had too little time to show him all that was really of interest.

On the 8th we had a Conference of Brigadiers, at which questions dealing with future operations were discussed.

On the 11th September, 1916, Guinchy was taken, and on the 11th an Army Order was published, according to which the shaving of the upper lip was made optional in the future.

On the 12th a Kite Balloon Conference took place, attended by all the Kite Balloon Commanders. I made detailed notes of what happened at this Conference. They are worth quoting as an instance of the kind of things that have to be dealt with in modern war, the kind of way work is done and the extraordinary number of small details that have to be attended to.

*September 12th,* 1916.—The Kite Balloon Conference, at the Third Brigade, was attended by the Kite Balloon Commanders: Cleaver, Boyle, Byng, MacNeece, and Wyse. Following is a brief summary of the Conference:

### Object of the Conference

To get into closer touch with the Kite Balloon Squadron Commanders.

To point out that as the War continues, and the scale of work increases, individualism, which has been a good thing and unavoidable in the past, will have to give way to uniformity. This does not mean that progress will cease, but that progress will work towards one uniform standard.

### Points Discussed

#### Rigging

*Boyle* thought guides ought to be made of cotton rope instead of hemp rope, because cotton ropes are easier to handle. He preferred the Caco Balloon to the old one. It can go up in a stronger wind, and is steadier.

*Byng* also preferred the Caco Balloon. He said it is steadier, and can work in a rougher wind, even in a 16-mile gusty wind. He considered the guides were not long enough and would like them thicker, not merely for the sake of comfort, but for safety. (Boyle here gave us to understand that this is what he had meant to say.) He did not care if they were changed to cotton. He said the Caco Balloon had done 4,800 feet with two passengers and ballast.

*Cleaver* had had no experience as yet of the Caco Balloon, (which should be spelt Caquot.) But he thought it was better, more stable and had a better lift. He was in favour of adopting the Caquot. He had nothing to say about the rigging. With regard to the handling ropes, he thought they could be shortened and a long cotton rope added to them. The G.O.C. suggested the pushed Bell handle rope. Squadron Commanders deprecated this as being likely to suffer from wet. Cleaver did not like the curve on the basket. He thought the lead on the metallic V might be shortened.

*MacNeece* thought the handling ropes should be softer and thicker. He agreed about the basket with Cleaver. He liked the Caquot.

*Wyse* thought the basket suspension too short. This could be remedied by putting slots (?); he also approved of cotton ropes for handling guides. He wanted ropes to be in one piece.

*Byng* wants a hole cut in the back of the balloon to let the air out quicker when on the ground.

*Boyle* raised the question of valve lines.

*Cleaver* used aeroplane cable on his suspension car, and preferred it as he said it doesn't chafe. This question does not arise in the Caquot balloon.

*Byng* wants a spare bar or hoop as the case may be.

WINCHES

*Cleaver* was in favour of the *Delahay* winch. He didn't know its power, nor its power compared with the *Scammel*. He thought the *Scammel* was not sufficiently powerful to pull down the balloon he has got now. Being asked by the G.O.C. whether he ever pulled down his balloon at top speed he said: "No, never except on a fine day."

*MacNeece* did not know the power of the winches either. He had hauled down at top speed.

*Wyse* had never had a *Delahay* winch. He knew nothing of their power.

*Byng* didn't think the *Scammel* powerful enough. He thought the

131

*Caquot* needed a more powerful winch. Asked why, he said because it works in a stronger wind and at a greater height.

*Byng* and *Boyle* agreed in thinking one should be able to pull down the balloon at top speed or 8,000 feet a minute in a 30-mile wind.

*Cleaver* thinks the *Scammel* winch too heavy and not mobile enough. He would like a *Caterpillar*. He didn't care how slow he moved. The *Scammel*, he said, needed a metal road.

*MacNeece* thought a *Caterpillar* would not stand a long advance. He advocated chains. He said the *Scammel* was more mobile in a wind.

*Wyse* said if winches are too light they are towed by the balloon. He said the *Scammel* loses ground going round corners. He was strongly against a *Caterpillar*.

*Byng* would like a petrol electric winch for changing gear while hauling down. He thought the most mobile winch would be the horse-drawn one. He was against a *Caterpillar*.

*Boyle* was in favour of chains and against a *Caterpillar.*

## TELEPHONES

Should they be in the hands of Squadrons or of Signals?

*Cleaver* voted for signals.

*Wyse* for Signals.

*Boyle* for Squadrons.

*Byng*, who had had experience of both, was indifferent.

## PARACHUTES

*Byng* did not like the cap, which he said comes off too quickly.

*Wyse* said the rubber band perishes.

*MacNeece* thought the parachute ideal, if the packing was all right.

*Cleaver* thought the rubber rings were not good.

No definite allowance of spare rubber bands is laid down. This was noted by Currin and Brooke-Popham.

The majority thought the parachute should not be fast- ened to the Balloon and to the observer, but ready for the observer to fasten completely at the last moment.

*Boyle* thought all fastening should be done, and that the only rea-son the observers were against this was because they were afraid of the parachute coming out, and being blown out themselves. He thought the rubber rings were not to be relied upon in all circumstances.

*Boyle* raised the question of the supply of gas. He said he had to send 40 miles each way for it. He suggested an advanced Depot at Fricourt. ,

*Byng* raised the question of red arrows being no longer painted on the tubes. This gives a lot of extra labour.

*Boyle* says his establishment is too small for the amount of paper work he has to do. He has no clerks, only one corporal. He wants typewriters.

On the 14th September, 1916, the general made a speech to the mechanics in the morning, and after luncheon he spoke to all the officers of the Squadrons belonging to the Ninth Wing, who were assembled in a shed. He told them about what was going to happen next day, that a big offensive was going to be made, that tanks were going to be used for the first time, and a great effort was going to be made to strike a decisive blow. The effect of this speech is well described in *An Airman's Outings*, by a pilot who was present, and who writes under the name of "Contact."

During the night machines were sent out with orders to drop bombs on the enemy's billets, railway junctions, aerodromes, and any other targets. This was done from every aerodrome in the Somme area. In the morning, before dawn, Ian Henderson left from No. 19 Squadron for special Contact patrol work—to follow and report on the movements of the infantry. He landed two hours later, his machine riddled with bullets, and came straight to our Headquarters. His face was glowing with excitement, and black with oil. He had seen our troops leave the trenches and go ahead. Only a few, he said, were held up. Selous, the son of the famous big-game hunter, took Ian Henderson's place. In the afternoon Selous came back with news of the tanks, and Ian Henderson was sent out again. He was a long time coming back from this second expedition, and we began to grow uneasy, but he landed all right with several wires and struts shot, and even his engine hit. He had seen one of the tanks capture a village at the head of a column of men walking beside it, cheering and waving to him as he flew over.

It was a terrific day in the air. It was not before a year passed that so much flying was done in the air again; 1,308 hours of flying were done; 24 German machines were brought down and 2 kite balloons. The troops on the Bapaume-Albert road and on the Bapaume-le Transloy road were scattered by machines flying low; Velu and Bapaume Stations were bombed and Provins Aerodrome Eight tons of explosives were dropped on Bapaume Station from a height of 200—300 feet. Near Cambrai, a bomb was dropped from 500 feet and blew up an ammunition train. I went to three Squadrons in the morning and to three in the afternoon. The Artillery Squadrons worked just as hard the day before.

*September 16th*, 1916.—Minding, a pilot in 34, had his main spar shot by a shell. Two-thirds of the main spar were shot out and the whole length cut. He signalled: "Have been stung by a wasp."

On September 14th, No. 34 never had less than six machines in the air: most of them did seven hours. Holt got bored with his registering, so went down to 1,300 feet and machine-gunned the battery.

Artillery co-operation had never been so great in volume, nor so effective.

In the Third Wing, on the 15th September, 1916, 96 shoots were carried out, including 70 on batteries; 43 batteries were engaged under the area call; 22 destructive shoots carried out on batteries. All the batteries engaged were active except two. Baines and Green (No. 3) went down and strafed a battery from 1,000 feet. This battery was firing four guns 300 yards from our infantry. They silenced the battery. Lynch did the same sort of thing. Roberts dropped a Hales bomb on a wrecked machine, scattering the people: when they collected again he strafed them with a Lewis gun. Sommers dropped two bombs on troops on the road: the men were in file. Transport was seen moving on the 16th from Pys to Grevilliers. Zone calls sent down, but they were out of range of anything but 6-inch. An observer came down low to strafe it with machine-gun.

On the 16th of September, 1916, the general sent me to No. 70 Squadron to take out anyone who wanted a rest for the day. The Squadron Commander (Lawrence) picked out a man called Drenon, and I took him to a round of Squadrons.

On the 15th we suffered one very sharp loss in the shape of Cruikshank, one of the most gallant pilots who ever flew. He was not only as brave as a lion but absolutely untiring. He had been fighting ever since the beginning of the war. And I think there was no one in the Flying Corps ever did so much work at a stretch. He had a sublime and, alas! as it proved, a mistaken belief that nothing could touch him or hurt him. He had told me himself a few days before he was missing that he knew he couldn't be killed in battle. When he saw a German machine he would see red, and pounce down on it nose-diving, whatever the circumstances. He was a great pilot, and we all loved him.

On the 17th, while I was showing a party of Russians round the aerodrome, someone casually told me that Raymond Asquith had been killed.

"Εἰπέ τις, Ἡράκλειτε, τεὸν μόρον."

What a waste people said, when they thought of his brilliant brain, his radiant wit, his mastery of language, his solid scholarship, and all his rare gifts. But it wasn't a waste, and never for one moment did I think so.

Raymond's service at the front was the crown and purpose of his life. A purpose fulfilled to a noble close.

He loved being in the army as much as he had hated being at the Bar. He went on with his life in the army where he had left it off at Oxford, and he died in a second miraculous spring; and by being in the army and being what he was, and doing what he did, in the way he did it, he made it a little easier for us to win the war.

On the 19th I heard Tower had been killed, who was one of the gayest and sunniest of pilots.

On the 20th of September, 1916, I went with the general to see a crack French Squadron at Cachi. There we saw Guynemer, the famous French pilot, who looked just like a young eagle. The general presented Commandant Pugo with his D.S.O., and from there we went on to another French aerodrome at Villers-Bretonneux. While we were there in the office a young observer arrived straight from an artillery shoot, and marked in the line on the map. The General was immensely impressed with the precision and straightforwardness of his work, as he also was with the whole organisation of the French photography and registration.

On the 23rd of September, 1916, a pilot in the Martinsyde charged a German and sent him to the ground like a stone, but in doing so his own ailerons were cut away. He got back over our line, but couldn't land and ran into a tree. He dislocated his shoulder. The fight had happened over Cambrai.

The fighting in the air which formed part of the big attack on September 15th made the general more and more anxious about the future. It would be strange if such a situation could last. So a memorandum was written which embodied the General's views. This memorandum was afterwards printed and circulated, and parts of it embodied later in a pamphlet called *Offence and Defence*. As it contains the main principles of our policy in the air, I quote it here. It contains nothing technical:

> Since the beginning of the recent operations the fighting in the air has taken place over the enemy's line, and visits of hostile aeroplanes over our lines have been rare. It is to be hoped that this state of things may continue, but as one can never be certain of anything in war, it is perhaps an opportune moment to consider what policy should be adopted were this state of affairs to change, and were the enemy to become more enterprising and more aggressive.
>
> It is sometimes argued that our aeroplanes should be able to prevent hostile aeroplanes from crossing the line, and this idea leads to a demand for defensive measures and a defensive policy. Now is the time to consider whether such a policy would be possible, desirable and successful.
>
> It is the deliberate opinion of all those most competent to judge that this is not the case, and that an aeroplane is an offensive and not a defensive weapon. Owing to the unlimited space in the air, the difficulty one machine has in seeing another, the accidents of wind and cloud, it is impossible for aeroplanes, however skilful and vigilant their pilots, however powerful their engines, however mobile their machines, and however numerous their formations, to prevent hostile aircraft from crossing the line if they have the initiative and determination to do so.
>
> The aeroplane is not a defence against the aeroplane. But the opinion of those most competent to judge is that the aeroplane, as a weapon of attack, cannot be too highly estimated.
>
> A signal instance of this fact is offered to us by the operations which took place in the air at Verdun.
>
> When the operations at Verdun began, the French had few machines on the spot. A rapid concentration was made, and a vigorous offensive was adopted. The result was that superiority in the air was obtained immediately, and the machines detailed for artillery co-operation and photography were enabled to carry out their work unmolested, but as new units were put into the line which had less experience of working with aeroplanes, a demand arose in some quarters for machines of protection, and these demands were for a time complied with. The result was that the enemy took the offensive, and the French machines were unable to prevent the hostile raids which the enemy, no

longer being attacked, was now able to make. The mistake was at once realised and promptly rectified. A policy of general offensive was once more resumed, and the enemy at once ceased to make hostile raids, all his time being taken up in fighting the machines which were attacking him. Superiority in the air was thus once more regained.

On the British front, during the operations which began with the battle of the Somme, we know that, although the enemy has concentrated the greater part of his available forces in the air on this front, the work actually accomplished by their aeroplanes stands, compared with the work done by us, in the proportion of about 4 to 100. From the accounts of prisoners, we gather that the enemy's aeroplanes have received orders not to cross the lines over the French or British front unless the day is cloudy and a surprise attack can be made, presumably in order to avoid unnecessary casualties.

On the other hand, British aviation has been guided by a policy of relentless and incessant offensive. Our machines have continually attacked the enemy on his side of the line, bombed his aerodromes, besides carrying out attacks on places of importance far behind the lines. It would seem probable that this has had the effect so far on the enemy of compelling him to keep back or to detail portions of his forces in the air for defensive purposes.

When Lille station was attacked from the air for the first time no hostile aeroplanes were encountered. The second time, this place was attacked our machines encountered a squadron of Fokkers, which were there for defensive purposes. This is only one instance among many.

The question which arises is this: Supposing the enemy, under the influence of some drastic reformer or some energetic leader, were now to change his policy and follow the example of the English and the French, and were to cease using his aeroplanes as a weapon of defence and to start a vigorous offensive and attack as many places as far behind our lines as he could, what would be the sound policy to follow in such a case? Should we abandon our offensive, bring back our squadrons behind the line to defend places like Boulogne, St. Omer, Amiens and Abbeville, and protect our artillery and photographic machines with defensive escorts, or should we continue our offensive more vigorously than before?

Up to now the work done by the Germans compared with that done by our aeroplanes stands, as we have seen, in the proportion of 4 to 100, but let us suppose that the enemy initiated a partial offensive in the air, and that his work increased, compared with ours, to a proportion of 30 or 50 to 100, it is then quite certain that a demand for protective measures would arise for protective squadrons and machines for defensive patrols.

One of the causes of such demands is the moral effect produced by a hostile aeroplane, which is out of all proportion to the damage which it can inflict.

The mere presence of a hostile machine in the air inspires those on the ground with exaggerated forebodings with regard to what the machine is capable of doing. For instance, at one time on one part of the front whenever a hostile machine, or what was thought to be a hostile machine, was reported, whistles were blown and men hid in the trenches.

In such cases the machines were at far too great a height to observe the presence of men on the ground at all, and even if the presence of men was observed it would not lead to a catastrophe. Again, a machine which was reported in one place would certainly, since it was flying rapidly, be shortly afterwards observed in another part of the lines and reported again, but the result of these reports was often that for every time the machine was sighted a separate machine was reported, leading at the end of the day to a magnified and exaggerated total.

The sound policy, then, which should guide all warfare in the air would seem to be this: to exploit this moral effect of the aeroplane on the enemy, but not to let him exploit it on ourselves. Now this can only be done by attacking and by continuing to attack.

It has been our experience in the past that at a time when the Germans were doing only half the work done by our machines that their mere presence over our lines produced an insistent and continuous demand for protective and defensive measures. If the Germans were once more to increase the degree of their activity even up to what constitutes half the degree of our activity, it is certain that such demands would be made again.

On the other hand, it is equally certain that, were such measures to be adopted, they would prove ineffectual. As long as a battle is being fought, any machine at the front has five times the value that the same machine would have far behind the lines.

If the enemy were aware of the presence of a defensive force in one particular spot he would leave that spot alone and attack another, and we should not have enough machines to protect all the places which could possibly be attacked behind our lines, and at the same time continue the indispensable work on the front.

But supposing we had enough machines both for offensive and for defensive purposes. Supposing we had an unlimited number of machines for defensive purposes, it would still be impossible to prevent hostile machines from crossing the line if they were determined to do so, simply because the sky is too large to defend. We know from experience how difficult it is to prevent a hostile vessel, and still more a hostile submarine, from breaking a blockade, when the blockade extends over a large area. But in the air the difficulty of defence is still greater, because the area of possible escape is practically unlimited, and because the aeroplane is fighting in three dimensions.

The sound policy would seem to be that if the enemy changes his tactics and pursues a more vigorous offensive, to increase our offensive, to go further afield, and to force the enemy to do what he would gladly have us do now. If, on the other hand, we were to adopt a purely defensive policy, or a partially offensive policy, we should be doing what the French have learnt by experience to be a failure, and what the rank and file of the enemy, by their own accounts, point to as being one of the main causes of their recent reverses.

Moreover, in adopting such a policy it appears probable that the Germans are guided by necessity rather than by choice, owing to the many fronts on which they now have to fight, and owing also to the quality and the quantity of machines they have to face on the Western Front alone. Nevertheless, one cannot repeat too often that in war nothing is certain, and that the Germans may, either owing to the pressure of public opinion, or the construction of new types of machines, or the rise of a new leader, change their policy at any moment for a more aggressive one.

September 22nd, 1916.

As we shall see later, the general's prophecy proved to be correct, for the Germans, both by the rise of a new leader and the construction of new types of machines, did change their policy for an aggressive and very effectually aggressive one.

CHAPTER 15

# The End of the Battle of the Somme and After

On the 22nd September, 1916, on our way to G.H.Q., we were kept waiting a long time at the Candas level-crossing, by trains, and on our return journey we found a block, and a seething confusion caused by two batteries, a column of infantry, a line of R.F.C. transport, a number of lorries, light-tenders, and touring cars and motor cyclists, all going in opposite directions. They had been there three-quarters of an hour. The general got out and gave a few orders, and made some of them stop and others move, and halt and move again, and in five minutes' time the tangled skeins of traffic were disentangled and moving on once more.

Further news of fighting came in the afternoon. We spent some hours at the Depot, where we were told that the hand starter epicyclic-gearing on the R.E.7, with the 250 Rolls-Royce engine, had gone wrong.

From a letter: September (undated). A sailor told me that when the zeppelin was captured in the Thames a dead German who was found inside it was given a naval burial in the rather shallow waters, and the parson was told (if he could) to say a few words of German. Some days after this burial the petty officer who carried out these instructions came to the officer in charge and reported as follows:

"Please, Sir, the 'Un's a-flood."

*September 23rd*, 1916. From my Diary: Three French officers came to the depot in the afternoon. Talking of the different makes of the Hispano engines, they picked out one maker as being the only good one. It was the one our pilots say is the only bad one, and the engine they clamour for is the one the French said was the worst.

*September 25th.*—Our wireless officer, Major Smith, has been made a Park Commander. I have addressed him the following lines on the subject:

*I hope one day Toc Smith will be*
*Sir Vincent Toc Smith, K.C.B.,*
*He thoroughly deserves the rank*
*For fitting wireless on a Tank:*
*For talking on a telephone*
*From Paris to the torrid zone,*
*From Lundy Isle and Salisbury spire*
*To Rome, without the aid of wire;*
*For making a transmitter weigh*
*A pound less than a pound of hay;*
*For making a receiver less*
*Than Staunton's pocket-book of chess.*
*For these and for all other things,*
*Toc Smith deserves the thanks of Kings.*
*But as there are no Kings to hand,*
*He'll get an Aircraft Park Command;*
*Commander of an Aircraft Park;*
*This comes of fiddling with a spark.*

*September 27th*, 1916.—Fighting at Thiepval.

*September 28th,* 1916.—The shock-absorber on the tail-skid of the Morane is too *fierce.*

*September 30th*, 1916.—Reading Pliny's *Letters.* He says that you often give offence in a letter by writing something which, if you said it in conversation, would give no offence at all. Conversation being helped out by look, gesture, and expression.

*October 2nd*, 1916.—The Maxim gun on the aerodrome has no washers.

*October 3rd*, 1916.—Tour round the Kite Balloon Sections. In No. 1 the gland for taking pressure in the balloon is unsatisfactory. The rope on the Caquot is different from the rope they repair it with.

*October 4th,* 1916. —Reading *King Lear.*

*October 6th*, 1916.—Finished Dante's *Paradiso, Canto* 17:

*Giù per lo mondo senza fine amaro.*

Just about this time Bron Lucas arrived in France, and was made a Flight Commander in No. 22 Squadron. The first time I saw him after his arrival was on the 7th of October. He had already flown his new machine, an F.E. 2.B. He wanted three valve rockers (old type) for the 120 Beardmore engine. We were able to provide him with these immediately, which surprised him, after being in England, where he said it was difficult to get a split pin out of anybody. Here in France, he said, you felt that everyone was out to help you. The next time I saw him was on October 11th. He had been over the line, and had been archied and a bit of his propeller had been shot off. His Squadron Commander said they could not keep him out of the air.

On the 14th he came to luncheon with us, and stayed the whole afternoon. We went to the aerodrome and watched the Sopwith machines flying. He had flown over the barrage lately, and he said it was the most marvellous sight he had ever seen.

On the 16th, Ridley, who had been a pilot in No. 60, arrived. He had landed in the German lines near Cambrai, where he had remained concealed for some weeks. He had then walked to Belgium, where he was once actually arrested on a tram. He hit the policeman in the face and jumped off the tram. He had walked about in the guise of a man with an earache. He couldn't speak French or German. He had a passport with his photograph on it given him by the German authorities. He gave me this photograph, which looks like the picture of an Englishman without a collar. He walked five miles to the frontier wires carrying a ladder; when he got there he climbed over into Holland. He had been away since August, and I had spent the morning with him before he started on this expedition. The chief gave him the D.S.O.

On the 22nd Mr. Balfour paid us a visit, and on the 24th I went with Neville Lytton to see Bron Lucas in his squadron. Afterwards I went on to Amiens.

*October 27th*, 1916.—From a letter: This afternoon we went to see the new naval squadron, and it was very wet and windy. A southerly gale blew all day, with drifts of gusty rain and ragged, fluttering clouds careering across the sky. We got back about four, and at half-past four, just as I was sitting down to typewrite, I noticed that the dark office was flooded with light, so I went out of doors to see what had happened.

We live at the meeting of five crossroads, and at their juncture there is a roadside chapel, and the roads are bordered with rows of trees. Through the trees and over the flat fields I saw that what had happened was this: the curtain of storm in the west had been lifted just a little, and underneath it and behind it, there was a sea of liquid light partly pale gold (the lower part) and partly a luminous sea green, and in this sea there were low islands and rocks and reefs of blazing fire.

But all this was nothing compared to what was happening in the East. Here the thick grey cloud was turned to purple by the reflected sunset, and right over all of it reaching from the earth to the zenith's height and then down again to the earth was the tallest and most perfect rainbow I have ever seen, all incandescent in the glory of the sunset and glistening in the rain. A marvellous sight. This is the second time I have described it today—I take it a symbol of hope, victory and peace—so much did it strike me. One seldom sees a perfect rainbow going all the way round and making an arch over the whole world.

Bron Lucas, who was flying over from St. Omer, crashed on the Candas Aerodrome. It was a cold and gusty day. He came in to tea with us, where he found Colonel Seely and Prince Antoine D'Orleans.

On the 29th we had a long and important conference with Colonel Barrès, Commander of the French aviation. The question of ordering *Hispano-Suiza* engines was discussed, also long distance bombing raids into Germany. Colonel Barrès said he intended to bomb the German towns, and did not want us to do it. His idea was to prolong the French long distance bombing. Rombach had already been evacuated. His aim was to force the Germans to evacuate all the factories on the Rhine. He thought bombing would not only put an end to war, but would finish the war. He said this was not a dream.

I finished *Coriolanus* and *Timon of Athens*. Besides these, during this month I have read *Hamlet*, *Othello*, *Macbeth*, and *Twelfth Night*.

On October 30th, 1916, I went to Bertangles and saw Bron Lucas. We walked across the aerodrome to Hawker's mess. It had poured with rain all day, but in the evening the clouds lifted over the horizon, leaving a low gold wrack, against which the sheds stood out black. Above there was a great tumult of clouds drifting and streaming and reflecting the light below, with here and there a rift. I said to Bron that it was like one of my pictures. He laughed and said "yes." I wondered what it meant.

On the 31st we were visited by the King of Montenegro, who wanted to fly over the line, but wasn't allowed to; and on the 2nd of November by the Prime Minister of New Zealand.

On the 3rd I went out with the general for a long tour round the Squadrons. We went to see seven squadrons. The wind was strong high up, but not on the ground. Just as we started he told me that Bron

Lucas was going to be given a squadron at once, and that he had written out the necessary telegram. We got back late, and for some reason I didn't look, as was my usual habit, at the table, where a whole array of telegrams told one the news from the brigades and whether any machines were missing. After dinner the general told me Bron was missing.

The next day Mr. McKenna came to see us, the day after Commandant Du Peuty, and the day after that Mr. Leo Maxse, and on the 9th a large party of French journalists, and on the 10th Sir Douglas Haig came to see the flying. Here are a few extracts from my Diary at this time:

*November 11th*, 1916.—We went to the Naval Squadron which is now attached to us, and which is on the same aerodrome as No. 32. They said they would like the oil used by No. 32 for machine-guns. It was better than their own *naval* oil. We then went on to No. 32.

They asked if they might have the *naval* oil, which they said was better than their own *military* oil. When the matter was investigated later there was found to be not the slightest difference between the naval and the military oil. The naval Squadron was short of gudgeon pins.

*Le feu se transforme en mouvement et le mouvement en feu et c'est là le monde.* (Heraclitus.)

*November 16th*, 1916.—Lord Milner and General Rawlinson came to the aerodrome.

*November 18th*, 1916.—Conference at the Third Army. Herds of generals. I am reading *The Mabinogion*, translated from the Welsh by Lady Charlotte Guest, lent me by Lawrence in No. 70 Squadron, and about King Arthur.

Somebody sent me a list of qualifications for a man who wanted to join the R.F.C. I threw the envelope into the fire before I read the letter, which said at the end: "I enclose his qualifications." I plunged my hand into the fire and rescued the qualifications, a little bit charred, but still readable and only partially destroyed. I took them downstairs to show someone, and left them for three seconds on the chimney-piece. During these three seconds, while I glanced at a newspaper, Corballis came in and threw the paper into the fire. I looked up and the deed was done. The qualifications were irremediably destroyed.

*November 20th*, 1916.—A German prisoner wrote a letter to ask another pilot to say he was all right. This letter was translated by the wing, and then sent *via* the brigade to the corps and then to the army. The army have sent it back here *to be translated*. The wing commander who originally sent it knows German better than he does English.

On the 21st we began to make arrangements for moving back to St. André. The battle of the Somme was over. I took an affectionate leave of the *Notaire* and his wife, in whose house I had been billeted. The *Notaire* gave a bottle of champagne, and Toc Smith and I presented them with a pair of bronze candlesticks representing victory and France triumphant.

*November 23rd, 1916.*—We left Fienvillers for St. André.

*Good night, the old year creeps towards the grave:*
*There are the young, and almost all the brave.*

On the 25th November we went to Cassel and spent the night with the Second Brigade, but on the way we stopped at the St. Omer Aircraft Depot, where we had a strenuous look round at the Repair Section and in the Stores.

Here are some points which were dealt with: There were no Sopwiths in cases at the Depot. Four Moranes were to go home. Throttles were not turned back on the R.E. The Rhone was short of nosepieces. Work was to be stopped on all machines without engines. The R.E. 8 was to be repaired. Gun drums were found to be going home with engine parts: they should be kept separate. There were no R.E. spares and no cocking handles on B.E. 125. Plug repair, field-glasses repair, and First A.D. leave were dealt with. Also the centre section on an R.E.8, which was not cut out near the fuselage for cellon. Mark 1. tuners were to go home, and old sets to be cleared out.

Wireless operators were to be taught German signals. No instructions had been received about the Hythe cameras. Camera plate-cases, brass clips, and the alterations in the new model aluminium camera were mentioned. A Nieuport had its number on the wrong side. A man was making washers. Sights for the single-seater Nieuport were being made at the depot. Two R.E.8's. were held up for wires and struts. A chute was being made for the R.E.7. No F.E's. and no R.E's. were to be repaired in the future if the bottom of the longeron has gone. Two F.E., 2 D's. were waiting for engines.

Scarfe gun-mounting and tail skids of Nieuports were discussed. It takes five hours and two men to clean the blue paint on the rotary engines. Rankin darts were to go home. There were 310 yards of Willesden canvas at First A.D., and 280 at Second A.D.; 300 cases were sent monthly to Pont de l'Arche. A superfluous number of magneto boxes was detected. No. 42 Squadron had asked for and taken 13 boxes of magneto spares. People add stray items to Gio. 98 (their standard list of what they should have); cushions for lorries had been indented for by No. 5 unnecessarily; 50 aluminium pistons for 90 R.A.F. came in October 2nd, and had not yet been used. Three special transmitters had been in store three weeks without being used. Metal belts hadn't been sent for. B.E. 2C. tanks were to be sent away. Twenty-five Kite Balloons were wandering about the country.

I have written down all these technical details, not from any hope that the reader will keep them clear in his mind, but because people used to talk glibly, and still do talk glibly, of the extravagance of the Flying Corps. The R.F.C. were extravagant no doubt. Flying and everything to do with it is an extravagant matter. The pilot is extravagant, the squadron is extravagant, even the equipment officer, even the technical sergeant-major was sometimes found to be extravagant but a lot of this extravagance was inevitable; what nobody knew or realised was that a perpetual effort was being made to check *useless* extravagance, and that even superfluous magneto boxes and an unnecessary indent for lorry cushions were noted.

On the 27th, I put the note about cutting down the reserve drivers which the general had given me on March 11th on his table. He acted on it immediately, and the reserve drivers were cut down.

On November 30th, we went to Paris to discuss questions of guns, machines and engines with the French. We saw Colonel Regnier on the following day, and also visited Nieuport's works. The next day we visited Darracq's works.

I got a telegram in the morning saying that it was now known that Bron Lucas, who had been missing since November 3rd, had been killed. As we afterwards heard, he had been shot in the neck, but had managed to land his machine and his observer safely. He was unconscious when the machine landed but still alive, and he died about six o'clock in the evening, and was buried near Bapaume. That night I read a *Canto* of Dante, and came across this line:

*Ove s'appunta ogni ubi ed ogni quando.*
(*Paradiso, Canto* 29.)
*There where every where and every when is determined.*

And never was there a *where* and a *when* more tragically fit and more mournfully appropriate than in the case of Bron Lucas's death.

So befitting and so appropriate that regret was lost in awe and wonder, and grief was silenced.

Bron was a wanderer by nature; his heart was above all things adventurous, and he went on seeking and finding adventures in spite of every handicap, in spite of circumstances, till he met with his last adventure fighting in the sky on his last errand. At Oxford he had rowed two years in the 'Varsity boat. He went out to the South African War as *Times* correspondent, where he was wounded. The wound, although not serious in itself, was followed by disastrous consequences and complications, and finally he was obliged to have his leg cut off, and for many months he was seriously ill. One would have thought this was the end of active out-of-door life and physical adventure as far as he was concerned, but not at all.

He was soon as active as ever, and rode and hunted and shot. Just before the war began he had a bad fall in a steeplechase. When the war broke out he was a Cabinet Minister, and I think the most difficult sacrifice he had to make in his life was not to throw up his work as a civilian and go out to France at once directly war broke out, or at least, prepare to go out. He was in the Yeomanry.

He stayed in the Cabinet until May, 1915, when there were changes. He was then released from his civilian fetters, and in July he went to Gosport to learn to be an observer. At first he found the new life very strange. He told me it was not only like going back to a private school, but to a foreign school. He was 39 years old, and most of his school-fellows were about eighteen or nineteen.

People who were with him then at Gosport told me that his keenness was electric in its effect on all the others. If a propeller was to be swung he would be the first to swing it. He learned to be an observer, and then he was not satisfied till he had learnt to fly. The idea was that he should have a Staff job in the R.F.C. when he had learned enough about machines. But this did not satisfy him. He went out to Egypt as a flying officer in No. 13 Squadron, and while he was there he took part in some long distance raids, and had one bad crash in the desert. He came back to England, and, after doing some instructor's work at Dover and having another bad crash, he was given a squadron, with a view to his being sent out to France with a squadron later. But this he would not do. As I have already said, he would not command a squadron in France unless he had first done the ordinary work of a pilot over the lines. And he threw himself into that work only too well.

These last weeks in France were, perhaps, the happiest of his life.

He was an undergraduate once more and an active soldier, as active, as athletic in the air as he had ever been on the ground. His youth had been given back to him with interest, and for his disabilities he had received a glorious compensation.

Apart from the work and his interest and whole-hearted keenness in the war, in his squadron, in his mechanics, and in his machine, he enjoyed himself with all the great gift of enjoyment and fund of gaiety with which he had enjoyed everything else in his life: his houses, his fishing, his pony-hunts, his steeplechases, his horses, his pictures, his dinner-parties, the performances of the Follies, or, as long ago, the days, whether of strenuous rowing or idle punting on the river at Oxford, and the musical supper parties at King Edward Street, where Donald Tovey used to explain the difference between Gluck and Piccini to a lot of rowing Blues, while others threw butter at the ceiling and slapped the ham. They could not keep him out of the air.

"He was too much of a tiger," his Wing Commander said. And his Squadron Commander said to me: "He is an air-hog." One could not help thinking with pangs what a great Squadron Commander he would have made, but even this regret was swallowed up in the thought that the most fitting crown to the example of his life was his, the splendour and sacrifice of his death.

The next day we went back to St. André, stopping at Chantilly on the way to have luncheon with Colonel Barrès at the Headquarters of the French aviation.

On December 10th, 1916, we went to London.

CHAPTER 16

# St. André Again—The Spring Offensive

We arrived back at St. André on the 2nd of January. We had to prepare for another year of operations and relentless fighting in the air. The lessons of the battles of the Somme were clear to us, and they were also clear to the Germans.

This is what General von Below wrote with regard to the air fighting during the battle of the Somme, in a Memorandum dated January, 1917, and which was captured later:

> The beginning and the first weeks of the battle of the Somme were marked by a complete inferiority of our own air forces. The enemy's aeroplanes enjoyed complete freedom in carrying out distant reconnaissances. With the aid of aeroplane observation the hostile artillery neutralised our guns, and was able to range with the most extreme accuracy on the trenches occupied by our infantry; the required data for this were provided by undisturbed trench reconnaissance and photography.
>
> By means of bombing and machine-gun attacks from a low height against infantry, battery positions and marching columns, the enemy's aircraft inspired our troops with a feeling of defencelessness against the enemy's mastery of the air.
>
> On the other hand, our own aeroplanes succeeded in quite exceptional cases in breaking through the hostile barrage and carrying out distant reconnaissances; our artillery machines were driven off whenever they attempted to carry out registration for their own batteries.

General von Below goes on to state the measures by which a gradual improvement was attained, and what measures he suggested should be taken to improve and increase this improvement. What he says can really be summed up in one sentence. We must exchange *defence* for *offence*, and do to the English what they are doing to us.

In order to achieve this end, the German air forces were reinforced, the organisation of *defensive* patrol barrages was forbidden, which could only lead, the general says, to *dispersal of strength*. "The main object of fighting in the air," he goes on to say, "is to enable our photographic registration and photographic reconnaissance to be carried out, and at the same time to prevent that of the enemy. All other tasks, such as bombing raids, machine gun attacks on troops, and even distance reconnaissance in trench warfare, must be secondary to this main object. So long as the execution of the main task is not ensured, all available forces must be employed for this purpose. All subsidiary tasks must be abandoned, even when the enemy's attacks are causing us considerable annoyance."

The Germans had made up their mind to do two things: to increase and strengthen their Flying Forces as far as possible and to abandon defensive measures, and attack. The question was: should we be ready as far as regards both quantity and quality of machines to meet their renewed efforts? should we have enough fast fighting machines to meet the enemy on equal terms? If by the time the spring offensive began we were not well supplied with an adequate number of fast fighting machines, we should be in a bad way if the Germans continued to make progress in their fighting material, and if their tactics in the air became anything like as vigorous as ours had been during the battle of the Somme. That the situation was foreseen clearly will be evident from the following extract from a Memorandum which was written in the winter, after the battle of the Somme:

> The only way in which this danger can be met is for our offensive forces to be strong enough to prevent the Germans from taking the offensive.
> During the Somme battle we had the advantage that any force actuated by offensive policy has over any force on a purely defensive policy. But now that the Germans have recognised the necessity of the offensive in the air and are putting it into practice, the only way to meet the danger and to. defeat it, is to double the output and to increase the efficiency of our weapon. In other words, if we are to fight the Germans successfully in the air during the coming operations we must have double the

number of our fighting machines. Otherwise we shall be necessarily reduced to a defensive policy, and our superiority in the air will be lost. And this will not only mean that our offensive far behind the German lines, which we know had a deadly effect on the German moral, will cease, and it will also mean that co-operation with the artillery and the infantry will be seriously hampered, since it has been proved in all operations so far, whether carried out by ourselves or by the French, that the only way to ensure this work being carried out without interference from the enemy is to be able to attack the enemy in his lines and thus prevent him from attacking.

It is this principle that the enemy have now realised and are now acting upon. *What we need to defeat their application of it is a sufficient quantity of efficient weapons; that is to say, a sufficient quantity of fast fighting machines.*

As far as we can tell, when the Spring does come, and with it new operations on a large scale, the policy that will actuate the German operations in the air will be an offensive policy and not a defensive one. And what is still more important, the Germans will have the means of putting such a policy into effect. They will be equipped with a sufficient quantity of fast fighting machines. Fighting in the air will, therefore, be on a larger and more deadly scale than it has ever been before.

It will be no longer a question of a group of machines losing one or two machines in a raid, but of a formation meeting another formation in battle daily and constantly. If we look back and remember the agitation and alarm caused by the appearance of the Fokker, which, it should be remembered, was a fast scout whose activity was confined to the German lines, and which succeeded in bringing down isolated British machines which were slower and less suitable for fighting, it is to be expected that the alarm and agitation caused by the appearance of this machine, which was out of all proportion to its potential mischief and peril to us, will be as nothing compared with the outcry which will come if in the Spring our lines are crossed day and night by large raiding parties of fast German fighting machines.

If by the Spring the Germans are able to do in the air one quarter of the work carried out by our air forces during the first months of the Somme battle, it is to be feared that the inevitable result will be a universal and irresistible demand for defence and protection; the abandonment of our offensive and consequently the loss of our superiority in the air.

If it be asked how it came about, if the situation was foreseen, that adequate measures were not taken to meet it, I believe the true answer to be this:

Those who deserve the blame for our being behind-hand in aircraft production are not the Government, nor the Air Board, nor this Minister nor that administrator, but ultimately and finally you and I, the public: public opinion, which would not have allowed any Government to spend enough money *before the war* to enable us by experiment, preparation and plant, to have the means *during the war* of swift and adequate production. It is a great mercy we had a Flying Corps at all. And the nation owes an eternal debt of gratitude to General Henderson and to those who fought the battle for the adoption of the aeroplane as a military weapon before the war, and to all .those who organised the original squadrons of the R.F.C. and the R.N.A.S. Other things which retarded our production were the disastrous interruptions and delays caused by the strikes.

From my Diary, 1917:

*January 3rd.*—An Army Commanders' Conference took place at Rollencourt. My India-rubber sponge has been eaten by rats.

*January 5th*, 1917.—We went to St. Omer to see a new Vickers single-seater pusher. The machine was flown. It was not thought to be a success. There was no view down out of it, and the gun was fixed. The reserve lorries were found not to be in a fit state, and there were no sockets for aileron-struts in the depot. We drove back from St. Omer to St. André in one hour and five minutes.

*January 8th,* 1917.—I went to the Fifth Brigade with the General, and to 5, 15, 32, 18 and 7 Squadrons. A long day in the rain, sleet, snow and mud. The general's cold is better; but everyone else has caught it, including the chauffeur. Brigades are to be warned to have housing ready for the Intelligence Officers who are about to arrive. No. 15 had no armourer's tools, and only 13 extension posts for double-drums, and complained of cracked cylinders.; 32's double-drums were not satisfactory. No. 7 want back-wheels for motor-cycles. The Lewis guns at No. 5 fired directly they arrived. They had no complaints. We lost the way coming home, because my servant, who was sitting on the box, got out and asked a man the way, and the man, a Frenchman, said,

I suppose, *gauche*, but my servant translated *gauche* as *right*, putting us wrong. (This, as Mr. Pooter would say, is rather funny.)

*January 9th*, 1917.—We went to the Third Army Headquarters, then to Squadrons 60, 13, 12, 11, and 29; the aerodromes were muddy. One man on a Nieuport did a roll, that is to say, he looped side- ways. We had luncheon in the car; the rug got muddy. I made it muddy by treading on it by accident. No. 60 want four more aircraft-tuners, and their silver dope has not yet arrived. No. 29 want big galvanisers.

*January 11th*, 1917.— Went to the Fifth Brigade, Naval Squadron 23, 19, 2 A.D. The Naval Squadron wants the Aldis sight. No. 19 want vacuum oil for the Spad. The Sopwith one-and-a-half strutters are to go to the first A.D.

*January 12th*, 1917.— Went to the First Brigade with the General and La Ferrière to 10, 16, 2, 25, 70 Squadrons. No. 16 cameras are not satisfactorily strung. No. 2 want carburendum stick and have not got the Norman-sight, and are short of a bicycle. No. 10 have only got two wireless mechanics. Six Portuguese officers are staying with them. No. 25 have the 20 inch camera mounted over the top. Nobody has told them how to fix up the big camera. No. 70 have run out of their supply of aluminium and are using cast-iron pistons.

*January 14th*, 1917.—It snowed hard last night, and it thawed hard today. The result is supremely disagreeable. We went to the Fourth Army. Luncheon with General Rawlinson, then to La Houssoye Aerodrome, where he saw Flechaire, a French star pilot, doing stunts. There was a thick mist, and he couldn't fly higher than 200 feet. In fact, he flew much lower, and he did "*le tonneau*" and other stunts. I was thankful when it was over. Beck was there and General Lambton. We took the less good road. I said it was the less good road. However, the general insisted on taking it. The result was we took two hours and three-quarters instead of one and a quarter hours. I looked patient and said every now and then: "We shan't be so very late."

*January 15th*, 1917.—We went to Cassel and Bailleul, and visited 42, 53, 1, 6, 41, and 46 Squadrons. We stopped the night at Cassel. It was very cold with snow. No. 42 have only four new type lighting-sets.

*January 18th*, 1917.—It is thawing, but there is still a lot of snow on the ground. Nothing is happening, and we can't go anywhere because of the state of the roads. The general has caught a fresh cold. William de Morgan, the novelist, is dead.

*January 20th,* 1917.—From a letter:

. . .Yesterday somebody asked me out to dinner by telephone to meet a Pole. I thought the message came from our Guest-House, the Flying Corps Guest-House, which is in the near vicinity. I said "yes," meaning "no," because it is impossible to say "No" *the first time* by telephone. Then, thinking better of it, I rang up to say I was very sorry, *but*—. The answer came that I had never been asked. I then realised that the message had come from the G.H.Q. Guest-House, which is 20 miles off. So I rang up the officer in charge of guests to say that I regretted but. . . . He was out, but his subordinate was in, and said he would pass on the message. He did, but he sent it to the commander- in-chief saying I regretted that a more important engagement prevented me from accepting his unkind but well-meant invitation.

"This I was unaware of till this evening at 8.30 a message came from the G.H.Q. Guest-House to know whether I had started as they were still waiting, and the Pole was so hungry that he was eating the matches. I tried to answer, but was put into direct communication with Monsieur Briand, who was entertaining guests at his Guest-House. So I rang off. I then tried again, and was told that *Maurice Guest* was out of print and the only copy on loan. However, I made a final effort, and the answer was Captain Guest was on leave. Then I gave it up. These are the advantages of the field telephone in war-time.

*January 21st*, 1917.—I dined with E. Mess. We had turkey to eat. One of the members of the mess had been sent a lot of malt-extract by his mother, who thought he was run down, so he gave it to the turkey. The turkey in consequence became fat.

*January 22nd*, 1917.—French Headquarters rang through to the general. He sent for me to find out v/hat it was about: it was to say he had been made *Commandeur de la Légion d'Honneur.*

*January 23rd*, 1917.—The water in my jug was frozen last night. The 2nd A. Depot are not fitting any more hot-air pipes. Vacuum-controls are not to go home. A mouse was nearly caught in the dining-room.

*January 26th*, 1917.—From a letter:

. . . a tragedy of far-reaching import happened today. Yesterday we started on a tour of a Brigade, including Kite Balloons, and incidentally we slept in the coldest house I have ever endured. The water froze while one waited. There was central heating and hot water pipes, but there was no coal, and the pipes had burst in the frost, being full of cold water. The floors and staircase were of solid stone. The doors of glass, and the windows of fine old cracked glass. The bedrooms, which had no fireplaces, had not been lived in since the twelfth century, and then only by serfs. There was no coal in the house, and a very little thin firewood such as is used by housemaids to lay a fire with. The house stood on the banks of a frozen river, in point of fact, the Somme. On the other side of the house was a marsh. The ground was covered with frozen snow. The wind cut like a razor. The thermometer registered 14 degrees of frost centigrade and 47 degrees according to something else.

Nevertheless, I enjoyed the outing. And, by drinking enough boiling whisky before going to bed, I was sufficiently unconscious to lose sight of the cold. The next day we spent looking at balloons. On our way back—and this is the tragedy—our luggage fell off the Rolls-Royce, the general's suitcase made of Willesden canvas, containing his razor, his new coat, his trousers, his shoes, his favourite buttonhook, and an advance copy of the *News of the World*, and my little *en tout cas* bought in St. Petersburg, which has been round the world and all over the Balkans, twice to Constantinople, and through the length and breadth of Russia, and the Central Empires. Messengers have been despatched to look for it, and I have hopes of its being found, as I have invoked St. Anthony, who has never failed me yet.

*January 27th,* 1917.—The wind cut like a knife. Today there was an Army Conference which lasted till 2.30. Our luggage was found on the road where it fell. Finished *The Ivory Child* and *The Holy Flower*, by Rider Haggard; likewise *The Red Morn*, by Max Pemberton.

*February 7th*, 1917.—The clock in the office struck over 250. Nobody could stop it.

From this time onwards we had a series of visitors. On the 28th of January a party of Russian officers arrived. They were shown the depot at Candas, and they played gipsy songs on the piano after dinner.

The day after a party of French journalists came and had a long talk with the general.

The only items I have on record for the month of January are, firstly, that the last captured German machine was not thought to be an Albatross because it had V shaped struts and a radiator on the centre-section and not on the sides as on the Albatross scout. It was therefore thought to be a Halberstadt. And secondly, that the Spad pump spindles in No. 19 Squadron were broken.

In February, 1917, we had more visitors, an Italian officer, Mr. Holt Thomas, H. Belloc, and Louis Belloc, his son, whom the general sent for from the line to dine and sleep, while his father was here. The general said that Louis Belloc was one of the few people he had met who talked sense about aeroplanes and observed points of real interest.

On the 17th the French commander-in-chief, General Nivelle, held an investiture and a review. So dense was the fog that the army was invisible, and seemed like an army of ghosts marching past to phantom pipes and an unearthly *"Marseillaise."* The general was decorated with the *Croix* of *Commandeur* of the *Légion d'Honneur.* General Nivelle pinned on the decorations himself and kissed the major-generals.

On the 20th of February, 1917, we went to Beauvais to see General Nivelle and to discuss future operations.

*February 20th* 1917.—From a letter:
His ante-room or anti-*chambre* was heated to fever heat. We waited standing a long time while various A.D.C's. flitted in and out of the room. Then a very nice sub-general came in and made conversation and was pleasant. Then an A.D.C. came and whispered to me where I was to sit at table. Then suddenly the general came in from an unexpected door and said 'How do you do' naturally and with energy, but did not break my fingers in the saying of it. Then another door was thrown open and a white-jacketed soldier said that the general was served, and in we went. I sat next to the other general. A lame Minister was also present. The general sat on General Nivelle 's left and the Minister on his right.

The Minister asked General Nivelle what was exactly the *Crise de l'aviation.* General Nivelle said that as long as there was aviation there would always be a crise in it. After luncheon we proceeded to business and maps, and had a most satisfactory discussion; and he gave the general a free hand with regard to future operations and thoroughly endorsed the offensive policy. Afterwards we saw Colonel Du Peuty, who was at that time practically commanding the French flying.

On the 25th of February, 1917, the general and I had luncheon with Sir Douglas, and went on to London. We got back on March 3rd.

*March 6th*, 1917.—Interviewed a Russian prisoner. He said he had been starved, but otherwise reported nothing of interest. Today the weather was spring-like. The snow has melted. The first message of spring was whispered.

*March 7th*, 1917.—The First Aircraft Park have no Vickers sparklets. No. 43 said their last machine came with packing in the cowling. No. 40 said their gun was never fixed but always loose.

*March 11th*, 1917.—A spring day, which began with a slight shower. Then it cleared and the air became warm, soft and grey, with fitful glimpses of sunshine. We drove to Beauvais, where we attended an Aviation Conference with Colonel Du Peuty and Commandant Pugo. We had luncheon there. Du Peuty said he always dressed up his observers as gunners. If they had to go and interview a gunner, he put a red stripe on their trousers. The gunners then believed what the observers said. The drive back took three hours and a half. It was a lovely evening: a soft sunset, with faint, pink clouds, and the trees bare against a silver twilight.

*March 13th*, 1917.—Bagdad has been taken.

*March 15th*, 1917.—The French Minister of War has resigned.

*March 16th*, 1917.—The Emperor of Russia has abdicated. One machine in No. 20. Squadron has been waiting three weeks for back centre-section struts.

*March 17th*, 1917.—Bapaume has been evacuated. A Zeppelin, that is to say reports of its movements, disturbed our sleep last night. It was brought down in flames at Compiègne.

*March 18th*, 1917.—Peronne has been taken.

*March 20th*, 1917.—Finished the *Awkward Age*, by Henry James, and reading some of his shorter stories. "*Things*," he says, "*that involve a risk are like the Christian faith: they must be seen from the inside.*"

*March 24th*, 1917.—From a letter:

Yesterday . . .I took the opportunity of going to the dentist. He was an English dentist who had the reputation of being the best dentist in Paris. He is now doing his bit. But it is a very different thing to go to a good dentist in war-time and to a good dentist in peace-time. In peace-time the good dentist is careful to hurt you as little as possible; in stopping a tooth he makes the hole gradually, using a whole series of files and drills, one finer than the other, and growing fine by degrees, and gradually less; and his conduct of the steel spike is nice. He says: 'A little tender there?' or 'Hold up your hand directly I hurt you.' He knows well if he does hurt you he will lose your valuable custom. In war-time how different.

Seizing hold of your head, he inserts a broad drill into your tooth, and goes on boring a hole with all his force, till the hole is made. No matter how much you struggle and scream and kick. I did all three, but it was no good. Holding my head in a vice, he dug the drill deeper and deeper into the tender tooth till the hole was finished. Of course, instead of taking half an hour it only took a few minutes, and that, when it is over, is an advantage.

*March 25th*, 1917.—General Henderson is staying with us. Basil Blackwood came to dinner.

*March 26th*, 1917.—Colonel Du Peuty came to have luncheon with Sir Douglas, but as he was late he had luncheon with us, and went to the chief's house later.

*March 28th*, 1917.—Finished Barine's *Life of Alfred de Musset. "Avec un esprit très gai, il avait l'âme saignante et désolée; association moins rare qu'on ne pense."* Musset has, she says, *"des vers de haut vol, de ceux que le génie trouve et que le talent ne fabrique jamais, quelque peine qu'il y prenne."*

*March 29th*, 1917.—The following description of an eminent personage: *"She has been told everything in the world, and has never perceived anything, and the echoes of her education respond awfully to the rash footfall—I mean the casual remark—in the cold Valhalla of her memory."* (Henry James, *The Death of the Lion*.)

*March 30th*, 1917.—A finer morning. We drove Philip Sassoon back from G.H.Q. to the chief's house. He said to the general: "I never saw you look so well." The general was scarlet. (The truth was he was sickening for an illness.) Bron Lucas' grave has been found intact near Bapaume (Map sheet 57, C.S.W.).

*March 31st*, 1917.—The general has got German measles, which is a relief as we all thought yesterday he was seriously ill.

*April 3rd*, 1917.—There was a violent snowstorm in the night, and snow drifts today. The general came down to luncheon. Reading

Pope:

*A strong expression most be seem'd to affect*
*And here and there disclosed a brave neglect.*

*April 4th*, 1917.—The chief's doctor came to see the general, and insisted on his going to bed; he says he is to stay in bed tomorrow. The Germans have cut down every rose-tree and every fruit-tree in the country; they spoiled the chairs with red-hot pokers. From a military point of view this surely must have been waste of time. German prisoners are now employed clearing up Nesle, which was left in a terrible mess.

*April 5th*, 1917.—Fighting in the air has begun. The general stayed in bed in the morning, but as soon as we were safely down at luncheon he got up and had a good rummage in the *operations* office.

*April 6th*, 1917.—The general stayed in; he has still got a very bad cough.

*In vain may heroes fight and patriots rave*
*If secret gold sap on from knave to knave.* (Pope.)

There is an air agitation going on in England in Parliament, etc. It cannot do us any good. No amount of agitation will give us one extra machine for the coming battle. *It is too late.* But it does do a lot of harm to the young pilots. And this occurs to nobody.

On April 7th the general sent me out by myself to see a lot of squadrons. The battle was now upon us. Fighting in the air on a battle scale had begun. We had not got the necessary number of fighting machines. One gap was, fortunately, filled by the French. Du Peuty gave us enough Nieuports to supply a whole squadron. It was evident that we should not get through the battle and do the work of the armies without severe loss.'

On the 8th of April the general decided to make a tour of the squadrons, and as there would not be time to visit all those he wished to see by road, he decided to go by air. He still had a touch of bronchitis, and did not seem fit for a journey by air. The doctor said it might either do him good or kill him. However we went. The General in an R.E.8 and I in a B.E.2.C. We saw eleven squadrons altogether. The general talked to all the pilots. While we were at the Le Hameau Aerodrome, Ball landed there, having followed us from Vert Galant. He wanted the General to let him keep his Nieuport machine instead of the S.E.2.5 he was now flying.

Afterwards he was very glad to have the S.E.2.5. Harvey-Kelly, whom we saw at Vert Galant, said the Germans he met in the air now were like floating meat.

On April 9th, 1917, the battle of the Vimy Ridge began. There was snow and rain, and the weather from the flying point of view was abominable. I went to St. Eloi in the afternoon.

The next day, which was intensely cold, with snow showers worse than the snow showers of March, we got news that 10,000 prisoners and 50 guns had been captured on the Vimy Ridge. I went to see the artillery squadrons at Brouay, which had done grand work during the fighting. The work of the army had been done in spite of the weather, in spite of our inferiority in machines, and in spite of the casualties.

*April 10th,* 1917.—In No. 16, Flight Commanders Bird and Perryman, in one machine, sent down artillery targets for three hours in the snowstorm, sometimes they were as low as 300 feet in our barrage. Stewart and Strut (?) did much the same thing on contact- patrol. The infantry let off all their flares at once and soon had none left.

The corps was pleased with No. 16's work. The neutralisation of fire was excellent.

*All sly, slow things with circumspective eyes.* (Pope.)

Our casualties were heavy, and had it not been for the indomitable pluck and spirit of the pilots we should not have been able to stand this ordeal.

On the 13th Ball came to tea with his Squadron Commander, Bloomfield. The general was delighted with Ball, and is giving him two machines: the S.E.2.5 for his ordinary work and a Nieuport for his individual enterprises. On one of these days, when he came home late after some strenuous fighting, he said it was lucky he was in his S.E.2.5 as the Nieuport would not have got him home.

Du Peuty wrote the general a magnificent letter, which was afterwards circulated in the squadrons;

10.4.17.

Dear General,

I do not know how to express to you all the admiration I feel, and the whole French Flying Service feels, for the British Flying Corps.

These results have not only contributed to the great success of your armies, but in close co-operation with our own efforts they have relieved us of a large part of the German aviation.

I hope to be able to teach what is left of the German aviation

that the French intend to apply the same methods and to follow the same principles in the same manner. I would be grate-
ful if you would let the troops under your orders know the
admiration which the French Flying Service feels for them, as
well as the feeling of comradeship they have for them.

Please accept my devoted respects,

Du Peuty.

It was especially in artillery machines that our casualties were heavy,
because we had not got enough fast fighting machines to deal with
the fast fighting machines of the enemy. We had been lent some Naval
Squadrons, and these did splendid work, and had among them some of
the best pilots we have ever had. In spite of our inferiority I can only
repeat again that the work of the army during the battle was done,
and our casualties in the air, although heavy, saved thousands of casualties on the ground, for there was no break in the artillery work. The
enemy's batteries were registered, and his trenches were photographed
unremittingly. The spirit of the Flying Corps was undefeated.

# CHAPTER 17

# Preparations for the Summer Offensive

*April 16th*, 1917.—The Naval Squadron at Auchelles want Aldis-sights. Reading Faguet's history of French literature. He says about Gautier:

> *Si un auteur n'était qu'un écrivain, Gautier serait un de nos plus grands auteurs, mais il ne faut jamais oublier qu'un auteur doit être un écrivain et aussi autre chose.*

*April 20th*, 1917.—With the general to the 13th Corps. Luncheon with General Haldane. Stopped at No. 13 on the way back. Powell says that A.C.N.F. (artillery signal meaning German battery firing) is better than Q.N.F. Du Peuty's letter is going to be circulated in the Squadrons. There are shy clouds in the sky, and the buds are beginning to open, and there is a blackcap's nest in the garden.

*April 21st*, 1917.—Cloudy. One tent party has arrived. Where are the two French Clergets for No. 70? A coarse-pitched propeller has been put on the Spad. Nobody knows why.

*April 22nd*, 1917.—We went to Laverville by air. The general in an R.E.8 and I in a B.E. 2. C. My pilot was Henley. When we got over the Aerodrome, Henley wasn't sure which aerodrome the general had landed on, as he got there before us, the R.E.8 being faster than the 2. C. We circled round. Then the general got impatient and fired Very lights. We went by air to 23—Leighton's Squadron; then to Fienvillers, where we landed with a bump. No. 23 say the valve comes off the water-regulator. Baldwin (at 55) said the D.H.4 had no ash longerons, only spruce.

*April 23rd*, 1917.—From a letter:

I went to look at the Boche machine that was so properly punished for circling over our garden this morning. The captured pilot said he thought our house was Buckingham Palace. That, he was told, was no excuse. When I say the captured pilot, there were three of them, two engines, a foot-warmer, a telescope, a periscope, a pack of patience cards, a concertina, a small printing press, for printing menus, a cocktail shaker, a bijou typewriter, and a green parrot, which says '*Hoch*' and '*Gott strafe England*,' if you scratch its head. They set fire to their machine on landing, or rather on being forced to land, and as the machine was full of bombs

> *They being of the dangerous sort*
> *exploded with a loud report,*

and the machine was partially burnt, but only partially; a lot of it survived. Ball has brought down another machine today. I believe that makes forty. . . . . There is a blackbird in the garden who is learning to sing quite nicely, but he can't, poor thing, learn to fly—he has no talent for aviation and always sideslips, do what one may. However, it has been settled that he shall be a *recording blackbird* and live in a nest.

*April 24th*, 1917.—We flew to Abeele. The fields were green, the woods were brown. Little puffs of cloud kept on arising out of nothing and disappearing, and then, at the edge of the world, a mysterious grey girdle—the sea? The general said that flying over my machine on this clear day it was impossible to see the marks on my planes. In the afternoon I flew to Candas with Norris. At Candas I saw a pilot, who told me he was "fed up" with flying. He had done 500 hours. He had had enough. He was sick to death of it. He didn't care. Then he paused and said: "But the general's a damned fine man to serve under." Reading Horace—*Eheu! fugaces*—Horace, Bk. 2.

> *Oh, Posthumus, the stealthy years, alas!*
> *The years, Dear Posthumus, they pass, they pass . . .*
> *Not all thy virtues will prevent*
> *Old Age, nor bid cold Death relent.*
> *Though hecatombs be slaughtered thrice a day,*
> *Yet Pluto, the untearful, claims his prey,*
> *Who holds in his dominion*
> *The triple-headed Geryon,*
> *And Tityos by the melancholy floss,*

*Which all who taste the fruits of earth must cross;*
*Though mighty monarchs they should be*
*Or painful sons of husbandry.*
*In vain we shun the grievous wounds of war,*
*The angry Adriatic's surge and roar;*
*And from the hot Sirocco hide,*
*That threatens us at Autumntide.*
*We must behold thy tide creep on apace,*
*Cocytus, and the shameful Danaan race,*
*And Sisyphus condemned to ply*
*A hopeless task eternally;*
*And bid farewell forever to the earth,*
*To wife and home, the land which gave us birth;*
*Of all thy trees none follow thee*
Except the hated cypress-tree.
*A worthier heir shall drain to the last lees*
*Those casks now guarded by a hundred keys,*
*And drench the floor with wine more rare*
*Than priests for festal days prepare.*

*April 25th*, 1917— Flew to the Fourth Army. My pilot was Buck-ridge, machine a B.E.2.C. The fields are scarred and charred up by shell fire, and the devastation on the ground beyond the Somme is past belief. Every single tree has been methodically cut down, every Virginian creeper. The damage to the roads has been for the greater part repaired.

We heard two shots in the air on the way there; on the way back, just as we were this side of the Somme, over the shelled area, a kite balloon was shot down and floated down into the river. We were looking at this; at that moment a scout appeared in the sky, and came swooping towards us. Buckridge pointed to the ground. I thought it was a German, and that we were going to land; looking down at the shelled condition of the ground I was terrified. It turned out to be an S.E. He told me afterwards he thought it was a German machine at first. It took us one and a half hours to fly back. It was bitterly cold: the earth looked like a photograph: a war photograph.

*April 26th*, 1917.—I cannot read any more, not another line of the *Golden Bowl*, by Henry James, after reading about half of it. Aladin the Russian and Barzani, the Italian correspondent, visited us.

*April 28th*, 1917.—The garden is full of oxlips and cowslips. The trees are red with sap. The hedges are budding.

*April 29th*, 1917.—We went to Vert Galant to see Harvey-Kelly, who commands No. 19 Squadron. When we got there we were told he had gone up by himself and one other pilot for a short patrol. We stayed there all the morning. By luncheon time he had not come back. He was due and overdue. When we went away the general said: "Tell Harvey-Kelly I was very sorry to miss him," but I knew quite well from the sound of his voice he did not expect this message would ever be delivered. Nor did I.

Harvey-Kelly never came back. He was the gayest of all gay pilots. He always took a potato and a reel of cotton with him when he went over the lines. The Germans, he said, would be sure to treat him well if he had to land on the other side and they found him provided with such useful and scarce commodities. He was the first pilot to land in France, as I have already described.

*April 20th*, 1917.—Went to St. Omer by air in the afternoon with Buckridge. Nearly crashed in the trees getting off.

*May 2nd*, 1917.—The trees are feathery and some of them slightly green. The pear blossom is out on the sun-baked wall in the kitchen-garden.

Reading Horace:

*O Fons Bandusiae*

*Spring of Bandusia,*
*Red wine and festal garlands are thy meed?*
*Tomorrow I shall offer thee a kid;*
*His waxing brow, his budding horns, prophetic,*
*Are ready for the war that goes with love;*
*But all in vain; the blood of this wild offspring*
*Thine icy waters must incarnadine.*

*The dogstar, and the incandescent days*
*Can parch thee not; and weary of the plough,*
*The oxen, and the silly sheep astray*
*Shall find in thee delicious, cool retreat.*
*Thou shalt be numbered amongst famous springs;*
*The rocks, the ilex, whence thy ripples fall*
*Tinkling, shall live forever in my verse.*

*May 3rd,* 1917.—Beverley, the H.Q. carpenter, blew up his hands by opening a bomb which someone had brought back as a souvenir.

It was not his fault. He was told to do it. It has blown off three fingers and a thumb from one hand and his thumb from the other. He was an admirable carpenter. It is most tragic, but it is to be hoped they may be able to make him artificial fingers at Roehampton. Reading Homer's *Iliad* with the help of Butcher and Lang (a crib). In many respects it is like a first-hand account of this war, or indeed of any war.

*May 6th*, 1917.—We got news that Ball is missing. This has cast a gloom through the whole Flying Corps. He was not only perhaps the most inspired pilot we have ever had, but the most modest and engaging character. His squadron, and indeed all the squadrons, will feel this terribly.

*May 7th*, 1917.—A Conference of Army Commanders.

*May 8th*, 1917.—Van Reyneveld now is commanding No. 45 Squadron, which fly Sopwith two-seaters. He has only one Ross-interrupter gear. The cowls on the 130 Clerget have been cut away because the pilots can't get at the plugs.

*May 9th*, 1917.—We flew to Vert Galant in the afternoon; I on the oldest B.E. in the world, which had been struck off strength. The engine cut out near Vert Galant, but recovered and we landed all right. The General's landing was terrifying to look at. The General went on to Fienvillers. My machine couldn't function; so I got another and went on to Candas. This second machine was likewise in a state of decay. I came home by road. The general got uneasy, and telephoned to know where I was. The wing sent back a flippant but reassuring message.

*May 10th*, 1917.—To Auchelles with the general to see 25 and the Naval Sopwiths. The "Spads" have been fighting the Sopwiths in the air: this has led to an acrimonious correspondence. Matters were smoothed. No. 25 are hard up for observers. Brommet (Naval) is two under strength. G.H.Q. (I) report that German captured documents speak of a new machine exactly like the Nieuport.

*May 12th*, 1917.—I went with Orpen to Auchelles. We saw five squadrons altogether. At the Naval Squadron the Nieuport was flown against the German Albatross; unfortunately the Albatross radiators burst. Little did some wonderful stunts on the Sopwith triplane and a tremendous dive. Orpen is going to paint the general, and some of the pilots.

*May 13th*, 1917.—Orpen came in the morning and painted the

general. The sitting took an hour and a half. The general went on working during the sitting, organising a bomb raid. There was never, I suppose, a stranger sitting.

The garden is thick with dandelions. The lilac is out, and the first lilies-of-the-valley. A hot thunderstorm made all this still more spring-like and beautiful.

*May 14th*, 1917.—General Henderson and Sir William Weir arrived at 11 . We took them to the depot at Candas.

"ἐν Τροίη ἀπόλοντο, φίλης ἀπὸ πατρίδος αἴης."

*They perished in Troy far away from their dear native land.* (Homer, *Iliad*, Book 2., line 163)...

*May 15th*, 1917.—General Henderson and Sir W. Weir went away. The General and I had luncheon with Sir Douglas Haig at Babincourt.

I went to Fienvillers late in the evening and slept at Candas at 2 A.D. Mess, to be ready for the visit of a herd of Italian Generals who are to arrive tomorrow. Reading the *Lawton Mystery*.

*May 16th*, 1917—The Italian generals were expected to arrive at 8, but they didn't arrive till 11. On arriving they were given breakfast. They then went to the Aerodrome Repair Section and to the stores, the 9th Wing, and the squadrons. They were entertained at luncheon at the 9th Wing Headquarters sumptuously. After luncheon the general came. Flying stunts and some perilous low flying took place, although the pilots had been entreated to do nothing of the kind.

*May 17th,* 1917.—We are staying at Avesnes, which we reached *via* Arras, where we were blocked by the arrival and passing of the King of the Belgians. After an exhaustive tour of Kite Balloon Sections we reached our billet.

*May 19th*, 1917.—From a letter:

A German was frightened down in the lines this morning. In his pocket he had a theatre ticket admitting him to a private box in the Theatre Royal, Cambrai. This he was on the point of destroying when the Intelligence Officer, with an eagle eye, noticed it and snatched it from him and had it translated into English. I am reading *Partners of the Night*.

*May 20th,* 1917.—We are back at St. André. Colonel Grant, an American officer, came to luncheon. Everyone is disturbed about the Russian news. Someone has written to me asking me to suggest a

Latin motto for the Tanks. I suggested *Nihil obstat*.

*May 22nd*, 1917.—A day with the Kite Balloons in the Second Army. The weather bad all the morning, but it cleared at 1 and the balloons rose into the air.

"Ὣς φάτο· τοὺς δ᾿ ἤδη κάτεχεν φυσίζοος αἶα,
ἐν Λακεδαίμονι αὖθι, φίλῃ ἐν πατρίδι γαίῃ."

(Iliad, Book 3, 213).

*So spake she; but they slept beneath the earth far*
*away in Lacedaemon, in the dear land of their fathers.*

H. Belloc came to stay with us on the 20th. After dinner there was an interesting discussion about the R.F.C., H.Q. war. Belloc said that one fine day the Germans would crack. Someone else said the strength of the local defensive was so great in modern war that we should never break through the German line. Belloc said, but supposing by their expenditure in men they were left with one man in their trenches, we should then get the better of the local defensive powers of that one man. Just about this time I received optimistic letters from the Russian Army without a hint in them of future trouble. Uneasiness about Russia was none the less being felt.

*May 29th*, 1917.—The general saw some asparagus and radishes in a shop window at St. Pol as we drove past. He said we must have some for our mess.

*May 30th*, 1917.—Thirteen pilots did 87 hours flying in one day in 46 Squadron. We hear that the people at Hythe have stoned the air mechanics because of the German raid. There is not one machine at Hythe capable of getting within reach of a German machine. They are school machines. June 1st, 1917.—A visit from some M.P.'s. June 2nd, 1917.—From a letter:

A certain Corps complained of some machines flying low over its line. So Bishop, a Canadian pilot, was given a free hand to deal with the matter as he thought best. He went to a Hun aerodrome and there he saw the Hun machines all spread out ready, starting their engines. This was very early in the morning. He flew down low as if he was going to land. He shot one mechanic, who was starting an engine, dead, and disposed of that machine.

Another, which had just got off, he drove into a tree, where it crashed; a third he brought down a few hundred yards from the aerodrome. Then he came home. He went down to about 20 feet. Think of the *audace* of it.

# CHAPTER 18

# The Summer Offensive

*St. Omer, June—July,* 1917.

On the 3rd of June we moved back to our original *château* at St. Omer. This became our advanced Headquarters. The remainder of the Staff and the bulk of clerks remained at St. André. Quite close to us were the Ninth or Headquarters Wing, which was not attached to any army, but was detailed for special fighting and directly under the orders of Headquarters. It consisted of three squadrons of fast scouts, Nos. 56, 19 and 70, which were stationed at Estrées-Blanches or Liétre, quite close to us, and of two squadrons of fast two-seaters, which were stationed at Boisdighem.

It was a hot June. The fourth was celebrated by Old Etonians.

*June 5th*, 1917.—From a letter:

"Last night there was an Old Etonian dinner at the Lord Roberts Memorial Hall. There were three hundred Old Etonians present. I knew about five by sight. All my contemporaries were lieutenant-generals They sang, accompanied by the Coldstream Band, and after dinner everything in the room was broken: all the plates, all the glass, all the tables, the chandeliers, the windows, the doors, the people. A bomb raid was nothing to it. Lord Cavan presided, and made a very good speech in Latin. It was answered by someone else, a scholar, in bad Latin. The guests spoke English. There was not one representative of the Julian and Billy Grenfell generation. They have all been killed. The rest were either much older than me. Or much younger than the war.

*June 5th*, 1917.—Baldwin (No. 55 Squadron) has only got six blast taps for the Lewis gun.

*The calm*
*And dead still water lay upon my mind*
*Even with a weight of pleasure, and the sky*
*Never before so beautiful, sank down*
*Into my heart, and held me like a dream.*

              (Wordsworth, *Prelude*, Book 2).

*June 4th*, 1917.—From a letter:

I was awakened this morning by the deafening roar of archies. In vain they shot. The Hun escaped them. One seldom gets a night's rest now, what with the telephone reporting penny balloons floating in the air near Dunkirk and the motor cyclists chatting in the yard, and the mosquitoes and the horse flies and the tapping of the telephone operator.

*June 7th*, 1917.—From a letter:

[1]Fighting is proceeding as you will have read in the newspaper two days before you receive this letter, and great things are being done in the air. One pilot flew down below the tents on the Boche Aerodrome and fired into the tents.

*June 8th*, 1917.—From a letter:

...You will have read the splendid news in the newspaper. It all went like clockwork, and the air reports read like a fairy tale. I think the Boches must be thinking long and bitter thoughts. The mine was like an earthquake. Or rather, the mines went up punctually at 3.15 a.m., and made no noise, but the hill of Kemmel shook. Punctually to the minute the barrage began, and aeroplanes went straight for the Boche aerodromes and fired into their sheds. No artillery machines were interfered with at all. It is all very gratifying.

Today we are having a little peace and quiet after the stress of the last few days, which have been beyond all understanding. It is hot, stuffy, and muggy.

*June 9th*, 1917.—From a letter:

As further news comes in about this victory the larger the event proves to be. It is the finest day in the air we have ever had. Our people entirely prevented the Boche Flying Corps from working, and our artillery work in co-operation with aircraft went without a hitch.

---

1. This was the news of the successful operation at Messines and Wytschaete.

It is hot. The summer is arriving in great strides, bearing in one hand a poppy and in the other a basket full of strawberries.

From my Diary:

*June 10th*, 1917.—The German prisoners were greatly astonished. They were told to hold the ridge at all costs. Basil Blackwood came to luncheon.

*June 13th*, 1917.—A new machine, The Dolphin, arrived and did its trials.

*June 14th*, 1917.—No. 2 Squadron tried the oblique camera which came from St. Omer. It was a failure.

*June 15th*, 1917.—Du Peuty and two other French officers visited us.

*June 16th*, 1917.—We had a crowd of people at luncheon. Among others two pilots who had escaped from Germany.

*And in the meadows and the lower grounds*
*Was all the sweetness of a common dawn.*
(Wordsworth, *Prelude*, Book 4.)

*June 17th*, 1917.—I went with the general to Calais and crossed in Sir Douglas Haig's destroyer with the chief, the C.G.S., etc. We proceeded to London in a special train.

*June 26th*, 1917.—We arrived back at St. Omer.

*June 28th*, 1917.—We had a Conference of Brigadiers in the morning.

*June 28th,* 1917.—One of the points discussed at the Conference referred to our artillery machines in the future. The general said that views on what artillery machines should be used in a year's time must be discussed now. After the Conference I went to the Fifth Brigade where I spent the night. Towards seven the Germans shelled the place. I saw two shrapnel shells burst, too high to do anyone any harm. Then it rained. Then a German machine flew over and was chased by five or more triplanes, but they could not see each other on account of the mist. Then we had dinner.

*July 3rd*, 1917.—A Russian pilot came here, and spent a happy morning at the depot. Finished Bourget's latest book, *Le Sens de la Mort*, a good story, spun out with needless comments. The Russian news is splendid.

*July 4th*, 1917.—At No. 55 Squadron we learnt that the oxygen apparatus for pilots is not turned on till a height of 5,000 feet is reached, and then it makes the throat dry.

*July 5th*, 1917.—From a letter:

I have been made a Major. I part with the title of Captain. A Captain is supposed to combine the fire of the subaltern with the discretion of the Field-Officer. Goodbye to the fire of the subaltern. The Queen came up to the aerodrome with Lady Airlie. Sloly did stunts. I sat up late in the depot mess listening to music. In the distance parachute flames shone on the horizon.

*July 6th*, 1917.—Conference with the Belgians and the French.

*July 7th,* 1917.—The King visited the aerodrome at 12. London was bombed by the Germans. We heard that Basil Blackwood was missing. There is a chance of his being prisoner or wounded.

These hopes turned out to be ill-founded. I had known Basil Blackwood since 1884. We were at the same private school. He had been wounded in 1914, and had to go home. Then he joined the Guards Brigade, in which he was a 2nd Lieutenant. He was killed on a patrol. He was an incomparable companion, and, as everyone knows who has read the books illustrated by B.T.B., *The Bad Child's Book of Beasts, Cautionary Tales for Children*, etc., an artist in black and white, of infinite humour and originality.

*July 9th*, 1917.—Monsieur Painlevé came to the aerodrome in the morning and was shown the wireless in deep detail. Being a mathematician, he understands what an oscillation means. The great mystery of propellers was discussed. Why does a propeller propel? Sloly and others did stunts.

*July 11th*, 1917.—Du Peuty came and spent the night. The question of German air-raids in England and how to deal with them was discussed. Du Peuty said that the only thing which would stop the Germans raiding London would be to raid their towns.

*July 12th*, 1917.—M. Pidou, who writes excellent war articles in the *Journal des Débats*, came to see the general. He was three-quarters of an hour late, and as the general had another appointment at 6, the officer who brought M. Pidou was bitten.

*July 14th*, 1917.—Went to Dunkirk. The Naval Squadron alter the Cowper-gear on the Camel in a different way. There are six French Nieuports at Dunkirk for the defence of the port, but they are not under Du Peuty's orders.

*July 16th*, 1917.—An exhaustive visit to the Ninth Wing: Squadrons 66, 70, 19, 56. The Sopwith Pups in 66 are short of integral propellers. On the Camels the cables for the elevators are going through the steel eye; in other words, the Camel is passing through the eye of a needle—a rare occurrence.

*July 17th,* 1917.—We went to see No. 1 Naval Squadron. Two Lighting-Sets have been offered by the army to the squadron in the Second Brigade. An excellent article in last week's *New Statesman* about the bomb-raid on London.

*July 18th*, 1917.—I went with the general to the French aerodrome at Bergues. We saw the pilots and had tea with them. The French like *Joly* plugs on the *Hispano-Suiza* engine. They don't think the *Eclair* propeller is good above 5,000 feet, unlike the *Gallia* propeller.

*July 19th*, 1917.—I dined with No. 56 Squadron. Ian Henderson, Bloomfield, Maybery, Bowman, Maxwell, Coote, Marson and Rhys-Davids were there. The squadron band played during dinner. The sergeant who conducted was before the war an important factor in the Palace Orchestra. The oboe belonged to the Coliseum in happier days. They played Mendelssohn's "Spring Song." One of the pilots said it was being played too slowly; and the conductor thought he said it was not being played slowly enough, and said: "Mendelssohn was played sprightly."

*July 24th*, 1917.—From a letter:

Yesterday we visited two French squadrons. The day before yesterday the commander-in-chief of the American Army and his Staff visited us. They were shown the Aeroplane Repair Section, the stores, the Balloon Stores, and three squadrons. Sloly, the pilot, flew to them, and did a spin down to within 40 feet of the ground. I felt sick. It was an accident. He was calculating by *glazomer*[2] and not by the instruments. But all is well that lands well. The day before yesterday, Ian Henderson's propeller came off in the air, jammed the controls and he had to plunge into the earth, having no control of his machine. It was broken into little bits. He himself received no scratch.

One of General Pershing's Staff, as we were driving through a cloud of dust, said: "I think I know the taste of this landscape now."

---

2. A Russian word meaning measuring by eye..

*July 27th*, 1917.—The Zeppelin sheds at Brussels were bombed by No. 27 Squadron. The pilots who did this came to tea.

*July 29th*, 1917.—A French pilot who bombed Essen came to luncheon. He said he enjoyed bombing Essen, but it took him two months from the day he began making preparations until the day he started. These preparations were necessitated partly by the engine and the machine, and partly by calculations of distance, time, drift, etc., it was necessary to make, and other kinds of practice.

CHAPTER 19

# The Second Summer Offensive

*July—October,* 1917.

We were on the eve now of another great offensive, and were all of us watching the weather with intense anxiety. The weather prophet's reports and charts were favourable and propitious, so was the glass. Nevertheless July 31st was a dull day. July 31st, 1917.—From a letter:

> It has been a thoroughly misty day, cloudy, that is to say, no sun and some rain, and in spite of this the machines of the Brigade flew down low through the clouds on to the Boche aerodromes, and shot at people driving in harmless motorcars and killed them. They also shot German machines in German aerodromes. In fact, they thoroughly enjoyed themselves, and if you could see the weather you would indeed wonder. Pritt, in No. 66, who claims to be 19, but looks more like 12, and is called the War-Baby, shot a fat German dead in his motorcar. The German had previously threatened him with a pistol, but in vain.

*August 1st*, 1917.—The rain continues to fall and fall in slow, thin torrents. This is most annoying from every point of view. It hampers the work which should be done.

*August 2nd*, 1917.—It is still raining.

*August 3rd,* 1917.—The rain is devastating. It goes on and on, stopping everything, especially aviators and aviation. They say there is a heat wave in America, and that people are dying of heat there.

*August 4th*, 1917.—Last night's dinner at the Communication Pilots' Mess on the aerodrome was great fun. No. 56 brought their band. Bowman played a solo on the drum. We sang and danced. Ian Henderson came. There is a faint hope of its clearing up, but it rained in the

177

night and in the early morning.

*August 7th,* 1917.—Copied the following from a novel by A. D. Sedgwick:

*He was clever; but there are some things cleverness cannot reach. What he failed to feel by instinct he tried to scorn. It was not the patrician scorn, stupid yet not ignoble, for something hardly seen, hardly judged, merely felt as dull and insignificant; it was the corroding plebeian scorn for a suspected superiority.*

On the 8th of August, 1917, the general, General Webb-Bowen, and myself went to see the Messines Ridge and Wytschaete. We wore steel helmets and took gas-masks with us.

*August 9th,* 1917.—From a letter:

The moment you walk into the battle zone the first thing that strikes you, or rather me, is the instant and sudden silence broken only by the noise of shells.

We walked to Messines, and as we walked the Boches were shelling some batteries to the right of us, and some batteries behind us, and the shells whistled over our heads like little trains. As or when we reached Messines itself the shells were falling on it, so we made a strategic movement to the left.

All the ground is pitted with huge holes, but it is all overgrown with tangled weeds and wild vegetation of every kind, mangel-wurzel and hemp and grass and concertina-wire, and every now and then a dead Boche's boots and bones. In one place there were the remains of what once had evidently been a garden. There was a fragment of a pergola lying about, and one rose tree in flower. In another place we came across a charred and derelict tank. We wandered on through devious ways to Wytschaete itself, now a heap of rubbish, and up a hill where a lot of bricks are, which were once a church. There we sat and watched big shells falling into Ostaverne Wood in front of us. Our batteries retaliating noisily also. All this was the quiet daily hate of an off-day as no fighting proper is going on there.

Then the shells . . it was a grey day, and no observation being possible . . . the Boche was just doing a round of registered targets . . . veered in our direction, and we retired in time to retire with dignity and not in an undignified fashion; and only just in time, as we watched from the other side of the road the shells falling on the place where we had just been sitting. Then we had luncheon at the roadside, and, after inspecting one of the vast mine craters, we returned once more to the land of the living.

*August 11th*, 1917.—From a letter:

There is a bird here which begins singing at dawn. It sings three notes wide apart, and at a sharp angle over and over again. The other birds follow its example. So far so good. You say how charming, but very soon motor bicycles join the concert, and aeroplanes and lighting-sets, and then the noise becomes irksome.

Yesterday a French colonel came here and pinned the Cross of the Legion of Honour on to my breast. It has two long and very sharp pins. He dug them into my not too solid flesh. I bore the pain for one second, but as I noticed that he was pressing the pins deeper and deeper into my breast I finally uttered a shrill squeak. Then he let go.

This colonel was Colonel Duval, who had been appointed Inspector of the French Flying Corps.

*August 11th*, 1917.—I went with the general to see the French Squadrons at Provins and Droglands. We saw the new Salmson machine. The French pilots asked the general if he would like to see it flown. He said no, on no account, as he knew that when a new machine is shown off something always happens. However, it went up. The engine cut out immediately, but it landed all right in a neighbouring field. We had, nevertheless, an anxious moment.

*August 16th*, 1917.—From a letter:

The War-Baby has been functioning freely this morning early. He visited some Boche aerodromes, set a shed on fire, destroyed two aeroplanes that were just getting off the ground, and silenced a machine-gun, besides attacking several trains. The glass is going up, and gleams of sunshine are struggling through the fluffy clouds. I am reading *Northanger Abbey*, by Miss Austen. I feel in the air the beating of the wings of Peace, but Peace is and always was a slow flier. The sun is at this moment actually shining through the clouds. Its rays can reach my head and illumine the keys of the typewriter.

*August 18th*, 1917.—Fairly fine, but clouds covered the sky after an early promise of a fine day. Today's great thought:

*Le temps passe, tout meurt, le marbre même s'use,*
*Agrigente n'est plus qu'une ombre, et Syracuse*
*Dort sous le bleu linceul de son ciel indulgent.*

(Hérédias.)

Reading the *Confessions of Alphonse*—Barry Pain.

*August 19th,* 1917.—It was fine all day, but the strong west wind is disastrous to our air tactics and favourable to those of the enemy, for it enables his machines to fly home quickly. Reading *The Loom of Youth*, by Alec Waugh.

*August 21st,* 1917.—Commandant Marmies came in the afternoon to give a *Croix de Guerre* to a pilot who had attacked Guynemer in the air. Guynemer had instantly shot back before he saw it wasn't a German, and wounded the observer in the leg. Guynemer flew home at once and reported that he had shot a British observer. I went to the hospital with Marmies. Finished *Northanger Abbey*. I am reading *Persuasion*, besides the *Iliad*, The *Prelude*, and *Pitman's Shorthand*.

*August 23rd,* 1917.—From a letter:

It is raining after a very sultry and hot day yesterday and a stifling night. Last night after dinner a Boche machine came over and bombed. The Archies banged at it. The searchlights flitted round it; the summer lightning flickered in the distance. We did not know till this morning that any bombs had been dropped, and I don't know now where they fell.

This morning I broke inadvertently the window of our motorcar, a Rolls-Royce. The window was half up, and I shut the door too emphatically. I did not bang the door, but the window vacillated and finally collapsed into a thousand fragments. Now we must needs get a new window, and this in war-time, as you know, is very difficult. Let us hope for the best. The sun is shining through the rain.

*August 25th,* 1917.—The bombs they dropped the other night demolished some small houses. Du Peuty told us some interesting things about the battle at Verdun, where he had been. The quality of the prisoners taken, he said, was bad. One French division, on being asked why they had taken no prisoners, said: "*Nous n'avons pas l'habitude d'en prendre.*"

*August 27th,* 1917.—The weather is atrocious.

*I wept not then,—but tears have dimmed my sight,*

*In memory of the farewells of that time,*
*Domestic severings, female fortitude,*
*All dearest separation, and terrestrial hope,*
*Encouraged with a martyr's confidence;*
*Even fates of strangers merely seen but once*
*And for a moment, men from far with sounds*
*Of music, martial tunes, and banners spread,*
*Entering the city, here and there a face,*
*Or person, singled out among the rest,*
*Yet still a stranger and beloved as such.*

(Wordsworth, *Prelude*, Book 9.)

*August 28th*, 1917.—A gale from the South-West has been blowing night and day, hurling the trees down like ninepins and scattering the telegraph wires like branches of honeysuckle over the fields and across the roads. The weather prophet says a new gale from the North is expected. We went to the French squadrons at St. Pol, and the general presented Guynemer with his D.S.O. Guynemer was covered with medals. He was natural and easy, but looked tired and ill.

*August 31st*, 1917.—Lord Cowdray arrived last night.

*September 2nd,* 1917.—It is as showery as in April, with rainbows and grey clouds.

*September 3rd*, 1917.—Last night there were three bomb raids over St. Omer. One bomb fell in the depot mess and killed three officers. The danger from falling anti-aircraft shell was greater than that from exploding bomb.

*September 4th*, 1917.—In the afternoon I went to Liétre, and had tea with No. 56 Squadron. No. 70 are very keen about going out on scouts against Germans at night. I told the general this. The general went at once to the Archie battery just outside St. Omer and asked them whether, if two of our scouts were to come over, they would be able to recognise them by the sound and not to shoot. They said it would be impossible for them to confuse the noise of a British scout with that of the twin-engine Gotha. We might think it easy to make a mistake, but they were trained by nightly experience.

Nevertheless, the general told them he would then and there have a Sopwith Pup with a Clerget engine flown over the battery. This was done at once. We went to G.H.Q. It was arranged that the general should have control over the A.A. Battery from 8 till 11; that they should not fire till he gave orders. The squadron was then told that they could send two scouts over St. Omer. At 9 o'clock the general took charge of the A.A. Battery, which was in direct communication by telephone with our Headquarters. Newall came over to dinner. All our lights were put out. The general sat at the telephone. Very shortly afterwards the two Sopwith Pups flew over. Newall said: "That's a Clerget engine," but everyone else thought it was a Gotha.

Telegrams poured in: "Hostile machine over Hazebrouck," "Enemy aircraft over this," "Enemy Aircraft over that." Someone said the throb of the twin-engine Gotha was unmistakable, but the general refused to take any action till 11, when he handed over the command to the Archie Battery. As 11 struck a deafening barrage began, which was repeated three times during the night.

The next morning there were 120 holes in the Bessonneau sheds on the aerodrome from the splinters of anti-aircraft shrapnel, but apparently only one German came over late in the night and dropped nothing. When the events of the night began La Ferrière was astonished at the silence in the house. He said: "This shows your discipline. If this had happened in our Flying Corps nothing would have prevented people chattering like magpies."

*September 5th*, 1917. —We were bombed again last night, and one bomb fell in a field opposite to the gate of our approach.

*September 6th*, 1917.—There was a thunderstorm last night, so there were no bombs and no anti-aircraft, so we were able to get a night's rest.

*September 7th,* 1917.—No. 27 Squadron have no red label ammunition.

*September 10th*, 1917.—I went to London with the general for one night.

*September 20th*, 1917.—News of more fighting.

*September 24th*, 1917.—Voss, the star German pilot, has been brought down. When we heard the news at luncheon the general sent me to No. 56 Squadron, where the pilots had brought him down, to get details. This was Rhys-Davids' account of the fight as he told it me himself:

I saw three Huns attacking one S.E.; one triplane, light grey and brown, with slight extensions, one red-nosed V.-Strutter, one green-nosed Scout. I never saw the green Scout again after the first dive. I then saw four S.E.'s. fighting the triplane and the red-nosed V.-Strutter. The triplane's top-plane was larger than the middle-plane. The engine was not a Mercedes, but I thought it was stationary. I wasn't sure. It had four guns. I thought the pilot was wearing a black leather flying-cap. Fired six or seven times and then went off to change my drum. The Hun either had armoured plates or else he was very lucky.

Last dive but one. I went for him. He came from the East. Not quite straight behind, fired from a hundred yards to 70 and emptied a whole drum. The triplane only turned when 20 yards away. I turned to the right, so did he. Thought situation impossible, and that there would be a collision. I turned left and avoided him. I next saw the tri-plane at 1,500 feet below gliding West. Dived again, opened fire at about 100. Got one shot out of the Vickers (My Lewis drum was empty) without taking sights off. Reloaded my Vickers.

Fired another twenty or thirty rounds. He over-shot and zoomed away. Changed drum, then made for the red-nosed V.-Strutter and started firing at about 100 yards. The V.-Strutter was flying at an angle of about 45 degrees across the front, and I came at him slightly above. We both fired at each other. He stopped firing. I dived underneath him and zoomed up the other side. I saw the V.-Strutter about 600 feet below spiralling North-West. I then lost sight of him and kept a good look-out low East, but saw no signs of him. During the whole scrap there were 11 to 14 E.A. higher East who made no attempt to fight.

McCudden said he saw a crash N.N.W. of Zonnebeck.

Maybery said:

I saw the triplane and went down after it. It was grey with slight extensions as far as I can remember. It was followed by a green Scout. Someone came and shunted the green Scout. After that I saw Rhys-Davids dive on the tri-plane, followed by the red-nosed Scout. I attacked the red-nosed Scout. I zoomed up over him and couldn't see anything of them. I saw a triplane going East, but this one seemed to be different and green.

Hoidge said:

I saw the bright green Hun going down on Maybery's tail at about 3,000 feet, and I fired with Vickers and Lewis at about 100 yards in order to frighten him. When about 30 yards away, the Hun turned South, and was flying directly in the line of fire.

I finished a full drum of Lewis gun at about 10 yards from him. He turned right over and went down in a short dive and turned over again. The last I saw of him was going straight down in a dive about 800-1000 feet. I stopped following him because the triplane was right up above him and I had an empty drum. I flew to the line climbing, and put on a full drum and came back and attacked the triplane from the side as it was flying nose on to McCudden. I attacked him four or five times, but I didn't see what happened after this. I never saw the red-nosed Scout at all. The green man didn't get a chance to scrap.

During dinner we received news that Dunkirk was being bombed, and that shells had fallen on the engine repair shed.

*September 25th*, 1917.—The propellers in No. 9 Naval Squadron (Admiralty design) give more revs. (1,150-1,350) near the ground, but don't climb as well. The Fourth Brigade say they have only one 20-inch focal length camera.

*September 26th*, 1917.—Yesterday was a splendid day in the air.

*October 1st,* 1917.—Last night there was a heavy bomb raid on St. Omer. Forty bombs were dropped on the town and the neighbourhood. Three hospitals were hit.

# CHAPTER 20

# St. Omer—Fienvillers—ST. André

*October—December,* 1917.

This is perhaps a suitable moment to pause and look back on the development of fighting in the air. On the 23rd of August another memorandum was written reviewing the principles of fighting adopted by the Flying Corps since the battle of the Somme. This was afterwards embodied in a further pamphlet and circulated to the Armies. I cannot do better than quote a part of it to make the reader understand how fighting in the air had developed and what principles the Flying Corps were following:

At the beginning of this year's operations, the principal elements in the new situation which we had to face were these:

(1) The Germans had realised that the offensive was as important in the air as it was on the ground.

(2) They were resolutely determined to act on this principle.

(3) They reorganised their Flying Corps and changed the command of it with this purpose in view.

(4) They increased the output of their machines and introduced as far as possible a rigid system of standardisation in types and material.

Besides this the general development and progress of aviation introduced several further new factors into the case which affected all combatants equally.

Firstly, the area of fighting extended upwards. Another story was added to the warfare in the sky. Aeroplanes fought at a height of 17,000—20,000 feet, as well as at 12,000 feet.

Secondly, as aircraft increased in quantity, formations took the place of single machines, and single encounters began to develop into battles of whole formations in the air.

The result of the operations of this year bore out and confirmed the lessons of the past, and soon a further new factor became apparent. Fighting not only extended upwards, but downwards; low-flying machines co-operated with the infantry, and attacked men, guns, trenches, transport, and hostile aerodromes, flying at a very low height. The Germans were obliged to follow suit. They have not yet imitated our low-flying raids on hostile aerodromes, but there is no reason to think they may not do so in future. They were behindhand in realising the necessity of the offensive, a year behindhand in realising the value of wireless in the air; but once they did realise by somewhat costly experience the effect of these tactics, they lost no time in adopting similar methods and applying them with thoroughness and energy.

The aeroplane is a new weapon in warfare; every fresh development brings with it an element of surprise which is bound to be looked on by other arms as something exceptional. Our aeroplanes attacked the enemy low down during the battle of the Somme. From captured documents and the reports of German prisoners we know that this new form of aerial fighting caused the greatest dismay among the enemy, and led their infantry to blame their flying forces for letting such a thing be.

The German Command retaliated in the only possible way. They did the same thing. They attacked our men on the ground; their aeroplanes co-operated with their infantry.

They at once realised and published in their orders that aeroplanes are powerless to prevent the operations of hostile low-flying aeroplanes. The aeroplane is not a defensive weapon even when flying high, owing to the unlimited nature and the dimensions of their fighting area. It is still less a defensive weapon against low-flying aeroplanes, owing to the impossibility of manoeuvring at a low height and the difficulty of visibility.

Defence against low-flying aeroplanes can only be carried out efficaciously by a well-organised system of shooting from the ground. But superiority and supremacy over low-flying aeroplanes can only be obtained by a superior offensive carried out by our low-flying aeroplanes in the enemy's area.

Low-flying aeroplanes as time goes on will become more and

more a permanent and integral feature and factor of fighting. Other arms will in time be no more surprised at seeing a low-flying aeroplane than they would be by the explosion of a shell; and just as no defensive measures against shells will enable us to master and silence the enemy's artillery, so no defensive measures either on the ground or in the air will enable us to defeat the enemy's low-flying aircraft.

The victory over such low-flying aircraft will be obtained, as is the case in other arms, by the superiority, the offensive superiority, of our own weapon. The task which lies before us now is to obtain that superiority, and the surest means to attain this end consists in a close and thorough co-operation between aircraft and other arms, especially the infantry.

The first thing which is essential is that our troops should be able to distinguish our aircraft from that of the enemy.

In the case of low-flying aeroplanes, this is comparatively easy with practice. But it has not always been found easy by either ourselves or by the enemy. One of our own aeroplanes works low, flying backwards and forwards over the trenches. The appearance of an aeroplane produces an instant moral affect. Troops do not know what it is doing. Supposing, they say, it is an enemy machine flying under false colours. Would it not be better to be on the safe side and to fire?

That the enemy have experienced this difficulty we know from documents repeatedly captured at different dates, in which the German Command reiterate that, so far, there has never yet been a case in which our machines had been found flying under false colours. Again, on the part of the pilots, it is essential that they should have a thorough knowledge of the trench line, especially when that line is being modified and changed from day to day. And it is hardly necessary to add that the co-operation of aircraft with the infantry in attacks can only be successful if complete harmony between the two arms as to timing, etc., is ensured.

Finally, it is important, when the two arms co-operate that each should realise the possibilities and the limitations of the other.

The Germans, at the beginning of these operations, knew they would have to face a powerful offensive on our part in the air, and they did their best to neutralise that offensive by doing all they could to try and force us to adopt defensive measures.

By bombing raids against London and in England they tried, trusting to their effect on public opinion, and to the political agitation which was bound to follow, to make us dislocate our flying forces in the field, and by concentrating their forces against our corps machines they tried to persuade us to adopt a system of protective escorts on the battle-front itself.

So far we have been able not only to resist the pressure which was bound to ensue, but to prove by carrying out our artillery and photographic work, in spite of every difficulty and disadvantage, that our principles were sound.

But it is still doubtful whether the soundness of these principles, which are clear to those who have first-hand experience of fighting in the air, and who are in possession of all the facts of the case, is realised by the rank and file in other arms.

They do not see our aeroplanes far over the enemy's lines. On the other hand, one of our machines which is brought down on this side of the line has twenty thousand spectators; and a low-flying German machine that appears over our lines now will naturally be thought to have been allowed to escape through a network of our aircraft which does not exist, and never could exist. The remedy for this is a closer co-operation between the two arms and a more widely-spread education with regard to the functions of the newer weapon.

As aviation develops further new factors are certain to arise. Aeroplanes will not only fight in formation, but formations will be led and commanded by one machine by wireless telephone or wireless signals.

But whatever new developments arise, one thing is sure and certain. The aeroplane is a weapon which has no other exact counterpart any more than a submarine, a cruiser, a destroyer, a gun, a tank or a horse; it has its own definite limitations and powers, but the principles which guide it in warfare, in order for it to be successful, are those which guide all other arms in all other elements of warfare, and the most important of these is the will and power to attack the enemy, to force him to fight, and to defeat him.

And here I will quote the report of a pilot showing their ordinary routine work to give the reader an idea of what kind of work was being done in the air at this time. This report was written by Lieutenant Maybery, in No. 56 Squadron. He was, alas, killed later on:

Left Estrées Blancheat 4.45 a.m. Crossed the lines over Ypres at 500 feet just underneath very thick clouds. Got into the smoke from the artillery barrage, and found it impossible to see ahead at all. Went South-East and found myself over Wervicq at 200 feet. Dived down to about 30 feet and flew straight along the road to Gheluwe. From there I went due East to Bisseghem. I could then see Courtrai and went North-East to strike Heule, but two German scouts appeared from over Courtrai and attacked me. I manoeuvred to try and throw them off, pulling down my Lewis gun and firing short bursts to try and frighten them away, but they would not be shaken off, so I made West again. Both Germans followed until I reached the lines South of Armentieres, when they turned South-East towards Lille.

I then turned North, striking the Canal at Comines, and again followed the same route to Bisseghem, when I saw a "Spad" just South of me firing at something on the ground, and flying West. It was now getting a little clearer, and I could see Courtrai more easily though the clouds were still at 500 feet. From Bisseghem I went North-East and immediately saw Heule Aerodrome. I zoomed up to just under 200 feet. Circling round the aerodrome, the only sign of activity I could see was one man lighting two smoke fires at the Heule end of the aerodrome. This man looked at me, but did not seem to take any particular notice. I then flew East, turned, and came back along the line of the southernmost sheds and dropped my first bomb, which hit the third shed from the East and exploded.

This caused immense excitement, and I could see people running about all round the sheds. Turning sharp to the left, I flew North along the line of the easternmost sheds and dropped another bomb, which hit the first shed from the South and exploded. Turning sharp to the West, I flew straight at the sheds at the Heule end of the aerodrome and dropped my third bomb, which hit the second shed from the East, and either went through the roof or in at the front, as I could see smoke coming out of the front and heard and felt the explosion, but could not see it. Turned North and again flew down the line of the easternmost sheds from the North.

As I came near a machine-gun opened fire from the back of these sheds. I pulled the bomb release, but nothing happened. Flying straight on, and still watching for the explosion, I found

189

myself approaching Courtrai Station, so pulled the bomb release again. The bomb fell and exploded between a goods train and a big shed.

Turned North again to Heule Aerodrome, and the same machine-gun and another, which I could not locate, opened fire. I dived at the former, shooting with both guns, and the crew dispersed. Turning to try and locate the second gun, it stopped suddenly. I then flew straight across the aerodrome at the southernmost sheds, firing both guns into the sheds from 20 feet. Changed Lewis drum and flew straight across the aerodrome from the West, firing both guns at the sheds in front and at one time actually touched the ground. Zoomed over the sheds and flew straight on to Cuerne Aerodrome, again attacking the sheds with both guns, driving back a machine which was just being got out.

Leaving the aerodrome saw two horsemen, who looked like officers. Attacked them, and their horses bolted. Turning West, I attacked a goods train going from Courtrai to Menin *via* Bisseghem. Saw a column of infantry, about 200 strong, on the road just West of Wevelghem, marching towards Menin, and attacked them with both guns. They scattered to both sides of the road. Changed drums. Turned back East and attacked infantry again; looking up saw one German two-seater at about 500 feet, just below the clouds making East. Zoomed up and got very close under the German's tail without being observed.

Pulled down Lewis gun and fired half a drum into the German, which started going down on a steep left-handed turn. The German straightened out again, and I followed, firing Vickers gun. The German crashed just North of the railway, South of the "G" in Wevelghem. Only one man got out. A small crowd started to collect, and I dived, firing both guns. The crowd either ran away or laid down flat. Saw a passenger train come in (towards Courtrai) and attacked, but Lewis gun ran out of ammunition and Vickers gun stopped. Flew West, recrossed the lines, South of Messines, and returned.

(Signed)          R. Maybery, Lt.

Here is another report from a pilot in a Naval Squadron:

Naval Squadron No. 3, attached 22nd Wing, R.F.C.
Sopwith Scout.                                    26-4-17.
Armament:Vickers Synchronised Gun.                7.15 p.m.
Pilot, Fit. Sub-Lt. Malone.                       Height 17,000 ft.
Locality: North of Cambrai City                   to ground.
    (Close to Cambrai- Arras Road).

### Hostile Machine: Albatross Scout

Flying in formation when leader dived at an hostile aircraft about 4,000 feet below. When leader pulled away from the combat with gun-jamb, I continued firing bursts at hostile aircraft as he dived whenever I managed to get in range.

At 7,000 feet three more hostile aircraft attacked me from above, and I could not get out. I tried to get away by diving, and when down to 3,000 feet was still followed closely. I decided to drive the hostile aircraft I first attacked to earth, thinking there was no chance of escape myself. He was still circling below me apparently going to land. I dived on him, and gave him a burst at about 60 yards' range. My tracers were entering the pilot's back and head.

This hostile aircraft nose-dived vertically and crashed head on in an open field. I was now down to 1,000 feet, and closely followed by the three hostile aircraft. I headed West, dodging as much as possible, but could not get away. I decided to feint a landing. Closing off my motor, I "S" turned over some tall trees in a field. Just as my wheels touched the ground I looked back and saw all three hostile aircraft about to land. One was almost on the ground, and the others were spiralling. Opening out my motor I climbed directly into the sun, and was followed by all three hostile aircraft, who could not catch me up. I crossed the lines at 2,000 feet, and the "Archie" and machine-guns fired from below and drove off the pursuing hostile aircraft.

                    (Signed)            J. J. Malone,
                                        Flight Sub-Lieutenant.

Our problems and our difficulties, it will be seen from the above, had changed. We were no longer behindhand in equipment. But flying had not only become higher but lower, and another important problem had arisen. London was being heavily bombed. The French towns and the places behind our lines were being heavily bombed also.

The problem which we had to face and solve now was how to defend England and how to attack Germany without interfering with the work of the armies, without diverting from the Armies of the Western Front such aircraft as was essential and indispensable in order to enable them to fight. The object of the Germans was to force us to disperse our forces, and to dislocate them, and to attempt to compel us to leave the work of the armies undone.

On the 2nd of October the general was summoned to London to discuss this question. He wanted to be in London by 12.30, so it was arranged we should go by air.

*October 2nd*, 1917.—It was a fine day, but slightly misty. We telephoned to Lympe to know what the weather was like, and they reported it unfit at 7, at 8, and again at 9.30. We missed the chance of going by boat, and we got into communication with Dunkirk to find out if a destroyer was available.

At 10 o'clock they still reported the weather unfit for flying in England. The general had a machine sent up from St. Omer to see what the weather was like. At 10.30 reports were still unfavourable. About 10.45 they reported clear weather at Folkestone and Croydon, but thick at Hounslow. We went up to the aerodrome at once. The general got into one R.E.8, Mayo piloting, I in a second, Reeves piloting, and Bates, the general's clerk, into a third.

We flew at about 3,000 feet. It was fine as far as the coast, but slightly hazy. Over the Channel it was quite fine as far as Folkestone. We flew along the railway line. I could see both the other machines. Then when we got near Tonbridge some small clouds began to appear in the distance like small pellets of cotton wool. More and more of them gathered, until suddenly we were enveloped in a thick wet blanket of white cloud. We lost sight of both the other machines at about 800 feet. Reeves went down quite low, and trees appeared out of the mist. He went down to 30 feet, reconnoitred the railway line and then went up again. We soon left the whole bank of cloud to the South-West of us.

We landed at Croydon safely; there were no signs of the general. About a quarter of an hour later the machine with Bates landed; there were still no signs of the general. I telephoned to Hounslow. No machine had landed there. Then to Lympe; no machine had landed there either. Then suddenly the air-raid alarm was given, and all further telephone communication became impossible. Machines were turned out and stood by. I waited about an hour and then I borrowed a car

192

and motored to London with the two pilots; we arrived in a deserted city. The population was sheltered from the supposed raiders. I went to the Hotel Cecil; it was quite empty, partly because of the alarm and partly because it was the belated luncheon hour. I could not find a single soul. I went down into the basement to the telephone exchange and asked if I could telephone to France. They got me on to our Headquarters at once. There I learnt the general had gone back to Lympe. He motored up, and I found him later at the Army and Navy Club. I was exceedingly anxious, especially as his clerk told me he had seen a crashed machine in a field and First Aid being brought.

The next day we drove back to Dover and crossed the Channel in a destroyer to Dunkirk. It appeared that we had caused the air-raid alarm. The noise of our engines in the clouds gave rise to a report of Gothas. There were no Germans in the air either near England or near the Coast.

It was settled that such machines as we could spare should be sent to aerodromes near Nancy and carry out raids on German towns whenever they could. For this purpose No. 55 Squadron was sent to the East of France, where it was joined later by a Handley Page Squadron and a Squadron of night-flying F.E.'s. This was the nucleus of what afterwards became the Independent Force. Colonel Newall was sent to Ochey to organise a brigade and carry out the work of making aerodromes, which should be ready to receive further squadrons in the Spring.

Preparations were now being made with the utmost secrecy for the big Tank attack. We none of us had any idea of these preparations, and the moves of the squadrons were made in a way that they thought until the last minute that quite different purposes were being aimed at.

During the month of October, 1917, I saw a great deal of the Ninth Wing Squadrons at Estrées Blanche, and especially of No. 56 Squadron, where I had a lot of friends. There were a number of brilliant pilots in this squadron, among others, McCudden, Rhys Davids, Maybery, Muspratt, Hoidge, Bowman, Coote and Maxwell. Ian Henderson and Ball had both belonged to this squadron.

One day I took Orpen, to visit them. Orpen beat McCudden at Ping Pong, and arranged to paint portraits of Hoidge and Rhys-Davids, which he did in the course of time. Rhys-Davids had only just left Eton, where he had been captain of the school. He was longing for the war to be over so as to go to Oxford. He had brought down about fifteen German machines, perhaps more. He told me he always carried a small volume of Blake's poems in his pocket in case he should come down on the other side. He also said to me one day: "The Buddhists have got a maxim, 'Don't be stupid:' that is all that matters in life."

I have already alluded to the wonderful string band which this squadron boasted of which was recruited in London by that prince of organisers, Bloomfield, who commanded the squadron. Towards the end of October I dined two or three times with the squadron, and on the 24th of October we had a wonderful evening of music, dance and song. The favourite tunes of the squadron at this time were "Hullo, my dearie," and "Someone has got to darn his Socks."

Shortly after this Bloomfield went home on promotion, and he came to say goodbye to us on the 27th of October. That same afternoon we heard that Rhys-Davids was missing. He had told me the last time I saw him that he was quite certain he would be killed.

I dined at the squadron again on the 29th. It was Bloomfield's farewell dinner. Everything was the same except that Rhys-Davids was not there. We kept up the pretence of saying we were certain he was a prisoner and would soon escape. As it turned out he was not a prisoner, and he was never able to read his favourite Blake on the other side of the line. He was passionately fond of books and poetry, and his mixture of scholarship, enthusiasm, fun, courage, skill, and airmanship made one feel that if these were the sort of pilots we had, whatever else might happen, we should never be beaten in the air.

On November 4th, two squadrons started for Italy, and we went to say goodbye to them.

On the 8th, I started with the general and La Ferrière for Newall's Headquarters at Ochey, where the general wanted to see the aerodromes which had been chosen for the coming bombing raids on Germany. We spent the night at Albert with the Third Brigade, and the next morning we started at 7 for Ochey, the general and La Ferrière inside, and I on the box. We started off so fast that the car very nearly got flying speed. An unperceived level crossing gave us a rude shock. We drove through Montdidier, Compiègne, and Coulommiers and had luncheon on the road beyond Coulommiers, thence through the Champagne country to Vitry-le-Francois and so to Ochey where Newall's Squadrons were. We arrived about 3 and went straight to the aerodrome, where we saw the Handley Page Squadron and the night flying F.E's, commanded by Christie. We then went on to Bainville, a little village where Newall lived. I was billeted in the village.

The next day we went to the squadrons, to No. 55, where we had luncheon, to the Aircraft Park at Vezelise, and then to the French Headquarters, where we saw Commandant Picard, and the general had an interview with General de Castelnau, who commanded the Group of Armies of the East. It was bitterly cold. When the conversations at the Staff were finished, we went to Rambervillers, where an aerodrome was being made out of what looked like a Scotch moor, with the help of some Indian troops. The ridge and furrow was so enormous, the ground so marshy that it did not seem possible, at this time, that this stretch of bleak sopping country could ever become an aerodrome. It did nevertheless.

The next day we stepped westward again, and stopped on the way and spent the night at Epernay, where we were billeted with Monsieur Moet, of Moet and Chandon, in a palatial house.

*November 10th*, 1917.—Mr. Moet received us with the utmost kindness and courtesy, and showed us over the Moet and Chandon Champagne Factory, where we tasted the embryo vintage of 1917, and the mature vintage of 1906. Most of the work is being done by women, and there is a great shortage of bottles. We had dinner at the hotel. Du Peuty and Ortlieb came. Du Peuty told us about the *Chemin des Dames* fight, where he led his men through the French barrage and took a farm and a great number of guns and prisoners. He told us that it was impossible to convince the French infantry that the French morning patrol of machines were not German machines. This is the description of what Du Peuty did at the *Chemin des Dames*, as it appeared in the Order of the Day:

*Citation à l'ordre de l'armée. Le Chef d'Escadron Du Peuty.*

*Officier de Cavalerie et aviateur hors de pair, venu aux 4 Zouaves sur sa demande, a pris a l'improviste, le 23 Octobre, 1917, sept minutes avant l'heure de l'attaque, le commandement d'un bataillon dont le chef et l'adjutant-major venaient d'être blesses.*

*Sous un violent feu de barrage est sorti le premier de la tranchée, suivi par tous les Zouaves électrisés par sa volontéet sa bravoure; a conqui d'un seul élan tous les objectifs assignés à ses unités, fait à la garde Imperiale plus de 500 prisonniers, capture 17 cannons et de nombreuses mitrailleuses.*

*Incomparable entraîneur d'hommes, chef de troupe accompli.*

This was the last time we were destined to see Du Peuty. He was killed leading his *Zouaves* in an attack in the operations of March,

195

1918, and with him the French lost a great soldier, and an example of the finest type of man that France can produce. He had all the noblest qualities of the French nation, and, as one of our pilots who knew him very well, said to me: "It makes one feel a worm to be with him."

The next day we went from Epernay to Compiègne *via* Soissons. At Compiègne we had an interview with Colonel Duval, the head of the French aviation, and luncheon at the French Aviation Mess. We stayed the night at Compiègne with the British Mission. The Forest of Compiègne was gorgeous with the last tints and faded glory of the end of autumn. On the following day we reached St. Omer.

*November 15th, 1917.*—From a letter:

It is cold and the war has not stopped, and ministries seem to be falling like packs of cards, and populations are peevish and whole armies are surrendering and Russia is having another revolution; in spite of all this I have seldom felt so optimistic. It is strange but true.

The chief events now were the revolution in Russia and the attack made by the Third Army with tanks. Reading Wordsworth's Prelude, I came across the following passage, which seemed to me completely appropriate to the situation in Russia:

*Glimpses of retribution, terrible,*
*And in the order of sublime behests:*
*But, even if that were not, amid the awe*
*Of unintelligible chastisement,*
*Not only acquiescences of faith*
*Survived, but daring sympathies with power,*
*Motions not treacherous or profane, else why*
*Within the folds of no ungentle breast*
*Their dread vibration to this hour prolonged?*
*Wild blasts of music thus could find their way*
*Into the midst of turbulent events;*
*So that worst tempests might be listened to.*
*Then was the truth received into my heart,*
*That, under heaviest sorrow earth can bring,*
*If from the affliction somewhere do not grow*
*Honour which could not else have been, a faith,*
*An elevation, and a sanctity,*
*If new strength be not given nor old restored,*
*The blame is ours, not Nature's. When a taunt*

*Was taken up by scoffers in their pride,*
*Saying, "Behold the harvest that we reap*
*From popular government and equality,"*
*I clearly saw that neither these nor aught*
*Of wild belief engrafted on their names*
*By false philosophy had caused the woe,*
*But a terrific reservoir of guilt*
*And ignorance filled up from age to age,*
*That could no longer hold its loathsome charge,*
*But burst and spread in deluge through the land.*

On the 21st of November, 1917 we moved our Advanced Head-quarters to Fienvillers again, so as to be in touch with the operations. Sir John Simon was now on our Staff, assimilating the problems of aviation with incredible speed. In all the operations in connection with the tank attack and the subsequent fighting at Bourlon Wood, aircraft paid an active part, although the weather was foggy and un-favourable in the extreme. Some of our machines attacking German aerodromes came down as low as 20 feet, and some of the pilots flying low got direct hits on lumber wagons on the road. One pilot, Browne, had his oil tank, his petrol tank, and the main spar of his machine shot away after obtaining direct hits of this kind. We went the round of these squadrons daily while this fighting was going on.

*November 24th,* 1917.—

*Their's is the language of the Heavens, the power,*
*The thought, the image, and the silent joy.*

(Wordsworth, *Prelude* Book 3.)

One day—the 25th—at No. 46 Squadron, a pilot, who was sitting next to me at luncheon, said he had made a forced landing among the infantry the day Bourlon Wood was taken. It was practically taken by the co-operation of tanks and aeroplanes. "I suppose you're pleased with us today," the pilot said.

"Oh! are our machines up?" the infantryman asked.

He said they were very good to him. "They credit us with all sorts of superhuman things we don't do, and they at the same time ask us to do the impossible," he said.

Never was a truer remark made. People who do not know what the possibilities and limitations of aircraft are, were continually asking the impossible, while at the same time they credited the pilots with fabulous powers. For instance, the fact of an engine taking a long time to start on a cold day would be considered a piece of carelessness, or due to the want of timely preparation on the part of the pilot by those who do not know what an engine is. At the same time a pilot in an aeroplane would be credited with being able to see from a height whether or not there were men in a thick wood.

On the 27th I went with the general to London, but we were summoned hastily back to France on the 1st of December by the news of the German counter-attack at Cambrai. We moved back to St. André on the 3rd.

*December 3rd*, 1917.—From my Diary:

*About the fields I wander, knowing this*
*Only that what I seek I cannot find.*
                    (Wordsworth, *The Excursion*.)

*December 4th*, 1917.—Winston Churchill came to dine and sleep. He said the war would last a very long time. "Of course if we gave in we could have peace tomorrow," he said. Reading Lord Morley's recollections. He talks of *The crystal lustre of Leopardi's unchangeable despair*.

*December 5th*, 1917.—Lord Lansdowne's letter is the great topic. Reading *Fantomas*, a detective story.

*December 8th*, 1917.—A Brigadiers' Conference

*December 11th*, 1917.—From a letter:

So Jerusalem has been taken again after an interval of 733 years, but Belloc says the Christians lost it in July, and *The Times* says October. This is the way historians disagree. It was very tactful of General Allenby not to shell it, and I expect he will refrain from all theatrical antics in the manner of his entry, so as to contrast with the behaviour of the German Emperor. The weather is again raw and far from pleasant.

*December 12th*, 1917.—From a letter:

I have just come in after an extensive tour. Nobody appears to have any wooden under-carriages in the R.E.8 yet, which is perplexing. I have a great longing to go to Jerusalem now that it belongs to General Allenby. But I suppose you would rather go to great Seleucia, built by Grecian Kings, or where the sons of Eden long before dwelt in Telassar. The weather is cold, but since noon fine.

*December 16th*, 1917.—From my Diary: I was in London for a few hours yesterday, but spent the whole time at the Air Office, and came back this morning. We went straight from Boulogne to the chief's house, where we saw Sir William Robertson.

*December 18th*, 1917.—It has been snowing and blowing. The roads are blocked and difficult. I went to Boulogne yesterday to fetch Mr. C. G. Grey, the editor of the *Aeroplane*, who is coming to stay with us. I bought a turbot, and waited for the boat which never came. It did arrive ultimately.

*December 19th*, 1917.—We are not quite snowed up. Our road is still open. Vehicles everywhere are stuck in the drifts and the ditches.

*That God who takes away, yet takes not half*
*Of what he seems to take; or gives it back*
*Not to our prayer, but far beyond our prayer.*

(Wordsworth, *The Excursion*, Book 6.)

There was, at this time, a panic in London about the Aerodromes at Ochey. It was thought apparently that not enough energy was being put into the matter. Gracious heavens, did they but know! The general thought he might have to go there, and we were ready to start. I was summoned hastily back from St. Omer, whither I had taken Mr. Grey. However, Commodore Paine was sent out from London to see the place, and he reported that the aerodromes would be ready long before we had one-tenth of the number of the machines which they were to accommodate, which proved to be more than true.

*December 20th*, 1917.—From a letter:

The countryside is still bound in snow, but it is less cold than it was. I foresee a thaw in the dim future far away and doubtful. I went out for a walk this afternoon in the snowdrifts and made a snow man. I then paddled in the snow and paddled on the frozen road. There was little motion in the air except the mill wheel's sound.

*The Eve of Christmas Eve,* 1917.—From a letter:

We started at 8 and got to the place where the Empress Eugenie used to give her famous little parties, at a quarter to 12. Then, after a quarter of an hour's conversation. . . . (This was Compiègne, and the conversation was with Colonel Duval.) we had luncheon. After luncheon, a Conference, which lasted till half-past two, and then we started home.

We reached a sharp turning when a *Camion automobile* ran into us, but the icy road on which we skidded saved us from the worst, and the axle was undamaged and the only damage done was to the mudguard. A little further on we met two lorries at right angles across a steep and slippery hill. We managed to get round them, but having done so, the wheels of the Rolls-Royce refused to turn round and we had to dig in, get stones and sand and chains and spades and ropes, and persuade the vehicle to go uphill, an arduous and long task. It was in the end successfully accomplished, but the result was we took five hours to get home. At dinner an allied major told me a long story, which was unfortunately interrupted long before the point had been reached. The cold is beyond all words.

. . . . Tomorrow is Christmas Eve, and one naturally wonders how many more Christmas Eves we shall have to endure darkened by the shadow of war and overhung by the threats of air-raids. Let us hope not many more. As for me, I am finished. My spirit is broken, my moral is deplorable, my feet are covered with chilblains, my fingers are stained with the nicotine of Virginian cigarettes, my hairs, which are grey and few in number, want cutting, my shoes, worn in the evening, have got holes in the soles of them, my boots pinch me and are as cold as vaults. Apart from all this, I am in very good spirits, and I think the war prospects are much better than they were last Sunday. Why? I cannot tell.

*December 27th*, 1917.—From a letter:

Christmas is over. We had tepid turkey and cold bread sauce and flat champagne and port made of furniture polish. After dinner there was a concert. The electric lighting was wonderful, as it was managed by mechanics and the best electricians in the world. It was better than Reinhardt or the Moscow Art-theatre or Gordon Craig. A strong man gave an exhibition of strength. But the assistants, who had ill rehearsed their parts, nearly killed him by stamping on the wrong portions of his body when he was trying to lift a dumb-bell weighing 2,001 lbs.

The ground is deep with snow. We intend to come to England for some days in a day or so.

It was now settled that the general was to go home as Chief of the Air Staff. On the 28th we went to say goodbye to the chief, but we were snowed up and we missed him.

On the 29th we started at 5 a.m. and went to Boulogne in the chief's train, arriving in London at 1.

The next day we took up our abode at the Hotel Cecil. The R.F.C. and the R.N.A.S. were now to be merged in one R.A.F.

This is the letter the general wrote to the squadrons on leaving:

All Brigadiers.

Wing Commanders.

Squadron Commanders.

Pilots and observers.

Officers on the ground.

Aerial Gunners.

N.C.O's. and men.

I have been appointed Chief of the Air Staff in England. This will, undoubtedly, interfere with my close personal touch with the Flying Corps in France, and therefore I would like to take this opportunity of thanking you all for the magnificent service which you have rendered to the great cause for which we are fighting during the past three years in which I have been actively concerned in trying to help and guide the work.

The splendid courage shown by pilots, observers and aerial gunners has been one of the outstanding features of this time. The fighting has been intense and hard, and casualties have sometimes been heavy, but I should like to put on record and impress upon everyone that what has been accomplished has been entirely due to the magnificent spirit shown by all.

The *moral*, which is a most important factor, has always been of the highest, and I would like to let everyone know that it is a great blow to me to sever my close personal connection with the splendid fighting force that I have had the honour to command.

I am perfectly certain that the honour recently conferred on me has been entirely due to the exertions of the officers under me, and I can honestly say that, although I would like to have continued to have served with you, I will do my best in my new post to try to help you to the best of my ability and to bring your efforts to a successful conclusion.

Good luck and good wishes to you all for 1918. I hope you will still look upon me as a personal friend who will do his utmost to help you.

7th January, 1918.            H. Trenchard,    Major-General.

And here is a copy of an Order of the Day of the French Army containing a translation of the general's letter, saying goodbye to the French Flying Corps. This letter was read out to the French Squadrons on parade:

*Au G. Q. G., 1 le 19 Février, 1918.*

*Grand Quartier Général Des Armées du Nord et du Nord Est.*

*État-Major Service Aéronautique.*

*L'Aide-Major Général, Chef du Service Aéronautique au Commandant Le Révérend, Commandant les G. C.*

*Officiers chargés de l'aéronautique dans Ies E-M des G.A.*

*Commandants d'aéronautique d'Armée.*

*Commandants des groupes de Combat.*

*Commandants des groupes de bombardement.*

*Commandants des Escadrilles.*

*Le Général Trenchard, ancien Commandant de l'Aviation Britannique en France, actuellement Chef d'État-Major du Ministère de l'Air a Londree, a envoyé à l'Aide-Major Général, Chef du Service Aéronautique au Grand Quartier-Général la lettre ci-après qui s'adresse à toute 1'Aéronautique française:*

*Mon Cher Colonel,*

*J'avais désiré pouvoir venir vous dire adieu, mais il m'a été impossible de le faire.*

*J'ai été en relations très étroites avec l'Aéronautique française pendant les trois dernières années et ce m'est une vive peine de sentir que ces étroites relations personelles vont être plus difficiles à maintenir mainte-nant que je ne suis plus en rapports intimes avec la France.*

*Je vous prierais de bien vouloir exprimer à l'Aviation française le sen-timent de dette profonde et la reconnaissance que j'ai à son endroit pour toute l'assistance qu'elle me donna pendant que je commandais l'Aéronautique en France. Je peux dire loyalement que ce fut l'exemple donné par les aviateurs français a Verdun et en d'autres grandes batailles que je m'efforcai de suivre si vigoureusement. Ce fut aussi des méthodes de l'Aviation française que je voulus m'inspirer et la perfection avec laquelle elle accomplissait les missions d'artillerie et de photographie fut la base sur laquelle je m'appuyais dans les travaux concernant nos missions d'artillerie.*

*Je souhaite qu'à tous les soldats de l'Aviation française que j'ai ren-contrés et connus, on dise qu'elle peine j'ai a sentir que dorénavant je serai plus loin d'eux que par le passé et que toujours je suivrai avec le plus grand intérêt et la plus vive sympathie leurs travaux et leurs exploits.*

*Je souhaite que quand nous aurons mené cette guerre à une fin victo-rieuse, il me soit donné de venir voir encore une fois,, en ami, quelques-uns de ceux que j'appelerai mes anciens amis, et que, si au cours de mon service, j'ai à me retrouver en France, je puisse avoir l'honneur de voir quelques-uns de mes amis de 1 'aviation française.*

*Votre sincèrement dévoué,*

Trenchard.

*L'aéronautique française a toujours trouvé, auprès du Général Trench-ard pendant qu'il commandait en France, un concours précieux et la plus cordiale sympathie. Les sentiments qu'il exprime dans sa lettre en sont un nouveau témoignage.*

*L'Aide-Major Général, Chef du Service Aéronautique lui a répondu en lui exprimant combien ces sentiments avaient été appreciés de tout le personnel de l'Aéronautique et en le remerciant de tout ce qu'il avait fait pour maintenir l'union la plus étroite entre les Aéronautiques al-liées.*

M. Duval

CHAPTER 21

# The Independent Air Force

*May—July,* 1918.

The general was appointed to command the Independent Air Force in May, 1918. We crossed over to France on the 16th of May, and went to the Headquarters of the R.A.F. at St. André.

Our old *château,* where he had spent so many months had been burnt down the night after we had left in December, 1917, and the Staff were now living in huts. We spent two or three days at St. André, and on the 20th we left for Paris, the general, his new A.D.C., Captain Ravenscroft, and myself.

*May 22nd,* 1918.—From a letter:

Headquarters, 8th Brigade.

We went to Paris and, of course, the shops were shut, as they always are if one goes to Paris for a day or a few hours. We dined at the Ritz. It was very hot. The next day we started for this place. Two thermos bottles were bought before starting, one by me and one by Ravenscroft. But scarcely had we travelled a kilometre before my thermos bottle, which was full of coffee, first began to leak peevishly but firmly, and finally broke and had to be thrown away. It cost 23 *francs.* We stopped for luncheon at a little dark hotel. . . . We arrived here about 6.30; it is a delicious *château* in a garden. In the flower beds there are potatoes instead of flowers, and it belongs to an old lady who is 81 and who walks about hale. . . .

*May 23rd,* 1918.—From a letter:

Yesterday we went the round of the squadrons. It did not take very long. The lady whom this house belongs to is 81. That is to say, she was born the year Queen Victoria came to the throne.

Not so very long ago.

*May 26th*, 1918.—From a letter:

> Headquarters, 8th Brigade.
> This house is delicious with untidy Louis XV *boiseries*, Empire
> furniture, the works of Walter Scott, and Goethe and faded and
> dignified classics of the thirties, and a nice untidy park-garden.
> Yesterday we went to look at a new *château* where we are go-
> ing to live. Looking round a new house with the general is a
> strenuous business, as he insists on seeing everything and know-
> ing everything.
> We saw General de Castlenau too, who is charming. It has been
> rainy and cloudy the last three days with storms.

At this time there were only four squadrons in the Independent
Force. The aerodromes which we had seen in the autumn, and which
at that time had looked like unreclaimable moorland, wore now wide
and smooth surfaces of grass. Thanks to Newall, the miracle, the impossible had been accomplished, and further Aerodromes were in the
process of making.

The Independent Force was in an extremely delicate position, as
we had not been recognised by the French Government, and we were
neither under the orders of the *Generalissimo* nor of Sir Douglas Haig,
therefore our unique and undefined position depended, as far as prac-
tical results were concerned, entirely on the goodwill of the French.
Luckily this goodwill was given to us in an overflowing measure by
General de Castelnau, the Commander of the Group of Armies of the
East. He and the general understood each other at once after their first
conversation.

General de Castelnau's name and exploits need no comment. They
will be written, and are already written in gold, in the history of
France, and in the *Gesta Dei per Francos*, as the victor of the Grand
Couronne and the restorer of the situation at Verdun. But it is perhaps
permissible to say a word or two about his personality.

He seemed to belong to a nobler epoch than ours, to be a native
of the age of chivalry, of that time when Louis IX, who is known
as Saint Louis, dispensed justice under a spreading oak-tree. He had
the easy familiarity, the slight play of kindly irony, the little ripple of
humour, the keen glance, the foresight and forethought, that *politesse
du coeur*, that complete remoteness from what is common, mean, base,
self-seeking, which are the foundation and substance of God's gentle-

men. His white hair, his keen eyes, his features, which looked as if they had been cut by a master-hand out of a fine block of granite, radiated goodness and courage and cheerfulness, a salt-like sense, and a twinkling humour. And his smile went straight to your heart, and made you feel at home, comfortable, easy and happy. When one had luncheon with him and the orderly said luncheon was ready he used to say:

"*A cheval, Messieurs*,"

and throughout his conversation there was always a rippling current of good-humoured, delicate and keen chaff. To hear him talk was like reading, was to breathe the atmosphere in which classic French was born, racy, natural, idiomatic, and utterly free from anything shoddy, artificial or pretentious. He was salt of the earth, and one felt that if Burke had met him he would have torn up his dirge on the death of the Age of Chivalry, for there it was alive and enjoying life and making others enjoy it.

The French had only to put the slightest spoke in our wheels, and our work became impossible, since every square inch of aerodrome, every arrangement for the transport of each gallon of petrol depended on their goodwill.

General de Castelnau was a keen believer in the power of aircraft, and he wrote an interesting memorandum on the subject, which he sent to the General. In this memorandum General de Castelnau advocated an offensive policy in the air and the utilisation to the full of American resources in machinery and mechanical agricultural implements in order to make the necessary Aerodromes and all else that was entailed by such an offensive. When London was bombed in the autumn of 1917 there was at once a clamour for reprisals, but the public did not realise that what was imperative was not to make reprisals but to get the maximum value out of the Flying Corps as it existed at that moment.

The importance of doing everything possible to stop the Germans raiding England, and of being able to carry the offensive in the air into Germany by bombing German factories or any other targets of importance had been fully realised months before; but the whole point of the question was that we could not by carrying out such raids sacrifice or impair the fighting efficiency of the Flying Corps at the Front, which was, of course, what the Germans wanted us to do.

We had to be able to carry out these raids without impairing our efficiency, and in order to do this we had to have enough machines capable of flying long distances.

In July, 1917, we had *not* got enough machines capable of flying long distances, to carry out raids into Germany without impairing the efficiency of the Flying Corps at the Front. That is to say, if we carried out raids into Germany then we should have to give up certain work, and this would vitally have affected the operations in the air and consequently those on the ground. As soon as we had enough machines we did *both*: we carried out raids into Germany without impairing our efficiency on the ground. Another point which it was difficult for the public to realise was to what a degree bomb raids and the possibility of carrying them out depended on the weather.

As I have already said, in the autumn of 1917 three squadrons were sent to Ochey to bomb Germany. But such was the inclemency of the weather that it took one of the squadrons ten days to arrive at the aerodrome which was the base of their operations.

The squadrons arrived at their base on the 16th of October, and from that day until the end of the month there was only one really fine day, when it was clear throughout the day, and besides this, only one day reported as "favourable for operations." On the remaining days there were snow, rain, haze, mist, fog, strong winds and banks of clouds. In spite of these circumstances, which could scarcely have been more adverse, 13 raids were attempted on factories and stations, out of which ten were carried out successfully and 12 tons of explosives were dropped.

And now, although it was summer, and the weather was to the outward eye fine enough, it was astonishing how rarely the circumstances were such as to make a long raid to Cologne or to Frankfort possible; and until the war was over the weather remained the determining factor as far as raids were concerned; and the weather will continue to remain the determining factor as far as flying is concerned until machines are constructed that can be guided through fogs, are impervious to wind and cloud, and can safely land in a mist.

On the 20th of May, we started on a long expedition to the R.A.F. Headquarters at St. André. We motored eleven hours at a stretch. From St. André we proceeded to Paris. On the road we met a long and melancholy procession of refugees, for the German attack had begun, and they had retaken the *Chemin des Dames* And in Paris on the 31st we heard that the Germans were ten miles north of Château Thierry. We met Sir Douglas Haig in Paris. An Inter-Allied Conference was going on. Also, if I remember rightly, an Aviation Conference, which we attended. As someone aptly quoted from the classics, we were chattering and the enemy was at the gates of Rome.

The French were angry with their Intelligence, who, they said, had expected the attack to be in the North and had seen no signs of preparations in the South. But the truth was the Germans had prepared the attack in the North and in the South simultaneously, some months before, and when they were making these preparations they had been observed and reported. Then the attack happened in the North in March, so this had put people off the scent.

Many people thought we should never see Paris again, and one looked at the beautiful buildings and the Champs Elysees, and the glittering dome of the Invalides, and the delicate trees which had just put on their fresh summer apparel, and one wondered whether in a fortnight's time all this would be one with Nineveh and Tyre, and Ypres.

General Duval, of the French aviation, told me that the situation would be restored to normal in three days, and he was not uneasy, but although one thought this would be the case, the question which lurked uneasily at the back of one's mind was, would the troops go on fighting? And the French authorities did not seem to be very confident of this.

On the 1st of June Big Bertha shelled Paris in the morning and in the evening, and a shell hit the Madeleine but nobody paid the faintest attention.

We started back again on the 2nd of June. The Germans were on the edge of Villers-Cotterets.

On the 4th of June we were back again at Froville, the Headquarters of the Ninth Brigade, and on the 6th we moved into our new Headquarters at Autigny-la-Tour.

Autigny-la-Tour is a lovely little village with square-squat white houses and red roofs, nested on a hill, and surrounded by still higher hills in the heart of the Vosges. Our *château* was right in the village; its gates forming part of the village street half-way up a hill. In front of it was a courtyard, down which there were two rows of acacia trees, flanked by two mediaeval towers with pointed roofs, and on one side of the yard an iron gateway led to stables and houses further up the hill; on the other a brick wall descended sheer into the garden.

The house faced the yard—a seventeenth century two-storied building—and formed an L, the long stroke of the L running parallel with a terrace, from which you went down by stone steps into a kitchen and flower garden. At the further end of it there was a long pond, surrounded by tall trees and full of immemorial carp. It was an ideally beautiful spot. The garden was looked after by an old gardener and his wife, who worked all day without stopping from six o'clock in the morning until eight o'clock in the evening.

*June 11th*, 1918.—From a letter:

We were days without a post. Then Gordon, the Chief of our Staff, happened to be looking for a map or a mouse, I forget which, in the attic this morning, and he found the mail bag, which contained all our letters and parcels and newspapers which had arrived two days ago. Today we are going to have the pond dragged in case there is another mail bag there. It is fine and hot after a day's coolness. The Concierge wound up the cuckoo clock yesterday, '*Pour distraire le Général.*' The beauty of our new *château* is great. It is nested on the top of a white, sun-baked village. It has a spacious terrace and a long pond, shaded by huge trees, in which the carp eat any mortal thing you choose to throw them.

*June 11th*, 1918.—From my Diary: Four days ago the gardener said it was la Saint Médard, and that if it rained it wouldn't stop raining for forty days. It didn't rain. The Staff is going through the feverish process of being taught its work.

*June 12th*, 1918.—We visited our depot at Courban. It is a gigantic depot, bigger than those of St. Omer and Candas. It is not yet finished. I have finished *Eminent Victorians*, by Strachey, and written a letter to the *Spectator* on his estimate of Lord Cromer, which I think is fantastic. He judges him from the book (*Modern Egypt*) in which Lord Cromer calmly looks *back* on his work years afterwards. He does not realise that while it was going on the strain, responsibility, anxiety, perplexity nearly killed him; also that in those days he had no great prestige or position to back him, but the book is brilliant. The springs of the Rolls-Royce broke, and no wonder considering the pace we had been driving and the roads we have been driving over.

*June 13th*, 1918.—It is hot. After having no mails for three days, four mails arrived yesterday. Tomorrow we set out once more on a three hundred mile drive—

*Cras ingens iterabimus aequor.*

The general's almanac was forgotten. The result was he dated his letters all wrong.

*June 14th,* 1918.—We started at 7 for Headquarters R.A.F., (St. André.) The car broke down as we left Autigny, so we got into another, and a slower one, and drove to the station at Gondrecourt, where we waited for the train. Just before the train started we learnt that the Rolls had been mended. So we waited for it. It arrived about half an hour later, and then off we spun, stopping in Paris for some tea. But as we arrived in the foodless hours we had to get tea from a Soldiers' Home. We arrived at St. André at 11.30 p.m.

*June 15th*, 1918 (H.Q., R.A.F.)—I went to see Bowman in his Squadron. At tea the pilots were discussing the new R.A.F. uniform; one of them asked another why the tie was black: "It's black because General Trenchard has left off being G.O.C. in the R.A.F.," said the others.

On the 16th we stopped the night at the French G.H.Q. at Provins. A beautiful little mediaeval town which suffered damage at the hands of the English Angevin Kings in days gone by.

*June 18th*, 1918.—From a letter:

One hundred and three years after the battle of Waterloo was fought. We arrived back last night after our terrific journeys. It rained yesterday for the first time for months. This has done a lot of good to the lettuce and strawberries, not to mention the onions. The next day we went to see General de Castelnau and reported to him the results of our journey and our conversations with the various authorities.

*June 19th*, 1918.—Twelve eggs, four ducks, one fish, a fox-rug, one doyly, four new blouses, one petticoat, and a pair of nail scissors have been stolen from a house in the village. A mechanic was seen leaving the house in the early dawn. A bedroom had been slept in and a whole candle had been burnt. The thief was thought, heaven knows why, to be a tramp. Sherlock Holmes has been sent for.

*June 20th*, 1918.—It rained slightly in the morning. We spent the day visiting the American squadrons. The general threw the end of his cigar into the pond and a carp ate it. It appeared to suffer from the effects.

From a letter: (date illegible)

We are having luncheon with General de Castelnau today. It is very fine. I am cheered by the Italian news. . . . The carp which ate the general's cigar, by mistake, is much better. It was able to swim to the surface of the pond yesterday. Bishop was sent for by the Canadian Government to go home, so before starting he went up into the air and shot down five Germans. Then he took the train for Canada *via* London.

*June 22nd*, 1918.—The mystery of the theft is still unravelled. The mechanic has accounted for his movements in a satisfactory manner.

*June 23rd*, 1918.—The stolen articles, with the exception of the nail scissors, were all put back in a parcel in the garden. Translated a memorandum, written by the general on bombing, into French.

This memorandum dealt with two points:

1. The most propitious time for long distance raids into Germany.

2. The methods which should be adopted in carrying out these raids.

By the question when is the most propitious moment to carry out these raids what was meant was this:

When does it cease to be necessary to concentrate all possible aeroplanes on the battle-front, and when is it possible to divert a certain number of them in order to bomb the industrial centres of Germany?

The answer being: when the flying forces of *each ally* were strong enough to hold and beat the German flying forces in the air. And the further conclusion: that British aviation was now strong enough to beat the German aviation in France and to attack the German centres of industry.

The general said that in June, 1916, he had asked for a certain number of squadrons to attack the German armies in France and for a certain number of machines to attack the Germans in Germany. The machines for attacking the Germans in Germany were to be considered as a *luxury* as long as we had not got a sufficient number of machines for dealing with the Germans in France. But as soon as we were provided with enough machines for that work it would then become a *necessity* to attack the Germans in Germany. That moment he considered had now come. One interesting point was made in this memorandum. I cannot quote it textually, as I have only my French version available, but it was to this effect:

If to ensure the superiority of a given arm you increase its forces beyond the necessary, you do not get the maximum effort from this superfluity of forces, but the superfluity is used to lessen the effort and to diminish the work of the forces you have already.

For instance, supposing you have 100 machines working on the front with an average of work of five hours per machine per day, and that you suddenly double this force, the result will probably be that the number of hours flown per machine will sink to three hours per day. Whereas if you employed these additional machines as a separate force for attacking the enemy from a separate base of operations their average work would still be five hours per day.

*June 25th*, 1918.—We had luncheon with General de Castelnau. He was perfectly delightful. Yesterday we had a tiring day at Courban. Dealing with various points such as messmen, spraying machines, for doping the Handley Page planes; coloured fabric; the mail at Courban; light railways; ferry pilots; test pilots; dynamos (30 kilowatt), where are they? work in the stone-sheds (too much); Handley Page salvage; tractors; spares from Dunkirk (they want sorting); Crossley ambulances; D.R.L.S. to Courban; tent party.

Today we received a telephone message from the R.A.F. Headquarters saying that Ian Henderson had been killed flying in Scotland.

On the 26th of June we started again on a long journey to the French G.H.Q. at Provins, where we stopped the night. We had dinner with General Pétain just outside the town. He looked white and tired. I thought he was what the French call *a pince sans rire*. A man who makes a joke or a cutting remark with an impassive face, and leaves you to laugh or to feel hurt as you please, but never bothers to underline, to explain or to apologise. We discussed during dinner, quite calmly and entirely theoretically, the advantages and disadvantages of the interference of civilian authorities with military operations at the critical periods of a great war. We might have been discussing the Punic War for all the emotion shown. We discussed the relative merits and demerits of the French and the English in this respect. Someone said: "After all we must not exaggerate. After all the worst the politicians do is to make the war a little more difficult."

General Pétain was undoubtedly in favour of the bombing of Germany.

*June 29th*, 1918.—From a letter:

Yesterday Baldwin and Landon, two squadron commanders, as they were driving back from dinner towards Ochey with two American officers, were fired at from the air by a Boche machine. The brake of their car went wrong, and they got out to mend it. As they were fiddling with it, two bombs burst on the road knocking them head over heels, wounding Landon in the head and Baldwin in the knee, smashing the car, and severely wounding the driver. This, one of those "little unremembered acts of anger and of hate" may happen to any of us when we go out to dinner, whether in London, Paris, Edinburgh, or Nancy. Such are the curious phenomena of modern warfare. Should it happen in Grosvenor Square, remember to lie down.

*July 2nd*, 1918.—From a letter:

The night before last we went to see the machines start and come back from the night expeditions to Hunland. It is quite uncanny to see the great monsters fly off into the sunset and disappear, and then you hear them much later humming in the darkness and circling round like great moths till they land. . . And how well they land! An electric light is turned on for a second from the control platform, and there is the machine safely on the ground.

*July 3rd*, 1918.—From a letter:

Last night there was a concert at the Y.M.C.A. tent given by an American lady and an American man. The man sang very well, and the lady was quite good, but the audience were a little slow to take her points as they did not understand them. General de Castelnau comes to luncheon with us at midday. Tomorrow we go to celebrate the fourth, not of June but of July, at the American G.H.Q. *Le ciel est couvert.* The strawberries are rapidly fading and the raspberries are not yet ripe.

*July 3rd*, 1918.—The mess had not understood that luncheon was to be at 12.30. A panic ensued. Fortunately the General had a short conversation with General de Castelnau before luncheon. This gave them time to cook luncheon.

*July 10th*, 1918.—From a letter:

It rained slightly yesterday after a prolonged spell of scorchingly hot weather. A tragedy of far-reaching import happened the other day in Paris. A great deal of glass had been broken by the German bombs, and if this were not enough damage done, my eyeglass was shattered by the string breaking. ... Sir Walter Lawrence has arrived. . . . . We have been to Paris for one night.

*July 10th*, 1918.—From my Diary: A happy day at the depot at Courban. Some American mechanics are being trained there, and Acting-Chief Mechanic Clarke, who is O.C. Carpenters' Machine Shop, had six men working under him, but no Americans. The same thing was found to be the case in other shops. Two coppersmiths were found in the Power-House, who had not yet been working at their own trade. The assembling of Handley Page planes was discussed and a quantity of other points.

*July 13th*, 1918.—From a letter:

I went to the city of Langres today where the pocket-knives are made and where there are a number of Renaissance houses. ...Yesterday one of the Chinese labourers engaged on making aerodromes was delivered of a child. This caused great surprise. It is unprecedented in the annals of labour and war work.

CHAPTER 24

# The French Counter-Offensive
# and After

The French counter-offensive began on July 15th. We received the good news during the course of the morning. In the evening at sunset there was a thunderstorm. An enormous rainbow appeared with a complete reflection round it. I had never seen a complete, unbroken reflection round a rainbow before. I have now seen a rainbow before each great offensive, but this one was by far the most perfect and the most hopeful.

We started off on a long expedition either on the 18th or 19th, but I have no record of it. We went to Paris. What we did and what happened I have forgotten, but on the way back, and while the battle was in full swing, we stopped at Marshal Foch's Headquarters, and had an interview with him. This was probably on the 20th of July, 1918. We started from Paris about 9 and motored to Marshal Foch's Headquarters. We arrived about 11, and went to General Du Cane's *château*. He took us to Marshal Foch's *château*. We saw General Weygand, the Chief of the Staff, and discussed affairs. Then we were taken into the Marshal's room. He was most affable. He said to the General: "*Nous savons que vous avez une position spéciale; cela nous gène pas. Continuez votre bon travail.*" While we were there he got a telegram to say things were going well, and he gave a cry of joy, and was for one moment transfigured by excitement, enthusiasm and hope.

This poem, which I translated from the French of Phillipe Desportes, came out in the *Times* of July 18th, 1918:

> *Icarus.*
> *Here fell the daring Icarus in his prime,*
> *He who was bold enough to scale the skies;*

*And here bereft of plumes his body lies,*
*Leaving the valiant envious of that climb.*
*O rare performance of a soul sublime,*
*That with small loss such great advantage buys!*
*Happy mishap fraught with so rich a prize,*
*That bids the vanquished triumph over time!*
*So new a path his youth did not dismay,*
*His wings but not his noble heart said nay;*
*He had the glorious sun for funeral fire;*
*He died upon a high adventure bent;*
*The sea his grave, his goal the firmament:*
*Great is the tomb, but greater the desire.*

*July 22nd,* 1918.—From a letter:

The Chinese have struck. This is the reason. They were supplied with American bread. It became impossible to supply them with American bread any longer, so they were given an equal quantity of *French* bread, which is better. They then struck because they said the French bread had holes in it. And therefore they lost on the transaction. . . . The news is good on land and sea and sky.

*July 27th,* 1918.—From a letter:

Lord Weir has been staying here and Sir Maurice Bonham-Carter. They were shown everything in three hectic days. General de Castelnau came to dinner on the 25th. He urged Lord Weir to give us plenty of machines. It has been pouring with rain, and is very cold. . . . The news is invigorating.

*July 28th*, 1918.—The Chinese strike is over. A man who spoke Chinese came and settled it.

*July 29th*, 1918.—The general gave a lecture on aviation and its difficulties to the American Staff College. We had luncheon with the British Mission. The lecture was unlike most lectures, and a great success. General Henderson is staying with us.

*July 31st*, 1918.—This morning we had a gloomy piece of news. No. 99 Squadron lost seven D.H. machines on a raid. The general sent for me and told me the news. He was very much upset. We went out to the squadron at once. The general spoke to the pilots, and told them that where we had the advantage over the enemy was that our spirit was such that we could face and get over our losses and go on in spite of them, and that the enemy couldn't. We had luncheon with the squadron.

*August 1st*, 1918.—From a letter:

The country is like a ripe plum: golden and delicious, and there is a slight mist over the wheat. I have just been for a walk round the village and up the hill. Wasps and hornets are buzzing about, and the old gardener has cut the grass in front of the house. The white raspberries are ripe, but the red currants, on the other hand, are over. We went to see a French squadron yesterday, and this so pleased them that they photographed us unawares and then sent us a pilot in a "Spad" to bring us the photograph, which was ready by tea-time. He flew over the house like a bird from Noah's Ark.

*August 3rd*, 1918—Soissons was taken.

Before the end of August five more long distance bombing squadrons had arrived. The bombing of Germany went on now by day and by night whenever the weather permitted. In July, the longest distance flown out and back was by day 272 miles, and by night 300 miles. In August the longest distance flown out and back by day was 330 miles, and by night 342 miles. Of all the experiences we had in connection with aviation I thought, personally, there was nothing more trying, more harassing, and more hard to bear for those who were responsible than waiting for these long distance raids to return.

The distances were so great, the possibilities of changes in the weather were so numerous and so various, the margin of safety was so narrow, the determination on the part of the pilots to attempt all there was to be attempted was so certain, that whenever one knew there was a big and long raid on hand one could not help being desperately uneasy till the machines had come back. It was not merely a question of losing one or two machines. One knew only too well that a change of weather might occur when the machines were at a great distance, and one might quite easily lose the whole formation.

As the general said in his despatch:

On several occasions machines with only five and a quarter hours' supply of petrol were out for that time; in one case a formation was out for five hours and thirty minutes, and only just managed to clear the front line trenches on its homeward journey. A miscalculation of five minutes would have lost the whole formation.

August 12th was a great day in the air for us. Frankfort was attacked from the air for the first time by twelve machines of No. 55 Squadron, under the command of Captains Silly and Mackay. They were heavily attacked by 40 Scouts on their way there and throughout the whole of the homeward journey. All the machines got back safely, but one observer was killed by machine-gun fire.

On the same day, Quinell, leading a formation of No. 104 Squadron, had a fight which lasted three-quarters of an hour, and when they had fought these Germans out of the air they flew to a German aerodrome and destroyed the machines which they saw on the ground. When Quinell was over the Rhine he wound up his watch and sang "We'll wind up our watch on the Rhine." The general sent me to see these squadrons. I had luncheon with Quinell. All the pilots were in tearing spirits.

On the 13th of August we spent a few fevered hours in Paris. The drive back the next day was very beautiful. The whole country was in the full mellow glory of summer, with long shadows falling on the golden cornfields and an air of ripeness and opulence, and the broad benediction of the harvest. We had a puncture—the fourth that day—in a little village between Chaumont and Neufchâteau. I commemorated the delay as follows:

*August 14th*, 1918.

> *August 14th.*
> *I hear the tinkling of the cattle-bell*
> *In the broad stillness of the afternoon;*
> *High in the cloudless heaven the harvest moon*
> *Is pallid as the phantom of a shell.*
> *A girl is drawing water from a well,*
> *I hear the clatter of her wooden shoon;*
> *Two mothers with their sleeping babies croon,*
> *And the hot village feels the drowsy spell.*
>
> *Sleep, child, the Angel of Death his wings has spread;*
> *His engines scour the land, the sea, the sky;*
> *And all the weapons of Hell's armoury*
> *Are ready for the blood that is their bread;*
> *And many a thousand men tonight must die,*
> *So many that they will not count the dead.*

A large bomb fell in our vicinity that night, shaking the house.

*August 15th*, 1918.—From a letter:

"The feast of the Assumption. The church was crammed. It is boiling hot and beautiful. Gold cornfields, large shadows. Gleaners, a haze of heat, a bloom of summer on everything, faint noises and tinklings."

*August 16th*, 1918.—From a letter:

There is at the Brigade Headquarters a very good-natured interpreter. Yesterday I had luncheon at the Brigade, and a young officer called X—— brought the interpreter a large bottle of Gregory powder. The interpreter asked what it was, and the officer said it was a refreshing drink called *Sherbet*, and must be taken with soda-water. So the interpreter took it to his room, and said he would take some before going to bed.

During this period we had a great deal to do with the American, the French and the Italian Aviation. The Italians had a squadron of Caproni machines quite close to us.

The Italians paid us a visit on the 22nd, but they arrived at rather a bad moment. They wanted some spare wheels for the Caproni. An important raid had been carried out on Frankfort and Cologne the night before. The general had sat up all night to see the machines come back, and had gone to the aerodrome at Autreville to meet them without telling a soul, by himself. He arrived back about five in the morning. Later on in the morning, just before the Italians arrived, he heard that No. 104 Squadron had lost seven machines. He was frightfully upset.

On the evening of the same day Marshal Foch's Aviation Officer, Commandant Polo-Marchetti, arrived from Headquarters to discuss the future of the Independent Force with the general. At dinner, it was said that it wasn't the Army or the Navy who had brought about the existence of a combined Air Force during the war. It was done in spite of them. It was never experts who decided things in public or private affairs. Take marriage, for instance; experts in population might be in favour of polygamy, but one doesn't have it all the same.

The next day there was a bad thunderstorm in the evening. The machines were out, but they all got back safely.

On the 26th we went a long tour of the squadrons, to Azelot and Xaffrevilliers. A lot of notes were made. We saw seven Squadrons and three new unoccupied Aerodromes. Here are some of the notes:

A roller is needed at the Frolois Aerodrome. There are no drains inside the *revetments* of the sheds. At Azelot, the anti-aircraft section is under strength. Their football-league is to be seen to. No. 55 have no radiators and no cowling. Baldwin had received no orders about not bombing Luxemburg. Ashes are needed in front of the sheds at Azelot. The *Gledhill* bomb-gear is incomplete.

Quinell wants 20 suits of Sidcote clothing, and is short of brackets (104) for baby-bombs.

No. 99 want an Armament Officer. No. 215, at Xaffrevilliers, want a. *Jack* for the 1,600lb. bomb; also an observer, and gun-layers for Handley Page Squadrons.

No. 97 have not received their *Aerodrome Officer*. The petrol system on Handley Page 0400 is cutting out. They want some well-trained observers. Six of their big cowls don't fit.

On the 27th we had luncheon with General de Castelnau. Before luncheon the general gave him an account of the raid on Mannheim, when two machines, in spite of searchlights and an intense anti-aircraft barrage, successfully carried out their bombing lower than the factory chimneys. This was one of the finest exploits carried out by the Independent Force. On their way back both the machines passed through rain and thick clouds, and there were thunderstorms the whole night. When they were over Mannheim the searchlights were turned almost horizontally, and the anti-aircraft batteries fired horizontally across the works and the factories.

During this month we had a constant stream of visitors.

*September 1st*, 1918.—From a letter: There is a place called Langres where there is a shop called Guerre. Guerre makes and sells knives. The knives are cased in tortoise-shell and have sharp blades. Among the blades they have a curved blade called *serpette*, useful and used for cutting flowers. The other day I went to Langres, and Sir Walter Lawrence gave me one of these knives.

Three days ago the gardener saw me cutting roses with my *serpette*, and he said the process would be more satisfactory if I used a *sécateur*. I said I was using a *serpette*, but that it had become blunt. He said 'I will have it sharpened for you.' I gave him the knife, and he had it sharpened on a whetstone. Yesterday I was using the back of the blade to cut the pages of a book, the book slipped from my hand and the blade was plunged into my thumb. I put five layers of sticking-plaster on it. And this morning I thought it must be healed, but to my surprise I found the cut was as fresh, as deep, and as new as ever, and spouting with blood as before. So I put on some more sticking-plaster. Sir Walter Raleigh arrives this afternoon, Sir John Hunter tomorrow, General

Brancker either tomorrow or the day after."

*September 1st*, 1918.—From my Diary:

Sir Walter Raleigh arrived at 5.

*And hope, too long with vain delusion fed,*
*Deaf to the rumour of fallacious fame*
*Gave to the roll of Death his glorious name.*

(Pope's *Odyssey*, 1, 216.)

*September 6th*, 1918.—From a letter:

There was a loud thunderstorm this morning mingled with hail. My thumb is better, but yesterday Wing-Commander Landon drove down a wasp on to my leg and it stung me through the cloth of my breeches. Blue-bag was administered, but it swelled to an immense size, and still is a little sore. It is intensely sultry. The news continues to be good.

*September 8th*, 1918.—From my Diary:

"I have just heard that Louis Belloc has been missing since August 26th. He was a pilot in a Camel Squadron."

*September 9th*, 1918.—From a letter:

The luncheon with the Italians was great fun. The general did not go, but I went with Colonel Baldwin. After luncheon a man played the violin, and the tune he played was called the *Intermezzo* out of *Cavalleria Rusticana*. You may have heard of it. He played it in one time and his accompanist played it in another time. Out of which grew an argument. The violinist saying it was four time, and the accompanist three, or *vice-versâ*. The argument grew fiercer and fiercer.

The pianist, who was a Neapolitan, turned white with rage, and someone else offered to bet and flung all his money on the table. Then the Neapolitan threatened to go and live somewhere else, but all the same was careful in the intensity of his fury not to take the bet. Finally they became calm, and went on playing the tune each in his different way, which was satisfactory to everyone except the audience.

After luncheon we were photographed in the pouring rain. This took an hour, because every time everything was quite ready I laughed, because I could not help it. This made the photographer, who was the Neapolitan, very angry, not with me, but with the others, who were standing behind me, be-

221

cause, he said, they were trying to make me laugh, as indeed they were. Owing to the pouring rain it was impossible to take an instantaneous photograph, which everyone in vain implored him to do.

On September the 12th the American offensive began. The Americans had been extraordinarily discreet about the actual date of the beginning of operations. So much so, that the day before we had had no news of it, and the first intimation we received of the battle was the arrival of an American officer at 2 a.m., who, by a happy fluke, walked straight into the general's bedroom.

About ten in the morning we drove to the Neufchâteau Aerodrome to see the French bombing machines start. The French had sent their *Division Aérienne*, which had been formed on the model of our old G.H.Q. Wing, but it was larger, to take part in these operations. We left our car on the road and walked across some fields to the back of the Aerodrome. Thirty-nine Breguet machines were on the ground, drawn up ready to start. We found the Squadron Commander in his office. A young smart captain called La Verque, and we strolled out with him and watched the machines starting their engines and going up into the air. The general said to him:

"Doesn't it make your heart beat every time a machine goes up?"

"Yes," said the squadron commander, "some people call aviation a sport; I call it *war*."

We stayed there watching until all the machines had started, and then we walked slowly down the bill. The machines had left the ground and were flying over our heads. as one machine—one of the last—came over the general said: "He's going to crash." The words were not out of his lips before the wingtip hit the ground. The machine burst into flames at once. The machine was in a blaze. Somehow or other the pilot and the observer were out. The machine was some way down the hill about 200 yards from where we were. I could not see clearly what was going on, but I saw the machine blazing like a bonfire.

Behind us there was stillness and nobody in sight. We could see the observer was running about, and he was crying out in pain. The general ran down the hill as fast as he could. I followed him. By the time I had reached the place I found a small group of men. The observer, the general, and some mechanics. Nobody had got a knife, and the general had cut off the observer's fur-clothing with a small gold Asprey penknife. An ambulance then arrived, and the squadron commander.

The pilot was lying on the ground insensible. He had been killed. The observer, when he saw the squadron commander, stood up and said he felt all right; but he was badly burnt, and his forehead had no skin on it. They put him into the ambulance and drove off. We walked on across the fields to meet our car.

The general said: "If the bombs in the machine go off, lie down." One of them went off, as we were walking towards the road, and as we got into the car the second bomb went off, making a louder explosion than the first one. The general's servant was on the box. He had seen what happened through field-glasses.

The general said to him:

"Aviation is *war*, Chalcroft, not a sport."

"Seems like it, Sir," said Chalcroft.

The next day I went to see the observer in the hospital; he had been badly burnt and had suffered terribly, but he recovered.

On the 13th we heard that the Americans had taken the Saint Mihiel salient. On the 14th we had luncheon with Commandant Goys, who commanded the *Division Aérienne*. He had escaped from Germany, after having made I don't know how many attempts. He ended by taking the express train to Cologne from Frankfort and travelling first-class.

On the 16th of September, 1918, we went to the Flying Hospital at Chaulmes. There was a pilot in the hospital called Dennis, who had been badly wounded on a long raid. The bullet had ricocheted inside him. His observer had been wounded too and collapsed. When he saw this he said: "I then felt bitter." He was determined to bring the machine home. He was 50 miles from the line. He brought the machine home and made a perfect landing: so much so that the squadron commander, who was looking on, didn't know that there was anything the matter. The doctor said he couldn't conceive how he could have managed to fly home with such a wound. When we arrived at the hospital he was hovering between life and death. The general said he wanted to give him the D.F.C., and asked if he could see him or whether it was impossible. The doctor said it might just pull him through. The general went in, gave him the D.F.C., and he was intensely pleased. He afterwards recovered.

*September 17th*, 1918.—From a letter:

I am re-reading *Les Dieux ont soif*, by Anatole France. I came across this remark, which seems to me profound. '*On n'est ja-*

*mais assez simplement mise,'* says one lady to another. *'Vous dîtes bien, ma belle, mais rien n'est plus coûteux en toilette que la simplicité. Et ce n'est pas toujours par mauvais goût que nous mettons des fanfreluches; c'est quelque-fois par économie.'* This is true about food, clothes, art, and everything else in the world.

*'Rien n'est plus coûteux que la simplicité.*

On the 25th we started at 6.15 in the morning for the R.A.F. Headquarters. We went *via* Senlis, and arrived at G.H.Q., Montreuil, about half-past four. The next day we went to the R.A.F. Headquarters, and the day after we went to London. The object of our visit was to discuss the future of the Independent Force. It was suggested that the general should command an Inter-Allied Bombing Force. We stayed in London till the 4th of October, during which interval Bulgaria withdrew from the war.

On the 5th of October we went to see General Salmond at his advanced Headquarters, and in the afternoon we went on to Paris.

*October 5th*, 1918.—From my Diary (*Paris*): Having nothing else to read before going to bed I read Dante's *Paradiso*, *Canto* 32.

*October 6th,* 1918.—Arrived at Autigny-la-Tour, from Paris. In the morning we heard the news of the German demand for an armistice. We had already heard of this the night before, as will be seen from the following letter:

*October 7th,* 1918.—From a letter (*Paris*, Hotel Ritz.):

The general and D. Henderson had gone upstairs. Sommy Somerset came in about 9 and found us. He said: 'There is a man from the *Gaulois* who says the Germans have asked for peace, and the news is going to be published tomorrow.' I said: 'Where is Belloc?' We were expecting him. Belloc arrived and we all went up to the General's room, where the General and D. Henderson were talking. (D. H. had been dining with us).

S. said: 'A man from the *Gaulois* . . .'

Belloc said: 'Do you know the story of the American who went to a séance?' He told it and we laughed.

S. said: 'It appears that the Germans . . . .'

The general said: 'That reminds me of a story they told at the Air Board . . . .' He told it and we laughed.

S. said: 'There is a rumour . . . '

David said: 'Have you heard the story of the pilot and . . .?' He told it and we laughed. S. gave it up.

On the 10th of October we heard that Le Cateau had been taken. On the 13th the news came that the Germans were willing to accept President Wilson's terms. At three I went with the General to see General de Castelnau. General de Castelnau thought this meant peace. We discussed the situation. He asked what President Wilson's 14 points meant. He was against a minor armistice followed by another. He was in favour of one final armistice and our occupying the left bank of the Rhine and the bridgeheads and letting Europeans settle their own affairs first.

On the 15th, a pouring wet day, one machine, following the river, reached and bombed a German aerodrome, to the intense astonishment of its inhabitants, who stood gaping till a bomb dispersed them. I saw the machine land in thick, dark rain.

On the 17th we received the false news of the German Emperor's abdication, which caused a good deal of discussion. A party of Japanese officers arrived on a visit.

*October 18th*, 1918.—From a letter:

We have some Japanese gentlemen staying with us. At breakfast Sir Walter Lawrence did the civil, and asked them several questions and made comments on the weather without getting any response from them. At last he said to one of them: 'Is the coffee to your liking?' The Japanese thought a little while, and then said: 'It's tea.' The weather has at last cleared up.

On the 18th we went to Paris for one night, and while we were there I finished reading the *Divina Commedia* of Dante. So I concluded the war had come to an end. I saw Monseigneur Duchesne, who said, talking of the Turks:

*Ils sont charitables, bons et hospitaliers, et ils sont bêtes, ce qui n'est pas une qualité a négliger.*

On the 22nd of October, 1918, we started once more on a long journey up North to the R.A.F. Headquarters. We went through Chalons, Rheims, Soissons, Braine, Compiègne, and Montdidier. We did not see the cathedral at Rheims, which was a disappointment. Compiègne was still deserted and very much in tatters from air-raids, but we found one small restaurant open, and had luncheon there. The sandwiches we had taken with us had been soaked in petrol on the way. Our route followed a trail of devastated villages and towns. We arrived at St. André about 5. The next day we went to Dunkirk to meet Lord Weir. And the day after, to Bapaume, where the advanced R.A.F.

Headquarters were living in a hut settlement made by the Germans. The next day we went to Paris, and got back to Autigny on the following day..

*October 28th*, 1918.—Commandant Picard, of the French Aviation, came to see us. He asked me when I thought the war would be over. I said very soon. He said he didn't think so; at any rate, he hoped not, because he was afraid if it was over soon it would mean that we shouldn't have made a job of it. This conversation took place in the General's room. I said Bulgaria being out of it meant Turkey and Austria *must* soon follow suit. While we were having tea in the ante-room, Sewell rang up from the French G.H.Q. and gave me the official message saying Austria was out of the War.

On the 9th of October, 1918, Prince Albert, who had been attached to the Staff of the Independent Force, arrived. The next day he paid a visit to General de Castelnau. On the 31st of October the Italian Minister of Supply visited us. He was so energetic and hardworking and efficient, although advanced in years, that one of his staff officers, who had been working with him since 2 in the morning as well as travelling, fainted after dinner. It was now settled and agreed upon that the general was to command the Inter-Allied Bombing Force. And some time—now I forget the exact date—the general was officially informed of this, and of the acceptance of the Allies.

On the 6th of November the general received an urgent message from Marshal Foch saying they wanted to see him at Headquarters. The general guessed what it was about, namely, a scheme for bombing South German towns and centres from Bohemia should the war continue, and for sending an expedition to Prague.

So when we arrived the next day at Senlis, the general had all his plans and maps ready. We arrived at Senlis at 3, and found the German delegates were expected at 5. They did not arrive, however, until 5 in the morning.

The next morning we went to Paris. In the afternoon we went to see the Czecho-Slovak Mission to arrange about sending machines and pilots to Bohemia.

The Czecho-Slovak Secretary, being asked if we could have some letters of introduction to the head of the Government at Prague, said there wasn't a Government, but he could let us have letters to the head of the *Movement*. We asked him if they had troops there. He said there were several *Gymnastic Societies*. We then asked which was the best way to get to Prague. He said there were two lines; one was safe and the other was dangerous, but the dangerous one was the more convenient.

The next morning we had an intensely busy time fixing up the details of this expedition. The people who were to go there had already arrived from London with special maps from the British Museum. A French pilot was to go and take charge. This was the advance guard: they were to report, and machines would be flown there if necessary.

We got back to Autigny on the 10th of November, 1918. News of the signing of the Armistice was telephoned to us in the night by the Italians, but it was not confirmed. The squadrons did a last bomb raid. All the machines got back safely.

The next morning we knew the Armistice had been signed. General de Castelnau came to see us. Prince Albert was entertained by the Italian squadron at luncheon, and by French squadrons in the afternoon, and made an excellent speech to them.

On the 16th of November we left for Paris at 7. Everyone came to see us off, and the road in the village and beyond was lined with officers and mechanics, who cheered the general.

*November 11th*, 1918.—From a letter:

A historic day. We returned last night from Paris. We had been summoned by Marshal Foch to his Headquarters two days before, and we arrived there just when the Delegates were expected. As you know, they were late owing to road trouble. We stayed at the British Mission one night, and the next day we went to Paris. Paris was very full. It was most exciting, with bits of news arriving every minute. We got the news of the Emperor's abdication there, the day before yesterday, in the afternoon. In the night there were manifestations in the streets. Last night we got the news of the Armistice and the official news this morning.

The Independent Force was at once demobilised.

On the 14th of November its squadrons came under the command of the Field-Marshal commanding in Chief the British Army in France.

LEONAUR

# ALSO FROM LEONAUR
### AVAILABLE IN SOFTCOVER OR HARDCOVER WITH DUST JACKET

**IRON TIMES WITH THE GUARDS** *by An O. E. (G. P. A. Fildes)*—The Experiences of an Officer of the Coldstream Guards on the Western Front During the First World War.

**THE GREAT WAR IN THE MIDDLE EAST: 1** *by W. T. Massey*—The Desert Campaigns & How Jerusalem Was Won---two classic accounts in one volume.

**THE GREAT WAR IN THE MIDDLE EAST: 2** *by W. T. Massey*—Allenby's Final Triumph.

**SMITH-DORRIEN** *by Horace Smith-Dorrien*—Isandlwhana to the Great War.

**1914** *by Sir John French*—The Early Campaigns of the Great War by the British Commander.

**GRENADIER** *by E. R. M. Fryer*—The Recollections of an Officer of the Grenadier Guards throughout the Great War on the Western Front.

**BATTLE, CAPTURE & ESCAPE** *by George Pearson*—The Experiences of a Canadian Light Infantryman During the Great War.

**DIGGERS AT WAR** *by R. Hugh Knyvett & G. P. Cuttriss*—"Over There" With the Australians by R. Hugh Knyvett and Over the Top With the Third Australian Division by G. P. Cuttriss. Accounts of Australians During the Great War in the Middle East, at Gallipoli and on the Western Front.

**HEAVY FIGHTING BEFORE US** *by George Brenton Laurie*—The Letters of an Officer of the Royal Irish Rifles on the Western Front During the Great War.

**THE CAMELIERS** *by Oliver Hogue*—A Classic Account of the Australians of the Imperial Camel Corps During the First World War in the Middle East.

**RED DUST** *by Donald Black*—A Classic Account of Australian Light Horsemen in Palestine During the First World War.

**THE LEAN, BROWN MEN** *by Angus Buchanan*—Experiences in East Africa During the Great War with the 25th Royal Fusiliers—the Legion of Frontiersmen.

**THE NIGERIAN REGIMENT IN EAST AFRICA** *by W. D. Downes*—On Campaign During the Great War 1916-1918.

**THE 'DIE-HARDS' IN SIBERIA** *by John Ward*—With the Middlesex Regiment Against the Bolsheviks 1918-19.

LEONAUR

# ALSO FROM LEONAUR

### AVAILABLE IN SOFTCOVER OR HARDCOVER WITH DUST JACKET

**THE 9TH—THE KING'S (LIVERPOOL REGIMENT) IN THE GREAT WAR 1914 - 1918** *by Enos H. G. Roberts*—Mersey to mud—war and Liverpool men.

**THE GAMBARDIER** *by Mark Severn*—The experiences of a battery of Heavy artillery on the Western Front during the First World War.

**FROM MESSINES TO THIRD YPRES** *by Thomas Floyd*—A personal account of the First World War on the Western front by a 2/5th Lancashire Fusilier.

**THE IRISH GUARDS IN THE GREAT WAR - VOLUME 1** *by Rudyard Kipling*—Edited and Compiled from Their Diaries and Papers—The First Battalion.

**THE IRISH GUARDS IN THE GREAT WAR - VOLUME 1** *by Rudyard Kipling*—Edited and Compiled from Their Diaries and Papers—The Second Battalion.

**ARMOURED CARS IN EDEN** *by K. Roosevelt*—An American President's son serving in Rolls Royce armoured cars with the British in Mesopatamia & with the American Artillery in France during the First World War.

**CHASSEUR OF 1914** *by Marcel Dupont*—Experiences of the twilight of the French Light Cavalry by a young officer during the early battles of the great war in Europe.

**TROOP HORSE & TRENCH** *by R.A. Lloyd*—The experiences of a British Life-guardsman of the household cavalry fighting on the western front during the First World War 1914-18.

**THE EAST AFRICAN MOUNTED RIFLES** *by C.J. Wilson*—Experiences of the campaign in the East African bush during the First World War.

**THE LONG PATROL** *by George Berrie*—A Novel of Light Horsemen from Gallipoli to the Palestine campaign of the First World War.

**THE FIGHTING CAMELIERS** *by Frank Reid*—The exploits of the Imperial Camel Corps in the desert and Palestine campaigns of the First World War.

**STEEL CHARIOTS IN THE DESERT** *by S. C. Rolls*—The first world war experiences of a Rolls Royce armoured car driver with the Duke of Westminster in Libya and in Arabia with T.E. Lawrence.

**WITH THE IMPERIAL CAMEL CORPS IN THE GREAT WAR** *by Geoffrey Inchbald*—The story of a serving officer with the British 2nd battalion against the Senussi and during the Palestine campaign.

www.ingramcontent.com/pod-product-compliance
Lightning Source LLC
Chambersburg PA
CBHW032051080426
42733CB00006B/229